...billasmes pour aller re...

...nt. General de la Pro[vince] ...

tres bien receus, il nous promi...

...y pour nous rendre Service

...primes congé deluy, et du...

...ection ou Mr dela chaise dire...

...ressurent tres bien, je leurs ___

...u ensuitte ou nous presenta...

...? heures nous nous retirames

...ance dans les Bureaux

...ge depuis paris jusqu'a la ___

...nt nous donner celle de ce pa...

A Company Man

A Company Man

The Remarkable French-Atlantic Voyage
of a Clerk for the Company of the Indies

A MEMOIR BY
Marc-Antoine Caillot

EDITED AND WITH AN INTRODUCTION BY
Erin M. Greenwald

TRANSLATED BY
Teri F. Chalmers

PUBLISHED BY
The Historic New Orleans Collection
2013

The Historic New Orleans Collection is a museum, research center, and publisher dedicated to the study and preservation of the history and culture of New Orleans, the lower Mississippi Valley, and the Gulf South. The Collection is operated by the Kemper and Leila Williams Foundation, a Louisiana nonprofit corporation.

Library of Congress Cataloging-in-Publication Data

Caillot, Marc-Antoine, 1707-1758.
    [Relation du voyage de la Louisianne ou Nouvelle France fait par le Sr. Caillot en l'annee 1730. English]
    A company man : the remarkable French-Atlantic voyage of a clerk for the Company of the Indies : a memoir / by Marc-Antoine Caillot ; edited, annotated, and with an introduction by Erin M. Greenwald ; translated by Teri F. Chalmers. -- First edition.
        pages cm
    Summary: "Caillot's 1730 memoir recounts a young man's voyage from Paris to New Orleans, where he served the Company of the Indies. An introduction and annotations provide historical context to this intimate examination of life in the French-Atlantic world"--Provided by publisher.
    Translation of an unpublished eighteenth-century manuscript acquired by The Historic New Orleans Collection in 2004.
    Includes bibliographical references and index.
    ISBN 978-0-917860-61-4 (hardcover : alkaline paper) -- ISBN 0-917860-61-6 (hardcover : alkaline paper) 1. Caillot, Marc-Antoine, 1707-1758--Travel--Louisiana. 2. Caillot, Marc-Antoine, 1707-1758--Travel--Louisiana--New Orleans. 3. Caillot, Marc-Antoine, 1707-1758--Travel--Atlantic Ocean. 4. French--Louisiana--History--18th century. 5. Indians of North America--Louisiana--History--18th century. 6. Louisiana--Description and travel. 7. New Orleans (La.)--Description and travel. 8. Ocean travel--History--18th century. 9. Clerks--France--Paris--Biography. 10. Compagnie des Indes--Officials and employees--Biography. I. Greenwald, Erin. II. Historic New Orleans Collection. III. Title.
    F372.C24A3 2013
    917.63'02--dc23
                2012032307

© 2013 The Historic New Orleans Collection
533 Royal Street
New Orleans, Louisiana 70130
www.hnoc.org

Priscilla Lawrence, *Executive Director*
Jessica Dorman, *Director of Publications*
Sarah R. Doerries, *Senior Editor*

Book design by Alison Cody
New Orleans, Louisiana
Printed and bound in China

Contents

Acknowledgments

This book would not have been possible without the assistance of the many individuals and institutions dedicated to the preservation and promotion of Atlantic and Louisiana history. The Historic New Orleans Collection—and, in particular, the membership of The Collection's Laussat Society—has supported this project in every conceivable way: from the purchase of *Relation du voyage* in December 2004, through the lengthy and painstaking translation and research phase, and finally into production of this book, The Collection has remained a faithful supporter. Current Collection board members, as well as the late Board President Charles Snyder, Executive Director Priscilla Lawrence, Williams Research Center Director Alfred Lemmon, Manuscripts Curator Mark Cave, and Publications Director Jessica Dorman, deserve special thanks. Each has played a critical role in making this publication a reality.

Teri Chalmers, who served as translator of Caillot's original French manuscript, was a valuable collaborator, acting—as good translators so often do—as a linguistic medium, navigating between past and present, French and English. I thoroughly enjoyed our countless back-and-forth conversations as we worked to conjure appropriate English-language equivalents to Caillot's sometimes difficult-to-parse eighteenth-century phrasings.

For helping to unravel the mysteries of the Caillot manuscript and its wily author, I thank Soeurs Odile and Marie Aimée of Malestroit's Augustinian community, Gilles-Antoine Langlois, and Myriam Provence in France; and David Mendel, archivist François Rousseau of Quebec City's Augustinian community, and archivist Pierre-Louis Lapointe of the Bibliothèque et Archives nationales du Québec in Canada. In 2008 a generous travel and research grant from the École nationale des chartes in Paris helped jump-start the initial research phase of this project.

My research and writing benefited from the insights of Kenneth Andrien, Hank Bart, John Brooke, Emily Clark, Shannon Dawdy, Nathalie Dessens, Lo Faber, Alan Gallay,

Virginia Gould, Gwendolyn Midlo Hall, Heidi Keller-Lapp, Phyllis Martin, George Milne, Larry Powell, Gordon Sayre, Dan Usner, Dale Van Kley, and Sophie White, all of whom offered advice, comments, and critiques that helped shape the content and tenor of my observations.

New Orleans archivists Lee Leumas of the Archdiocese of New Orleans and Sarah-Elizabeth Gundlach of the Louisiana State Museum Historical Center provided gracious assistance with my research queries. In the reading room of the Williams Research Center, Siva Blake, M. L. Eichhorn, Daniel Hammer, Jennifer Navarre, and Eric Sieferth bore the brunt of my many requests to use microfilms and reference materials from The Collection's holdings. Their patience and professionalism will not be forgotten.

Many thanks to the archivists and research associates at the Archives Nationales and Bibliothèque nationale de France in Paris; the Archives nationales d'outre-mer in Aix-en-Provence; the municipal archives in Lorient and Paris; and the Archives départementales des Hautes-de-Seine (Nanterre), du Morbihan (Vannes), and de Seine-Maritime (Rouen). Curator René Estienne and archivist Jy Le Glouahec of the Sérvice historique de la Défense, Fonds de la Marine, in Lorient went out of their way to make sure I had access to all necessary record groups pertaining to the French Company of the Indies.

In preparing *A Company Man* for publication, the editorial staff at The Historic New Orleans Collection proved invaluable. Sarah R. Doerries, Jessica Dorman, and Dorothy Ball deserve full credit for the difficult work they do every day in making the written word look its best upon the page. Thanks also to book designer Alison Cody and to my colleagues John H. Lawrence, Teresa Devlin, Mary Mees Garsaud, Rachel Gibbons, Howard Margot, Lauren Noel, and Anne M. Robichaux for tolerating and even encouraging my enthusiasm for this project over the last five years.

Illustrations for *A Company Man* were made possible thanks to photography from the Archives nationales d'outre-mer, Bibliothèque nationale de France, Château des ducs de Bretagne–Musée d'histoire de Nantes, Fonds de la Marine (Lorient), John Carter Brown Library, Newberry Library, Peabody Museum of Archaeology and Ethnology at Harvard University, and Special Collections Research Center at the University of Chicago. At The Historic New Orleans Collection, photographers Keely Merritt, Melissa Carrier, and Tere Kirkland provided much-appreciated assistance, scanning the entire Caillot manuscript for reference and ensuring access to high-quality images of all manner of items from Collection holdings.

Lastly, I thank my parents, Charles and Sandy Greenwald, for their continued encouragement. My husband, Vasy McCoy, remains my most valuable sounding board. He listens to, reads, and comments on all phases of my works in progress, often with our daughter Acadia standing by, waiting for the opportunity to inject comic relief into our discussions. I thank them both for enriching my life and work.

Erin M. Greenwald

List of Illustrations

Figures

Plates

The watercolor, pencil, and ink drawings from *Relation du voyage*, including those Caillot incorporated into his title and section pages or embedded in his narrative, appear in galleries one and three as full-color plates. Gallery two features supplementary images intended to contextualize Caillot's life and travels.

Gallery 1
Following page xliv

Gallery 2
Following page 64

Gallery 3
Following page 144

Introduction

In 2004 The Historic New Orleans Collection, under the guidance of Manuscripts Curator Mark Cave and Williams Research Center Director Alfred Lemmon, acquired an unpublished eighteenth-century manuscript entitled *Relation du voyage de la Louisianne ou Nouvelle France fait par le Sr. Caillot en l'année 1730* (*Account of the voyage to Louisiana, or New France, made by Sieur Caillot in the year 1730*). The manuscript's author, Marc-Antoine Caillot, was an employee of the French Company of the Indies.[1] He recorded his travels to and residency in Louisiana from 1729 to 1731. During his sojourn in the colony, Caillot documented events of both major and minor import, ranging from an account of the 1729–31 Natchez war to his own cross-dressing escapades during a 1730 wedding turned Lundi Gras celebration along Bayou St. John. Caillot returned to France in the spring of 1731, when the company relinquished its Louisiana charter and the colony reverted to the Crown; he closed his narrative with an account of his departure on the slave ship *Saint-Louis* in May 1731.

Relation du voyage represents an important new source for students of colonial Louisiana history and may be the field's most significant find in well over a century. As an unpublished, illustrated manuscript likely prepared for an intimate circle of friends, rather than for administrative or military officials, Caillot's account was never subjected to censorship by the company or king, making it an exceptional example of a fully narrative account, unhindered by the literary conventions of polite society. *Relation du voyage* provides a detailed—and often irreverent—window on an Atlantic

---

1. On the French Company of the Indies, see Philippe Haudrère, *La Compagnie française des Indes au XVIIIe siècle, 1719–1795*, 2 vols. (Paris: Les Indes Savantes, 2005); Philippe Haudrère and Gérard le Bouëdec, *Les Compagnies des Indes* (Rennes: Editions Ouest-France, 2005); Erin M. Greenwald, "Company Towns and Tropical Baptisms: From Lorient to Louisiana on a French Atlantic Circuit" (PhD diss., The Ohio State University, 2011); and Cécile Vidal, "French Louisiana in the Age of the Companies, 1712–1731," in *Constructing Early Modern Empires: Proprietary Ventures in the Atlantic World, 1500–1750*, ed. L. H. Roper and B. Van Ruymbeke (Leiden, Netherlands: Brill, 2007), 111–33.

world circuit made possible by the trade, military, and administrative networks of the French Company of the Indies.

From the late seventeenth through the eighteenth century, the French Atlantic stretched outward from Paris to France's eastern and southern seaboards, south to Africa, and across the Atlantic to the Caribbean, Louisiana, and New France. Caillot illustrates with astounding clarity the interconnected nature of seemingly disparate sites across the Atlantic, while his larger life story hints at the global nature of the trading networks that undergirded the Atlantic economy.

Relation du voyage is unique in that it begins not with the ocean crossing, as was the tradition with most published travel narratives, but rather with the author's overland journey from Paris to the coast. Only after tracing his trek to the company town of Lorient did Caillot shift his attention to the wooden world that bore him across the sea. More accustomed to pushing paper in the company's Paris offices than enduring the distinct discomforts of eighteenth-century life at sea, Caillot provides a description of a transatlantic crossing marked in turn by wonder, horror, desperation, and hope. Once settled in Louisiana's swampy, ill-fortified capital, he struggled to make a place for himself. This struggle, and the company's fight (and ultimate failure) to make Louisiana a worthwhile venture, play out upon the pages of Caillot's memoir. Through it all, his sharp tongue and fervent desire to impress his audience—whether through feats of daring or cleverness—are evident. His is a story that aims to draw readers in. That he succeeds in doing so more than two hundred fifty years after his death, in 1758, is a testament to the enduring quality of his words and the keenness of his observations.

Travel Writing, Reading, and Publishing in Eighteenth-Century France

Until the mid-1700s, literature of the voyage was just as likely to be read in manuscript form as in print. French publishing houses released far fewer travel narratives in the first half of the eighteenth century than their colonizing counterparts did. Indeed, the first printed French travel account of note, Robert Challe's three-volume *Journal d'un voyage fait aux Indes orientales*, did not appear until 1721, long after memoirs by roving Englishmen, Dutchmen, and Spaniards were popularized in the sixteenth and seventeenth centuries.[2] And Challe's journal made it into print only after three decades had

---

2. Robert Challe, *Journal d'un voyage fait aux Indes orientales*, 3 vols. (Rouen: Jean Baptiste Machuel Le Jeune, 1721). On divergences between Challe's manuscript and print versions of *Journal d'un voyage*, see Jacques Popin,

passed from the time of his original travels to the East Indies. Until publication, *Journal d'un voyage* existed in the form of multiple manuscripts. The version published anonymously in 1721 was scrubbed clean of political commentary, and the author's casual tone was formalized, presumably in advance of the censors' review. Ancien régime editors wielded far more discretionary power to significantly alter authors' manuscripts than twenty-first-century editors do, often engaging in preemptive censorship and sometimes embellishing an author's tale beyond the limits of truthfulness.

Challe's literary endeavor, along with the distinct turn toward scientific inquiry that marked the emergence of Enlightenment thought, sparked an outpouring of scientific and pseudo-scientific travel memoirs, whose authors aimed to expand the state of knowledge surrounding little-known and far-flung locales and entertain a growing number of readers eager to transport themselves via others' adventures. Some of these accounts were published, often decades after an author's return to France. Others were never published but enjoyed wide readership in some circles; still others languished in travelers' trunks, never circulating beyond the author's own household. During Caillot's lifetime *Relation du voyage* probably circulated within a small circle of his intimates as an informative and amusing account of his experiences.[3] Caillot's descriptions of life at sea on board the company ship *Durance* and his criticisms of company personnel—especially of the *Durance*'s captain, whom he accused of withholding provisions for his own profit—would not have made it past company or Crown censors.

Eighteenth-century travel narratives grew out of France's attempt to evaluate and exploit the resources and inhabitants of its colonies, but they were also vehicles for the Enlightenment push to measure, count, and classify, and otherwise contribute to the production of fact-based knowledge. No less significantly, many of their authors employed storytelling techniques more frequently associated with picaresque novels than with official reports, in an unconcealed attempt to draw readers in.[4] The outcome is a hybrid genre best described by the French term *histoire*, which, according to

---

"Le *Journal de voyage* destiné à Pierre Raymond: Ecriture et Réécriture," in *Autour de Robert Challe*, ed. Frédéric Deloffre (Paris: II. Champion, 1993), 49 62; and Frédéric Deloffre and Jacques Popin, "Le *Journal de voyage* de 1721," in *Journal d'un voyage fait aux Indes orientales* (Paris: Mercure de France, 2002), 71–88.

3. On the history of manuscript circulation in ancien régime France, see François Moureau, ed., *La Communication manuscrite au XVIIIe siècle* (Paris: Universitas, 2003); Moureau, "La littérature des voyages maritimes, du Classicisme aux Lumières," in *La Percée de l'Europe sur les océans vers 1690–vers 1790*, ed. Etienne Taillemite and Denis Lieppe (Paris: Presses de l'Université de Paris-Sorbonne, 1997), 223–64; and Moureau, *La plume et le plomb: Espaces de l'imprimé et du manuscrit au siècle des Lumières* (Paris: Presses de l'Université Paris-Sorbonne, 2006).

4. Robert Challe, always the trendsetter, was among the first to combine nautical and ethnographic observations with personal musings, revealing his "taste for fighting, gambling, [and] strong drink." Moureau, "La littérature des voyages maritimes," 252.

anthropologist Shannon Dawdy, "should be understood in its double meaning as both 'story' and 'history.'"[5]

Histoires documenting newcomer experiences in the Louisiana colony were often a mixed bag of natural and administrative history, astronomy, fashion and culinary critique, and good old-fashioned storytelling, in which the tall tales spun by the writer were at times self-serving aggrandizements or, worse, gross distortions of reality. Yet regardless of any specific content reflecting the writer's disposition or personal tastes, *histoires* tended to follow a formulaic model. Standard features included detailed descriptions of the Atlantic crossing; the promotion of a sort of colonial boosterism, often detailing progress made by colonizers in the arenas of architecture, engineering, and agriculture; and descriptions of natural history, including commentary on New World natives.[6]

Caillot dedicated more than half of his account's 184 pages to his journey from Paris to New Orleans. For him, as for many Atlantic World travelers, time in motion—the period spent traveling through time and space toward a final destination—proved just as noteworthy as time actually spent in a destination. Indeed, as soon as Caillot reached the end of his waterborne travels, the narrative structure and content of *Relation du voyage* changes, from one of recorded experience to one marked by the conventions of Enlightenment travel writing. Like his contemporaries, Caillot followed an established model of what sorts of details should be included in travel memoirs, though his observations are often more perfunctory than informative, suggesting that he felt compelled to include them for their status as travel-narrative requisites rather than for a sincere personal interest.

Another shared convention employed by eighteenth-century French travel writers was to openly address the audience. In *Relation du voyage* Caillot begins his narrative with a direct appeal to the reader:

It having been proposed to me to share with you, in an abridged form, a brief account of the particulars of my journey to New France, I feel I must warn you about the bad style of the author before carrying this to fruition. I must also advise

---

5. Shannon Lee Dawdy, *Building the Devil's Empire: French Colonial New Orleans* (Chicago: University of Chicago Press, 2008), 50.

6. On pre-nineteenth-century travel writing as a genre, see Mary Louise Pratt, *Imperial Eyes: Travel Writing and Transculturation* (New York: Routledge, 1992); Moureau, "La littérature des voyages maritimes"; Sophie Linon-Chipon, *Gallia Orientalis: Voyages aux Indes orientales, 1529–1722: Poétique et imaginaire d'un genre littéraire en formation* (Paris: Presses de l'Université Paris-Sorbonne, 2003); Jean Viviès, *English Travel Narratives in the Eighteenth Century: Exploring Genres* (Surrey, UK: Ashgate Publishing, 2002); and Philip Edwards, *The Story of the Voyage: Sea-Narratives in Eighteenth-Century England* (New York: Cambridge University Press, 1994). On travel accounts dealing with colonial Louisiana, see Dawdy, *Building the Devil's Empire*, 25–61.

you about faults that I may have committed here due to my lack of ability. But, on the other hand, those who will read this account will do me honor to give credence to it, since to my knowledge I have not said anything untrue. Indeed, I am a long way off from using certain exaggerated digressions, as many historians have done in their works for the purpose of ornamentation and to attract to themselves the applause of a few people who are infatuated with their fable. (1)

After excusing himself in advance for any stylistic weaknesses, Caillot stressed the intended truthfulness of his account, hoping to convince prospective readers of his integrity. He did not limit acknowledgment of his reading public to prefatory remarks in his introduction; in multiple instances, throughout the manuscript, Caillot addressed the reader directly (see, for example, pages 97, 100, and 119–120), each time in order to express particular concern that he not bore the reader or try his patience with too many minute details. Sometimes his abrupt shifts from one topic to the next must have jarred readers, leaving them to wonder if Caillot was trying to avoid boring himself as much as them.

There is only one instance in the manuscript to suggest that Caillot wrote with a particular reader in mind, and even then the allusion—a casual reference to "seigneur" on page 140—is so vague that one can surmise only that his intended audience was male. If he possessed a noble patron or intended to use *Relation du voyage* as a way of impressing a specific individual, he never named him. Nor did he dedicate any of the twelve watercolors included in his manuscript to any particular individual. Indeed, the author was almost as vague regarding his own identity, signing his account only "Sieur Caillot." To be fair, he also included an impossible-to-untangle cipher on some of his watercolors, but both the cipher and last-name-only signature helped veil his identity from unintended readers. Caillot's identity was uncovered, at least for twenty-first-century readers, only after years of careful archival research.

Marc-Antoine Caillot and the French Company of the Indies

Marc-Antoine Caillot was born June 4, 1707, in Meudon, France, a small village located two leagues (one league equals roughly 2.4 miles) from Paris and a short carriage ride from the Château de Versailles. His father, Pierre Caillot, held the office of first footman in the Château de Meudon (see fig. 1), the royal household inhabited by Louis XIV's eldest son and heir, Louis de France (known more commonly as Monseigneur le Dauphin). His mother, Marie-Catherine Blanche, was the daughter of Pierre Blanche,

Figure 1. Château de Meudon by de Fer, detail from *Parc, jardins, château et bourg de Meudon*. Paris: G. Daniel, 1708. (Courtesy of the Bibliothèque nationale de France)

a longtime officer in the Maison du Roi, or king's household, the institutional entity to which the king's clerical, religious, military, and domestic personnel belonged. His uncle and godfather also held official posts in the Maison du Roi: François Caillot worked side by side with his brother as a footman, and Marc-Antoine Balligant served as an *officier de la bouche*, charged with overseeing food service in the dauphin's household.[7]

Meudon was one of eighteen royal French residences whose household staff fell under the purview of the Maison du Roi.[8] With the exception of the highest-ranking posts,

---

7. All genealogical details and information regarding titles and offices held by members of the Caillot family in Meudon derives from the sacramental records of Meudon Parish, which are housed in the Archives départementales des Hautes-de-Seine (ADHS), série 4E, régistres paroissiaux et d'état civil, 1 MiEc, Meudon.

8. The other royal households were the Châteaux and Palais de Bellevue, Choisy, Compiègne, Fontainebleau, Le Grand Trianon, Louvre, Luxembourg, Madrid, Marly, Montreuil, La Muette, Rambouillet, Saint-Cloud, Saint-Denis, Saint-Germain, Saint-Hubert, and Versailles.

which were often honorific and filled directly by the king, offices within the Maison du Roi were either purchased or passed down from father to son. Offices were divided into three categories, based on social rank, with members of the high nobility at the top of the household hierarchy. Gentlemen attendants of the *noblesse de robe* (those ennobled by office rather than heredity) typically filled intermediary posts, including specialized offices such as master of ceremonies, falconer, and horseman; while commoners, including members of the bourgeoisie, merchants, and tradesmen, took up all manner of duties at the lower end of the hierarchy. Because Pierre Caillot reported to the horse master (*grand ecuyer*), an office held by a member of the high nobility, his position as first footman likely placed him in an intermediate position within the Maison du Roi.[9]

From a twenty-first-century perspective, the idea of nobles serving as footmen, cupbearers, and waiters may seem unlikely, but these were individuals in daily contact with the king, or dauphin in the case of Meudon. They clothed him, fed him, and prepared his carriage. They taught his children to dance, delivered messages to his mistress, and loaded his musket at the hunt. Their physical proximity to the king and his heir required a certain level of social distinction. "The king's household," noted French historian Roland Mousnier, "was an agency of social mobility."[10] Membership in the Maison du Roi allowed the sons of bourgeois personnel to attain nobility, the newly ennobled to solidify their positions, and members of the high nobility to gain even greater social currency through their nearness to the monarch.

The number of posts in a royal household ranged widely depending on its size and importance. The Châteaux de Fontainebleau and Marly, for example, were both used primarily as hunting lodges and had far fewer personnel in the first decade of the eighteenth century than the royals' year-round residences at the Palais de Versailles or Château de Meudon had. Members of the Maison du Roi filled every post needed to keep the households running, from the constant companions who attended the royals' *toilettes* to those who cared for animals in the king's menagerie.

Known collectively as *les domestiques commensaux*, or the live-in nobility, members of the Maison du Roi benefited from distinct privileges in exchange for their service, including the *droit de manteau* (wages provided to individuals clothed by the king); exemption from direct, royal, and local taxation; legal protection from creditors; and exemption from wartime military service.[11] Perhaps more importantly, the live-in

---

9. On the offices overseen by the horse master and social hierarchy within the ranks of the Maison du Roi, see Roland Mousnier, *The Institutions of France under the Absolute Monarchy, 1598–1789*, vol. 2, *The Organs of State and Society*, trans. Arthur Goldhammer (Chicago: University of Chicago Press, 1984), 116–17, 121–23.

10. Ibid., 122.

11. Sophie de Laverny, *Les Domestiques commensaux du roi de France au XVIIe siècle* (Paris: Presses de

nobility and their families profited from the patronage of royals. Historian Sharon Kettering has shown the intergenerational impact of patron-client relationships in the noble households of seventeenth- and early-eighteenth-century France, stressing that those who served in them "frequently became clients of the household head because of their proximity and positions of trust as companion-attendants and household officials"; they "received gifts in cash and in kind and patronage opportunities for themselves and their families in addition to room, board, and an annual salary."[12] Patron-client relationships between *domestiques commensaux* and the king or his heir proved most beneficial, with service in the Maison du Roi often guaranteeing not only patronage opportunities but also pension payments from the Crown. For Marc-Antoine Caillot and his siblings, their father's and grandfather's service to the dauphin did result in patronage opportunities and pensions, but not in continued membership in the Maison du Roi.[13]

On April 14, 1711, Monseigneur le Dauphin succumbed to smallpox. His eldest son, Louis, duc de Bourgogne, died the next year; his youngest, Charles, duc de Berry, in 1714; and his father, Louis XIV, in 1715, at the age of seventy-seven. The series of deaths visited upon the Bourbon clan in the four years between 1711 and 1715 wreaked havoc on the households operating under the Maison du Roi. The new heir, Louis XV, was only five years old at the time of the succession. His regent, Philippe II, duc d'Orléans, eschewed residency at Versailles or Meudon in favor of consolidating power in Paris, within the walls of his family home at the Palais Royal.

The absence of heirs and their courts at Meudon relegated the château to hunting-lodge status and significantly diminished its importance in the Maison du Roi's hierarchy. Had Meudon maintained its place as home to French royalty, Marc-Antoine, his brothers, and his cousins would likely have followed in their fathers' footsteps in service to the Maison du Roi, but its transition to an occasional residence made a fully staffed household unnecessary.[14] Indeed, many of those already in service at Meudon saw their functions shift. Some attendants remained at Meudon to oversee upkeep of the château or fulfill whatever roles its temporary residents required. Others, including

---

l'Université de Paris-Sorbonne, 2002).

12. Sharon Kettering, "Patronage and Kinship in Early Modern France," *French Historical Studies* 16 (1989): 418.

13. Four of Marc-Antoine's siblings—three sisters and a brother—received lifetime pensions in the name of their father's service in the Maison du Roi, while Marc-Antoine and at least two of his cousins, Hyacinthe and Louis-Christophe Caillot, received patronage opportunities in the form of overseas clerkships. "Pensions de la Maison du Roi," Archives Nationales (AN), série O1 Maison du Roi, carton 670.

14. In October of 1718, Marie Louise Elisabeth d'Orléans, duchesse de Berry and daughter of the duc d'Orléans, took up residence at Meudon, but she died in July of the following year. The château remained a Crown property until the French Revolution, but after de Berry's death it was only an occasional residence of the royal family. On the Château de Meudon, see Paul Biver, *Histoire du Château de Meudon* (Paris: Jouvé et Cie, 1923).

Marc-Antoine's father, who became a tax collector in the Norman village of Andelys, were offered offices elsewhere.

Despite the changes at Meudon, former members of Monseigneur le Dauphin's household continued to reap patronage benefits for themselves and their offspring well into the eighteenth century. Sometime in the fall of 1728, the twenty-one-year-old Caillot received his first overseas commission with the French Company of the Indies. Before that, however, he likely served as a *commis*, or clerk, in the company's Paris offices. Both appointments were made possible by his family connections to the Maison du Roi.

Situated at the corner of rues Vivienne and Neuve-des-Petits-Champs, the U-shaped structure that was home to the company in France served as gateway to its global network of *comptoirs*, or trade outposts.[15] Each year, dozens of literate and well-connected (but cash-poor) young men cycled through the company's ground-floor copying division, quill in hand, to fill the lowest available clerical positions.

The full extent of Caillot's training in Paris is unclear, but if he followed the typical model for young men hired by the company, he likely started as a copy clerk, moving on to a more specialized department once he had the requisite training. After gaining experience as a copyist, some clerks were placed in bookkeeping offices; others migrated upstairs to one of the half dozen offices charged with site-specific correspondence. These work spaces, divided by region, served comptoirs in China, India, Senegal, the Mascarenes, and the Americas—as well as outfitting offices in Lorient, France—and were typically the last stop for clerks before they received an overseas commission.

Paris was the training ground for clerks and administrators alike, but comptoir service was often the ultimate goal for those in the company's employ. Service abroad, especially in the more lucrative trade zones, in the East Indies, brought opportunities for advancement and increased wealth. The path was relatively well defined: two years as a *commis* in Paris usually led to a commission, perhaps to an outpost the clerk had corresponded with in his time in the central offices. Not all comptoirs, however, were equal. When Caillot received his commission to Louisiana, as a bookkeeping clerk in New Orleans, he may have envied those among his former Paris officemates who had received commissions to far more profitable outposts, in India and Southeast Asia, where a brisk trade in textiles, spices, tea, ceramics, and other goods facilitated sideline profiteering.

---

15. Built in 1635, Hôtel Tubeuf became part of the Palais Mazarin in the 1640s. It was acquired by John Law in 1719 and served as company headquarters until the 1780s. On April 30, 1803, Hôtel Tubeuf hosted the signing of the Louisiana Purchase treaty. The building now houses the Bibliothèque nationale de France's Richelieu site.

Of all the possible sites in the company's vast global trade network, New Orleans—and Louisiana in general—was among the least desirable. Louisiana's trade in 1729 still revolved mainly around peltries (deer, bear, squirrel, buffalo, and beaver), naval stores (tar and pitch), and poor-quality tobacco. Many in France viewed the colony as inhospitable, corrupt, and dangerous—opinions formed largely on the basis of word of mouth and on Louisiana's association with John Law's failed financial scheme[16]—and Louisiana offered limited opportunities to young bureaucrats anxious to advance their careers and increase their personal fortunes. Yet for all the economic disadvantages of a commission to Louisiana, the colony remained enough of a curiosity in the metropolitan imagination that a young, relatively inexperienced clerk felt compelled to record his experiences traveling and residing there during the last years of company involvement in the Americas.

Relation du voyage begins with an account of Caillot's departure from Paris on February 19, 1729. With two companions—a fellow Paris-trained clerk named De Troyes and another unnamed employee (likely a bookkeeper named De Bussy)—Caillot made his way from the French capital to the coastal Breton town of Lorient, home port of the Company of the Indies. Traveling mainly on horseback and keeping pace with the mail coach, the trio passed through small towns, villages, and bustling urban centers. They outwitted gamblers in La Flèche, ridiculed Breton dances "with the most bizarre steps" in Ingrande, and attended the plays of Molière and Philippe Néricault in Nantes (10–11). When they reached the coast in early March, they boarded the *Durance*, a five-hundred-ton merchant vessel helmed by a twenty-eight-year-old captain from Le Havre.[17]

On March 16 the *Durance* charted a course for the voyage that took Caillot, his fellow passengers, and the ship's forty-eight-man crew across the Atlantic to Saint Domingue, through the Gulf of Mexico to the Balize (a fortified outpost at the mouth of the Mississippi River), and finally up the Mississippi to the port of New Orleans. Sixteen weeks after its departure from Lorient, the *Durance* dropped anchor in the Gulf

---

16. From 1716 to 1720, France rolled out a series of financial reforms under the direction of Scotsman John Law in an attempt to stabilize an economy drained by decades of continental wars. The reforms, which included the creation of a national bank, issuance of paper money, and a stock scheme premised on investment in the newly formed Company of the Indies in general, and the Louisiana colony in particular, culminated in a spectacular stock-market crash, known as the Mississippi Bubble, in 1720. On John Law, his financial schemes, and the Mississippi Bubble, see Greenwald, "Company Towns and Tropical Baptisms," 39–56; Jacques Cellard, *John Law et la Régence: 1715–1729* (Paris: Plon, 1996); and Antoin E. Murphy, *John Law: Economic Theorist and Policy-maker* (Oxford: Oxford University Press, 1997).

17. Armament of the *Durance*, 16 March 1729, Fonds de la Marine à Lorient, Service historique de la Défense, (FML), 1P168-244, 2P2-23, no. 624.

of Mexico. Contrary currents prevented the ship from approaching closer than two leagues' distance from the Mississippi's mouth, forcing passengers to load themselves and their trunks into shore-bound pirogues. The first people the travelers encountered in Louisiana were not fellow Frenchmen or Native Americans but rather enslaved African boatmen owned by the Company of the Indies. Africans bore them ashore, half rowing, half carrying the small boats over sandbanks and mud lumps, maneuvering their charges through the tangle of dead cypress and tupelo trees that obstructed their passage to the Balize.

Though it was the gateway to Louisiana, the Balize was only a stopover, a place where travelers took brief respite en route upriver. After gathering provisions travelers faced a week or more of difficult maneuvering against the river's current before reaching New Orleans. Plagued by oppressive heat, devoured by mosquitoes, and often suffering from nutritional deficiencies from their time at sea, some new arrivals survived the overseas crossing only to perish during the thirty-five-league ascent to the capital.

The slave ship *Vénus* arrived at the Balize from the company's Senegal concession with a cargo of 320 bondsmen and bondswomen in late June, at roughly the same time as the *Durance*. Caillot and the other recently disembarked company employees faced the added responsibility of overseeing boats full of these newly arrived African captives. As a white male representative of the Company of the Indies, Caillot found himself deputized as an impromptu overseer, tasked with supervising the captives' transport to the company plantation across the river from New Orleans (in present-day Algiers Point). Within hours of setting off from the Balize, "four Negroes died of scurvy, which," according to Caillot, "ordinarily strikes most of them when they leave the ships to go on land" (70).

Finally, on July 13, 1729, Caillot reached Louisiana's capital. His journey from Paris spanned fifty-one days and more than six thousand miles, but the eight days it took to ascend the Mississippi were more exhausting "than the whole crossing from France" (68). His relief at reaching New Orleans was clear: "From then on we were done with the war, plague, and famine we had faced during this little trip. War, because it had been necessary for us to have stick in hand to keep the Negroes under control; plague, for the stench that the scurvy-ridden people had given us; and famine, because as a rule we had nothing to eat" (74).

Caillot spent two years in New Orleans as a bookkeeping clerk. He passed his days in the compound of newly constructed buildings known as *la Direction* (see fig. 2), which filled the entire block bounded by the quay on one side and Chartres, Saint-Pierre (St. Peter), and Toulouse Streets on the others. The headquarters were, according to Caillot, "very well built, both grand and spacious" (78), with living quarters for

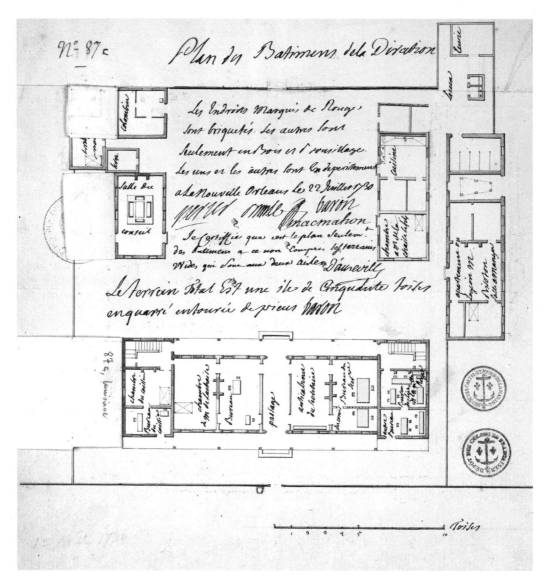

Figure 2. Floor plan of the company's Louisiana headquarters (*la Direction*) in New Orleans. Caillot likely worked in the bookkeeping offices, seen here at lower right. *Plan des batimens de la Direction*, signed by Etienne Périer, Antoine Bruslé, Pierre Le Baron, and Laurent MacMahon, 22 July 1730. (FR. ANOM. Aix-en-Provence. 04DFC 87C)

Director General Jacques de La Chaise and his family, a great meeting hall decked out with a tapestry as well as the requisite crucifix and portrait of Louis XV, and three offices. The first office was occupied by superior council staff, namely a secretary and two assistants. The second housed the special accounts of the old *régie*. These were, in effect, accounts leftover from the previous regime, including those established by former governor Jean-Baptiste Le Moyne de Bienville, who was recalled to France during the company's reorganization in 1723.[18] A staff of seven managed the previous administration's affairs with an eye toward merging the old accounts with the new. Last were the company's bookkeeping offices, headed by François Chastang, who oversaw a staff of eight subordinate bookkeepers and clerks—Caillot, De Troyes, and fellow *Durance* shipmates Gontier and De Bussy now among them—in the New Orleans offices.

Here clerks tracked inventory reports from the company's multiple storehouses, balanced incoming and outgoing receipts, and maintained credit and debit sheets for colonists and Indians trading with the company. The company oversaw nearly a dozen comptoirs during its tenure in Louisiana from 1717 to 1731, including outposts in the Illinois country; at the Balize; in the Mobile, Natchez, Natchitoches, and Wabash settlements; and among the Alabama, Missouri, and Yazoo Indians. Clerks stationed outside the capital all reported to the central offices in New Orleans. Maintaining correspondence—both with outlying trading posts and company offices in Paris and Lorient—represented a large portion of a clerk's daily duties.

In the evenings Caillot retired to a room at the inn kept by Anne and Louis Jarry, whose Royal Street lodgings were favored by company employees and visiting ships' officers alike. Lodgers took full advantage of the couple's hospitality, sharing meals and swapping stories at their landlords' table. Given the inclusion of the year 1730 on Caillot's stylized title page, he likely began compiling notes and drafting *Relation du voyage* in New Orleans while a guest at the Jarrys' inn. From the capital, where he had access to reports, maps, and official correspondence at the office, and word of mouth from fellow guests at the inn, Caillot was able to paint a picture of life in Louisiana that went beyond his own personal experiences. That is not to say that Caillot's day-to-day experiences earned no place in *Relation du voyage*. They did, especially those related to his endless pursuit of members of the opposite sex. But he, like other contemporary observers of colonial life, did not limit himself to personal narrative alone, choosing instead to expand his topical and geographic scope to Louisiana writ large.

For Louisiana, the period coinciding with the company's tenure was one of tremendous growth, despite the colony's negative image in France. In 1712 the colony was home to no more than four hundred nonnative individuals. Less than twenty years later the colonial and enslaved African population had swelled to more than four thousand. Not surprisingly, as the population grew, French settlements expanded beyond the area immediately adjacent to the Gulf Coast. With growth came company investment in

18. Louis XV issued the order to recall Bienville on October 15, 1723, but Bienville lingered in Louisiana until June 1725.

infrastructure (forts, tobacco works, mills, processing facilities, et cetera) and the military officers, administrators, and engineers responsible for overseeing it. Such investment in educated (or at least literate) personnel perhaps helps explain why the period of company tenure produced more *histoires* and epistolary accounts than any other period in Louisiana's colonial history.

Antoine-Simon Le Page du Pratz's three-volume *Histoire de la Louisiane* is arguably the best known and most frequently cited eighteenth-century Louisiana *histoire*. He, like Caillot's other quill-toting contemporaries, came to Louisiana during the company period; he eventually became overseer of the company's west bank plantation. Even the young Ursuline novice Marie-Madeleine Hachard, whose letters to her father were published at his urging in 1728, found herself and her fellow Ursulines in New Orleans due to company machinations. And Jean-François Benjamin Dumont de Montigny and Jean-Charles de Pradel (also known as the Chevalier de Pradel), too, had clear connections to the company in Louisiana; both arrived in the service of the colonial military (whose presence was financed by the company), and both provided accounts of their lives in Louisiana: Dumont de Montigny in an *histoire* published in 1753, Pradel in letters to his family that were eventually published in 1928.[19] Given that Le Page du Pratz, Dumont de Montigny, and Caillot were all resident in the colony at the same time, it is probable that they read or—at the very least—discussed each other's accounts, sharing notes and swapping stories. There are echoes of similarity among all three narratives, though there are also divergences.

Caillot's narrative focus ranged well beyond New Orleans, from the Gulf of Mexico to the Illinois country, though the French settlement at Natchez (now Natchez, Mississippi)—established in 1714 and located ninety leagues upriver from the capital

---

19. Antoine-Simon Le Page du Pratz, *Histoire de la Louisiane*, 3 vols. (Paris: De Bure, l'aîné, 1758); Marie-Madeleine Hachard, *Relation du voyage des dames religieuses Ursulines de Roüen à la Nouvelle-Orléans, parties de France le 22 février 1727 et arrivez à La Louisienne le 23 juillet de la même année* (Rouen: A. Le Prevost, 1728); Jean-François Benjamin Dumont de Montigny, *Mémoires historiques sur la Louisiane* (Paris: C. J. B. Bauche, 1753); Dumont de Montigny, *Regards sur le monde atlantique, 1715–1747*, ed. Carla Zecher, Gordon M. Sayre, and Shannon Lee Dawdy (Quebec: Septentrion, 2008); and Jean-Charles de Pradel de Lamase, *Le chevalier de Pradel: Vie d'un colon français en Louisiane au XVIIIe siècle d'après sa correspondance et celle de sa famille*, ed. A. Baillardel and A. Prioult (Paris: Maisonneuve frères, 1928). See also the accounts of ship captain M. Valette de Laudun, *Journal d'un Voyage à la Louisiane, fait en 1720 par M.****, capitaine de vaisseau du Roi (The Hague: Musier, Fils et Fournier, 1768); Jesuit Father Antoine Laval, *Voyage de la Louisiane* (Paris: Jean Mariette, 1728); and the Chevalier de Pradel Papers, The Historic New Orleans Collection (THNOC), MSS 589. On source-sharing among Caillot's contemporaries, see Gordon M. Sayre, "Composing the History of French Louisiana" in his article "Natchez Ethnohistory Revisited: New Manuscript Sources from Le Page du Pratz and Dumont de Montigny," *Louisiana History* 50 (2009): 433–36.

in the midst of one of the colony's most powerful, populous Indian groups—drew his attention more than any other. Caillot was not alone in his fascination with the Natchez Indians and the neighboring, eponymous French settlement. While New Orleans served as Louisiana's administrative capital under company rule, the lands surrounding Natchez's Fort Rosalie (est. 1716) served as fertile ground for the company's economic aspirations. Natchez, observed Caillot, "is the place where they grow good native tobacco" (89). Efforts to encourage tobacco cultivation in the area began in 1718, just after John Law's Company of the West (predecessor of the Company of the Indies) secured a lucrative monopoly over the production, transport, distribution, and sale of tobacco within the French Empire.

The Natchez tobacco enterprise got off to a slow start, despite initial company claims that the colony would be able to satisfy demand throughout the French Atlantic by 1723. In 1728 Louisiana exported its largest tobacco crop yet: 150,000 pounds. Much of it was of poor quality. The previous two years had been worse, with less than 100,000 pounds shipped during both years combined. (In contrast, the Chesapeake exported nearly 30 million pounds of tobacco per annum in the 1720s.) Year after year, projections for Louisiana tobacco cultivation topped 300,000 pounds, but each year brought far more disappointment than tobacco.

Despite less-than-ideal yields, settlers and plantation managers in pursuit of the tobacco dream poured into the area. From 1719 to 1729 the European population in Natchez grew from fewer than fifty to approximately four hundred. The enslaved African population rose apace—more than five thousand Africans arrived in Louisiana during this period—as did company investment in the infrastructure needed to establish Natchez as the nexus of tobacco production in the French Atlantic. Company slaves, trained by skilled Germans from the Rhineland and Frenchmen from Clérac (both tobacco-growing regions), prepared fields for planting, sheds for drying, and casks and flatboats for shipping, while concession holders and prospective planters actively sought to expand their land holdings.

Back in New Orleans, company administrators sang the praises of Natchez's prospects to directors in Paris, conveniently sidestepping any discussion of rising tensions between the area's settlers and namesake inhabitants. In fact, the establishment of a French settlement in the midst of the Natchez nearly proved Louisiana's undoing. The close proximity of the Indians and their French neighbors produced daily opportunities for frontier exchange, with each group relying on the other for access to trade goods and provisions. Yet their nearness, combined with settlers' hunger for additional land, threatened the colony's stability. Louisiana Governor Etienne Périer's appointment of the hot-headed military officer de Chépart as commandant of Fort Rosalie in 1728 aggravated an already tenuous situation.[20] Less than a year after taking up command, de Chépart moved to confiscate Natchez lands at White Apple village in order to carve out tobacco plantations for himself and Governor Périer. He ordered the Natchez to decamp, but the Natchez chiefs convinced him to delay eviction until after the fall harvest.

The Natchez responded to de Chépart's attempt to push them off their lands by mounting a coordinated attack against their French neighbors. Beginning on November 28, 1729, the Natchez set in motion a plan to destroy the French: they set fire to tobacco fields, drying sheds, warehouses, forts, and houses; scalped and killed more than 200 soldiers, settlers, and indentured servants, including 138 men (de Chépart among them), 35 women, and 56 children; and took captive the remaining French women and children and all of the African slaves. To further undermine the French, Natchez warriors confiscated a recently arrived half-galley filled with more than 300,000 livres' worth of goods intended for the Indian trade.

In early December 1729, Caillot and a group of friends were walking along the levee in New Orleans and "saw a little pirogue coming down the river," carrying a group of people (123). As the pirogue landed, they and other onlookers rushed toward it, "surprised to see some of these people completely naked, others in their drawers, maimed," looking "pale and disfigured" (123–24). These "poor wretches," wrote Caillot, brought news from upriver, where "everything was on fire and covered in blood" (123–24). The bedraggled colonists arriving in New Orleans via pirogue were among only a handful of survivors not taken hostage by the Natchez.

In the weeks and months following the initial attack, which Caillot deemed "the most noteworthy thing that happened while I stayed in that colony" (122), company business ground to a halt as Périer diverted available resources and manpower into a retaliatory campaign. A total of just twenty letters and memoirs were received in France from the Louisiana offices in 1730, less than half the volume received in each of the two previous years. Caillot and his office mates were channeled into one of four newly formed militia units intended to patrol the capital while French forces and their Choctaw allies routed the Natchez. When not on guard duty, Caillot reported that he and his office mates were "bored to death" (134). But he did manage to entertain himself despite the somber shadow cast over New Orleans, as his description of masking on Lundi Gras 1730, just months after the initial attack, makes clear.

Given Caillot's status as company clerk—and one who frequently fraternized with visiting ships' officers bearing rumors from across the Atlantic—he must have sensed an impending shift in company policy in Louisiana. French and Choctaw forces had

---

20. To date, de Chépart's first name, which does not appear in official company records, has eluded historians.

managed to recover most of the hostages, and had tracked down and killed or enslaved hundreds of Natchez Indians. But the economic damage had been done. The company had invested millions in its efforts to create a tobacco economy in Louisiana. From 1723 to 1729 company ships had delivered thousands of enslaved Africans to labor in the fields; most were sold on credit to planters and farmers, who were in debt to the company to the staggering tune of 4.4 million livres. The company had sent skilled tobacco workers to train laborers and planters in producing Chesapeake-style tobacco, and had used its own slaves to clear settler lands surrounding Fort Rosalie. Company funds had financed the creation of an operational support system that relieved planters of the burden of curing, processing, packing, and shipping the crop from Natchez to New Orleans, then across the Atlantic to Lorient, and had underwritten expenses incurred in the Indian trade that was so vital to maintaining peaceful relations.

In the end, it was all for naught. In less time than it took a pirogue to make its way downriver from Natchez to New Orleans, the foundation of the Company of the Indies' Louisiana operations had been destroyed. Marc-Antoine Caillot saw the writing on the wall: as soon as Périer declared victory in his campaign against the Natchez, Caillot put in for a transfer. He left New Orleans on April 1, 1731.

Even if Caillot had remained in Louisiana, he would not have stayed for long. After evaluating the debt owed by Louisiana's colonists, the debt incurred in building a tobacco infrastructure, and the losses sustained by the destruction of both infrastructure and tobacco in the Natchez war, the French Company of the Indies signed a deal relinquishing control of the colony to the king, on January 23, 1731.[21] Caillot's return to France that spring presaged a wave of departures that followed news of the retrocession. By October most company officials and staff had withdrawn from the colony, leaving behind only a handful of midlevel clerks to collect debts owed the company.

After disembarking in Lorient the first week of July, it is unclear whether Caillot remained in Brittany or returned to Paris. Presumably he used the time between his arrival and his departure seven months later—this time for India—to complete the draft of *Relation du voyage*. In any case, on January 14, 1732, Caillot boarded another ship, the *Atalante*, a five-hundred-ton frigate bound for the East Indies.[22] He headed

---

21. On the terms of the retrocession of Louisiana, see "Arrêt du Conseil d'Etat du Roy, concernant la retrocession faite à sa Majesté par la Compagnie des Indes de la Louisiane et du pays d'Illinois," 23 January 1731 (Paris: Imprimerie Royale, 1731), THNOC, MSS 268, folder 18.

22. Armament of the *Atalante*, 14 January 1732, FML, 2 P 3 I.

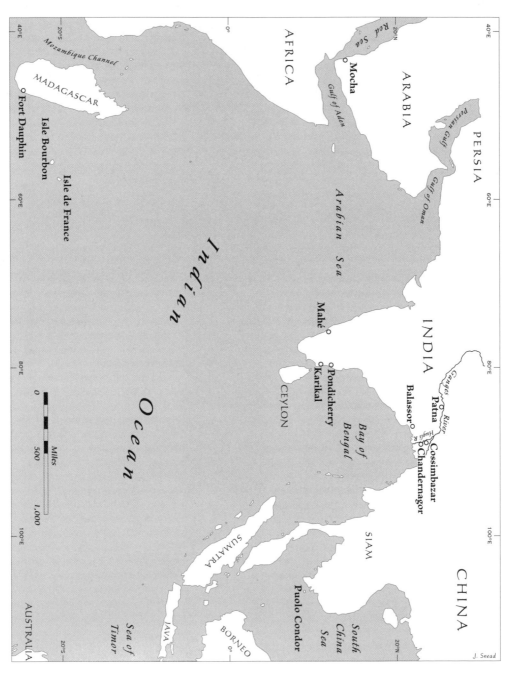

Figure 3. Company-controlled outposts in the Indian Ocean, 1729 (Map by John Snead)

for the ship's last port of call, Pondicherry (now Puducherry), where he assumed a new clerkship in the company's Indian Ocean headquarters.

If company employees viewed New Orleans with skepticism—or outright disdain—Pondicherry must have seemed like the Promised Land. Indeed, the profitability of the company's comptoirs in India—and the corresponding opportunities for personal (illegal) profit—stood in stark contrast with those in Louisiana. When Caillot arrived in August 1732, trade was booming.[23] The previous year, in the 1730–31 trading season, a total of sixteen company ships had hauled merchandise weighing more than 4.9 million livres to France from the company's Indian Ocean outposts (see fig. 3). Their cargos—including thousands of pounds of Indian textiles and cowrie shells destined for the African slave trade—fetched a combined 10,974,000 livres at market. In the year of Caillot's arrival, profits nearly doubled, to 19,421,000 livres, and that despite a 19 percent reduction in the number of ships operating on the East Indian circuit.[24] This was a market worth investing in.

Caillot's professional and financial fortunes shifted dramatically in India. After starting in Pondicherry as a clerk in 1732, he moved quickly through the company's administrative ranks. In 1736 he married into the company equivalent of royalty when he wed Marie-Claire Lucas.[25] Lucas was the great-niece of Pierre de Saintard, who served first as a syndic, from 1723 to 1738, then as a director—the highest attainable post in the company hierarchy—from 1739 to 1759.

Though his wife died days after giving birth to the couple's only child—a girl, Marie-Madeleine Caillot—in 1737,[26] Caillot continued to reap the professional benefits of his association with the Saintard family. His first major promotion, in 1738, can be directly attributed to those ties. In a letter dated January 18, 1738, company directors in Paris recommended that the superior council of Pondicherry "recognize that he is related to M. de Saintard, one of us."[27] Within months the council had promoted him from head clerk to assistant merchant-trader, or *sous marchand*, sending him to Chandernagor (now Chandannagar), in northeast India's Bengal region.[28]

---

23. Disarmament of the *Atalante*, 4 May 1733, FML, 2 P 25 I.

24. Greenwald, "Company Towns and Tropical Baptisms," 225.

25. Marriage of Marc-Antoine Caillot and Marie-Claire Lucas, 23 January 1736, AN, registres de l'état civil, Outre-mer, Pondichéry, 85 Miom 1218.

26. Baptism of Marie-Madeleine Caillot, 12 June 1737; internment of Marie-Claire Lucas, 15 June 1737, AN, registres de l'etat civil, Outre-mer, Pondichéry, 85 Miom 1218.

27. Company directors to the Pondicherry Superior Council, 18 January 1738, *Correspondance du Conseil Supérieur de Pondichéry et de la Compagnie*, ed. Alfred Martineau, vol. 2 (Pondicherry: Société de l'histoire de l'Inde française, 1927), 254.

28. Members of the Pondicherry Superior Council to the Chandernagor council, 30 September 1738, *Correspondance du Conseil Supérieur de Pondichéry avec le Conseil de Chandernagor*, ed. Alfred Martineau, vol. 2 (Pondicherry: Société de l'histoire de l'Inde française, 1927), 40.

Caillot remarried in 1740, wedding Marie-Anne Coquelin, widow of a fellow *sous marchand* and daughter of a company ship captain.[29] Two years later he was again promoted, this time to director of the Balassor comptoir, an outpost at the mouth of the Ganges River, which, as a provisioning outpost and home to river pilots, played a role similar to Louisiana's Balize.[30]

With improved professional prospects came new routes to wealth. Caillot wasted little time establishing profitable trade connections. By 1743 he had amassed enough personal profit to purchase and outfit his own brigantine, the *Cheval Marin*, and was using the ship to run goods up and down the Ganges on his own account. A company inquiry into his activities that year seems to have been exclusively for show: he was never penalized for engaging in these trade activities, which were in direct violation of company policy. In fact, within a year of the inquiry, the superior council of Pondicherry began using Caillot's ship to shuttle company correspondence back and forth between subordinate comptoirs.[31]

Caillot remained in Balassor until December 1744, when he sailed south on board the *Neptune* with his daughter and two domestic servants to visit members of the Saintard family on the Isle Bourbon (now Réunion). Their stay in the Mascarenes was followed by a two-year sojourn in France, presumably for Caillot to tend to personal affairs and allow his then ten-year-old daughter to get acquainted with her Meudon relatives.[32] It is unclear whether his second wife joined her husband and stepdaughter in France.

When Caillot returned to India in 1747, the Pondicherry Superior Council named him a supernumerary member of the Chandernagor Administrative Council, awarding him an annual salary of twelve hundred livres in addition to remuneration he received as a merchant-trader. Repeated incursions by members of the Hindu Maratha Confederacy,[33] beginning in 1744, had left the company's comptoir at Cossimbazar, located forty-six leagues north of Chandernagor, vulnerable to attack. Caillot's appointment allowed the Pondicherry Superior Council to place him in command of

---

29. Caillot was thirty-three and Coquelin was thirty-four. The couple married in Chandernagor, though her family hailed from France's Picardie region. Marriage of Marc-Antoine Caillot and Marie-Anne Coquelin, 1 November 1740, AN, registres de l'état civil, Outre-mer, Chandernagor, 85 Miom 1209.

30. Caillot maintained his status as *sous marchand* in Balassor, picking up additional duties as head (*chef*) of the comptoir there. 28 April 1740, *Correspondance du Conseil Supérieur de Pondichéry avec le Conseil de Chandernagor*, 2:128.

31. Ibid., 4 April 1743 and 4 March 1744, 272 and 311.

32. Members of the Pondicherry Superior Council to company directors and syndics in Paris, 28 November 1748, *Correspondance du Conseil Supérieur de Pondichéry et de la Compagnie*, vol. 3 (1918–19), 36–37; Rôle du *Neptune*, 1743–46, FML, 2 P 33-II.6.

33. The Maratha Confederacy was a political and military alliance formed by supporters of the western Indian kingdom of Maharashtra and its leader, King Sahu. During the mid-eighteenth century the Maratha Confederacy pushed eastward and northward, expanding its power into central India and Bengal.

Bengal-bound French troops without sacrificing any of Chandernagor's six permanent council members.[34]

Caillot's leadership of troops in Cossimbazar led the Pondicherry council to recommend his transfer back to Chandernagor and permanent appointment to its council in 1750, but as late as December 1751 he was still awaiting a fully commissioned seat. His patience was ultimately rewarded the following year when, instead of receiving a seat on the Chandernagor council, he ascended to the company's highest administrative body in the Indian Ocean—the Pondicherry Superior Council—though his tenure did not last long.[35]

In 1756 a war that began in Europe between age-old continental rivals spilled over into the warring powers' colonial territories. The Seven Years' War (known more commonly in American history as the French and Indian War) reached Chandernagor in March 1757. In the course of less than two weeks, British forces, under the command of Colonel Robert Clive, sacked the French fort and settlement there, forcing a near-complete evacuation of the colonial population; the British claimed the conquered territory as their own.[36] Caillot, who was active in the defensive campaign, was wounded during the siege and unable to evacuate with the majority of the population. He remained at his home in Chandernagor until early 1758, when he boarded a Portuguese vessel, the *Nossa Senhora dos Prazeres*, presumably to seek asylum in one of France's remaining Indian Ocean territories. The *Nossa Senhora dos Prazeres* never reached its final destination. Instead, it sank, with all its passengers, crew, and cargo, off the coast of India.[37]

After traveling the globe for nearly thirty years as an employee of the French Company of the Indies, Marc-Antoine Caillot died in a shipwreck on February 24, 1758. He was fifty-one. His second wife had preceded him to the grave, but he left behind a twenty-one-year-old daughter and a considerable fortune.[38] From having nothing but a meager salary and solid family connections when he began his career in 1728, Caillot had propelled himself upward—seizing opportunities and exploiting relationships—to

---

34. Members of the Pondicherry Superior Council to company directors and syndics in Paris, 10 January 1748, *Correspondance du Conseil Supérieur de Pondichéry et de la Compagnie*, 4:389, 457; Members of the Pondicherry Superior Council to the Chandernagor council, 11 July 1748 and 28 November 1748, *Correspondance du Conseil Supérieur de Pondichéry avec le Conseil*, 3:25, 36–37.

35. Company of the Indies nomination of Sieur Caillot to the Superior Council of Pondicherry, 1752, Archives nationales d'outre-mer (ANOM), Col E 59.

36. After gaining control of Pondicherry, Chandernagor, and Karikal during the war, England returned these territories to France during the peace settlement of 1763.

37. Marc-Antoine Caillot Quittance, 13 May 1761, AN, Minutier central des notaires, Cote ET XXXV, 708.

38. Internment of Marie-Anne Coquelin, 26 August 1756, AN, registres de l'état civil, Chandernagor, 85 Miom 1210.

become one of the wealthiest, highest-ranked men in the company's Indian Ocean network. At the time of his death, his net worth was valued at more than 74,000 livres. As part of his succession, his daughter and son-in-law, Claude St. Michel, both of whom then resided in Paris, inherited liquid assets in the amount of 17,239 livres. Real estate holdings in Chandernagor composed the rest of his fortune.[39] To date, no succession or inventory of Caillot's moveable goods has been found, though one surely exists somewhere in the recesses of the French national archives' notarial records.

Two Hundred Fifty Years in the Life of a Manuscript

Completed sometime between Caillot's departure from Louisiana in 1731 and his death in 1758, *Relation du voyage* was inaccessible to the public until 2005. Its whereabouts during the first two centuries of its existence are unclear, though its early-twentieth-century history suggests it may have been kept for a time in a convent in the small Breton town of Malestroit, France. It is not known if the manuscript remained in France when Caillot sailed for India or was carried back there during his trip home in the mid-1740s. It is unlikely that it descended through his daughter, who lived out her life in Paris following her father's death. More likely, it remained in company circles, given that it eventually turned up in a Breton convent less than sixty miles from the company's home port at Lorient.

The first printed mention of *Relation du voyage* appeared in August 1939, when Mother Superior Yvonne-Aimée de Jésus and Assistant Superior Marie-Anne de Jésus, both members of an Augustinian convent in Malestroit, traveled across the Atlantic to Canada aboard the *Empress of Australia* to help commemorate the tercentennial of Augustinian presence in Quebec City.[40] They brought with them the Caillot manuscript, which had, according to Mother Yvonne-Aimée, come "from an old, noble French family" who bestowed it upon the Augustinian convent at Malestroit.[41]

Before the French Revolution, this particular convent had been home to a group of Ursuline nuns who ran a small, private hospital catering mainly to ships' officers and white-collar employees en route from the company's port in Lorient to its administrative headquarters in Paris. It is tempting to think that Caillot may have written

---

39. Real estate values, Chandernagor, 13 January 1757, ANOM, C 2 93, fo. 41v; Marc-Antoine Caillot Quittance.

40. *L'Action Catholique* (Québec), 19, 21, 27, and 29 August 1939.

41. Translation my own. Damase Potvin, "Un intéressant document," *L'Action Catholique* (Québec), 28 August 1939.

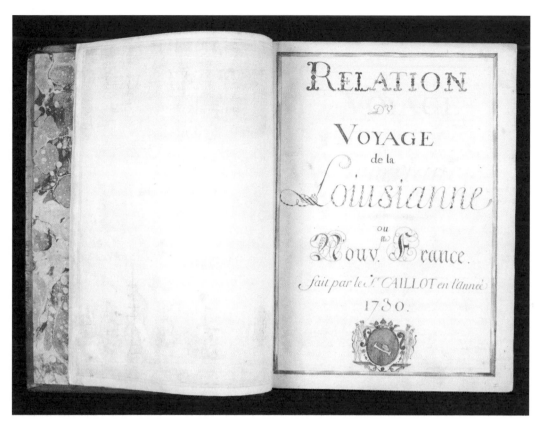

Figure 4. Title page of *Relation du voyage*, by Marc-Antoine Caillot, between 1729 and 1758 (The Historic New Orleans Collection, 2005.0011)

Relation du voyage during a convalescent stay with the Ursulines on his way back to Paris in 1731, but there are impediments to such a thesis. The Ursulines were expelled from Malestroit in 1792, their possessions confiscated and sold in the midst of France's revolutionary fervor. The convent then sat empty for nearly forty years before its purchase by an order of La Mennais Brothers in 1828. Not until 1866 did the Augustinians take possession. It is unlikely (though not impossible) that the manuscript remained within the convent's walls over the course of multiple nineteenth-century property transfers. A more plausible possibility is that *Relation du voyage* was in fact donated to the Augustinians of Malestroit sometime during the late nineteenth century, after having sat for some years on a shelf in a personal library. Whatever the backstory, there are no extant records—no correspondence, no receipts, no surviving nuns' tales—related to the Caillot manuscript in the Augustinian archives in Malestroit.

The paper trail truly begins only in 1939, when the two Augustinians from Malestroit carried the manuscript with them to Quebec City. The manuscript's title page, bearing the words "Relation du voyage de la Louisianne ou Nouvelle France," must have led the Malestroit Augustinians to believe it held some intrinsic value to the keepers of Québécois history (Nouvelle France, or New France, was the name most frequently associated with French Canada) (see fig. 4). On the surface this seems like a fair assessment, though a quick scan of the document reveals that the author employed "Nouvelle France" in its broadest sense, applying the label to all of France's American possessions rather than exclusively to Canada. In an interview with the Quebec newspaper *L'Action Catholique*, Mother Yvonne-Aimée expressed her desire to sell the manuscript "to a Canadian or American archive" to help raise money for her order's good works.[42] The Nazi invasion of Poland on September 1, 1939, prevented her from personally carrying out this wish. Instead, Mother Yvonne-Aimée and Sister Marie-Anne returned to France, leaving *Relation du voyage* in the care of their Québécois counterparts. The Quebec City Augustinians sold the manuscript to Quebec's provincial government in February of the following year, with the intent that it be housed at the Musée de la province (now the Musée national des beaux-arts du Québec), then under the direction of Curator Pierre-Georges Roy. In a letter dated March 8, 1940, Deputy-Provincial Secretary Jean Bruchési authorized payment to the Malestroit Augustinians in the amount of 9,000 French francs, or approximately 3,900 dollars in today's currency.[43]

What happened to the manuscript after its 1940 purchase is unclear, though at least one typescript version was made and deposited in the Quebec provincial archive. The 1960s were a tumultuous period for Quebec's archival materials, which were moved out from under the provincial museum umbrella in 1961 and maintained as a stand-alone provincial archive until 1971. That year, the provincial archive joined Canada's national archive system as the Archives nationales du Québec. From 1940 to 1964 no further mention of the Caillot manuscript was made, and the volume does not seem to have been formally accessioned. In 1964 the archive's new director, Bernard Weilbrenner, noted its existence as one of several nongovernmental "collections worth mentioning by name."[44]

In 1967 Weilbrenner exchanged a series of letters about the Caillot manuscript with New Orleans–based researcher Henry Pitot, in which Weilbrenner authorized the

---

42. Translation my own. Ibid.

43. Copies of invoices and receipts dated 16 and 28 February 1940, and a letter to Pierre-Georges Roy dated 8 March 1940 from the Secrétariat de la Province du Québec were provided by the Bibliothèque et Archives nationales du Québec (BAnQ) in 2008. In 1939 one US dollar equaled 37.8 French francs. Modern-day dollar equivalents are based on data from the Consumer Price Index (CPI) calculator, United States Department of Labor online, Bureau of Labor Statistics, accessed April 10, 2012, http://www.bls.gov/data/inflation_calculator.htm.

44. Translation my own. Bernard Weilbrenner, "Les Archives du Québec," *Revue d'histoire de l'Amérique française* 18 (1964): 11. This 1964 reference is unique in the history of the *Revue d'histoire*, which was first published in 1947. There is also no mention of Caillot or his manuscript in the *Bulletin des recherches historiques*, which served as the official publication of the Quebec provincial archives from 1923 to 1968.

copying of the complete typescript for Pitot's personal use, but when pressed about the whereabouts of the original document, Weilbrenner wrote, "The manuscript, I believe, was loaned to the Quebec Archives some years ago by a French Hospitalière Sister for copying."[45] Weilbrenner's response raises some serious questions about the document's past: What happened to the original manuscript between 1940 and its reappearance at auction sixty-four years later? Was it ever officially incorporated into the Quebec archives, or was it, as Weilbrenner suggested, only loaned to the archives for copying?[46] And, if that was the case, what was the purpose of Quebec's provincial government's authorizing payment of nine thousand French francs to Mother Superior Yvonne-Aimée? These questions remain unanswered.

Relation du voyage resurfaced in the fall of 2004, when it was put up for auction through Christie's New York.[47] That December the manuscript was purchased by The Historic New Orleans Collection. The seller was anonymous at the time of the sale and remained unidentified at the time this publication went to press, in October 2012.

When the manuscript arrived in New Orleans, Collection staff members carefully recorded its condition—noting stray pencil marks, tears, water stains, and evidence of previous conservation efforts. Staff photographers then digitized the entire document, making page scans available to researchers for the first time in the document's more-than-two-hundred-fifty-year history. The manuscript itself, bound together with an unrelated item published in the late eighteenth century, was put on display in the museum's Louisiana History Galleries until it was sent to the Conservation Center for Art and Historic Artifacts (CCAHA) in Philadelphia for conservation and repair in early 2012.

The work undertaken by the CCAHA included restitching the manuscript's spine and repairing minor tears throughout. CCAHA conservators also cleaned all of Caillot's watercolors, using a combination of manual cleaning with soft brushes and targeted scrapings of accumulated dirt. Four of the watercolors suffered from prior conservation efforts that employed acidic adhesive tape, which was commonly used in manuscript repairs during the first half of the twentieth century, before its damaging qualities were fully understood. Despite the delicate nature of the watercolor medium, CCAHA paper

---

45. Bernard Weilbrenner to Henry Pitot, 21 March and 13 April 1967, THNOC, Henry Pitot Papers, folders 352 and 354, MSS 400.

46. The BAnQ's current catalog also states that the Archives nationales du Québec "purchased a copy of this collection in 1940 from the Reverend Mother Yvonne-Aimée Beauvais, Mother Superior of the Augustinians in Malestroit, France, through sisters from Quebec's Hôtel-Dieu," Fonds sieur Caillot, ZF56, Description fonds, BAnQ (translation my own).

47. Lot 299, *Fine Printed Books and Manuscripts Including Americana*, Christie's New York Auction Catalog, 16 December 2004, 138–41.

conservators were able to remove much of the adhesive residue (see fig. 5). The result of this specialized, careful conservation is that Caillot's text and watercolors have been stabilized and preserved for future generations.

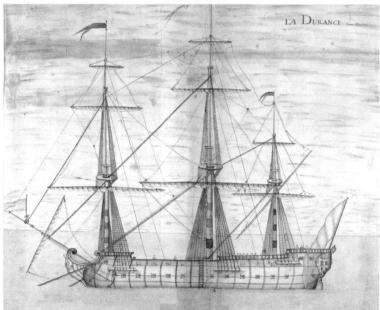

Figure 5. Pre- and postconservation photos of Caillot's watercolor depicting the *Durance* (Photos courtesy of the Conservation Center for Art and Historic Artifacts, Philadelphia)

Editor's Note

In editing *Relation du voyage*, I made every effort to cleave as closely as possible to the spirit of Caillot's original manuscript. In order to render the text more accessible to modern readers, I have made certain changes: the most significant reflect stylistic shifts in both the English and French languages that have occurred in the more than two and a half centuries since Caillot wrote his manuscript. Sentences—which sometimes ran to more than twenty lines—have been broken throughout, as have paragraphs. Punctuation and capitalization, too, have been standardized and modernized.

The fluidity of eighteenth-century French orthography, in particular when it came to names, presented another challenge. For clarity, all proper nouns—including names of people, places, and Indian groups—have been standardized to their most commonly accepted spellings. Thus "Biloxcis" was changed to "Biloxi," "Chartre" to "Chartres," "D'Hautherive" to "d'Hauterive," and so on. In the rare cases when a name could not be corroborated by other sources, Caillot's original spelling was retained.

Caillot separated his manuscript into two parts: "An American Journey," in which he recounts his travels from Paris to New Orleans, and "An Account of the Mississippi Country and the Indians Who Inhabit This Land," which details life in the Louisiana colony. Within each part, Caillot made further subdivisions, which have been reproduced typographically, closely following Caillot's original written signals, which include larger, heavier type, line spaces, subheadings, and asterisks.

Of the thirteen watercolor illustrations in *Relation du voyage* (reproduced here in galleries one and three), Caillot signed four, initialed two, and dated six. Ten appear to be his original creations, and three are of questionable origin: *Plan du Fort Sauvage des Natchez* and *Plan de la guerre des Natchez* are notably similar to contemporary plans drawn and painted by anonymous artists or engineers that can be found in various repositories in France, including the Bibliothèque nationale de France in Paris and Archives nationales d'outre-mer in Aix-en Provence; and the depiction of the mouth of the Mississippi River, titled *Carte particulière de l'embouchure du Fleuve Mississipy* [*sic*], is strikingly similar to a detail included on an anonymous 1723 map now housed at the Newberry Library in Chicago. Whether Caillot based these three illustrations on others' work, or vice-versa, is unclear.

Readers interested in viewing the original Caillot manuscript may do so at The Historic New Orleans Collection. To facilitate research, original folio page numbers appear in brackets throughout this edition. Each bracketed page number indicates the beginning of the corresponding folio page.

Caillot occasionally provided his own explanatory notes to help readers understand technical terms. In both the original manuscript and this edition, Caillot's notes are marked with asterisks. These notes appear at the bottom of the relevant pages, just above the editor's numbered footnotes.

Erin M. Greenwald
June 7, 2012
New Orleans

Translator's Note

One of the earliest meanings of the Latin word "*translatio*" was the removal of holy relics, usually the remains of a saint, from one location to another. There is some truth in that definition today, for certainly the job of a translator is to remove the meaning of a text written in one language and transfer it to another language as faithfully as possible. It is inevitably an imperfect job, because so much of meaning has deep roots in culture, place, and time.

I have attempted to accomplish three things in my translation of Marc-Antoine Caillot's manuscript. The first, of course, is to make sense of the text and allow it to flow in a natural way for modern readers of English. The second is to give the text a slightly antiquated feel, by using certain period words and phrases and avoiding current expressions. And the third is to occasionally use phrasing that might suggest a Frenchman, not completely fluent in English, attempting to express himself in this language.

Caillot himself had to choose words carefully when referring to things that were unknown in the Old World. In some cases, he appropriated Native American words, such as "calumet" (ceremonial pipe) or "*boucané*" (a method of smoking meat), and at other times he used Old World words incorrectly to describe novel, New World creatures, such as "crocodile" for "alligator," or "tiger" for "cougar."

I left words in French only if there was no acceptable English equivalent, such as the titles "*sieur,*" "*monsieur,*" "*madame,*" and "*mademoiselle,*" as well as historically significant terms such as "*petites nations*" and "*comptoir,*" both duly noted and explained by historian and editor Erin Greenwald. Some word choices were not so easily resolved. It took much thought, time, and collaboration with others to decide what terms to use for "*nègre*" and "*sauvage.*" Though today "Negro" is commonly considered a derogatory descriptor, it was a neutral term in previous centuries, so I left the term in its literal form. The word "savage" used to describe a Native American also has negative connotations; many readers may not remember that the idea of the "noble savage" was in vogue during the Enlightenment. "Indian"—though geographically incorrect, and recently considered politically incorrect—was the term most widely used to describe Native Americans during previous centuries, so it was chosen for its slightly antiquated undertones. The word "savages" does appear in the translation, though it is translated from a different word, "*barbares*." I chose "savages" rather than the more literal "barbarians" because of the cultural and geographical context.

I found it especially rewarding to learn about the earliest inhabitants of the region, most of whom are either long gone or reduced to a few hundred members; we know them today mainly as toponyms: Illinois, Arkansas, Alabama, Yazoo, Biloxi, Natchez, Tunica, Bayagoula, and Houma, to name just a few. Many other geographical features retain their eighteenth-century names, albeit in English: Horn Island, Ship Island, Bayou St. John, and Santa Rosa Island, among others. In the translation, Native American names appear in their English forms, as do place names.

I am grateful to The Historic New Orleans Collection for having entrusted this translation to me. I especially extend my thanks to Harry Redman, who recommended me for the project; Jessica Dorman, who believed in me and encouraged me throughout the project; and Erin Greenwald, who never tired or complained during the back and forth of working out details, and who provided encouragement and much-needed suggestions in areas of the text that were awkward or poorly phrased. I also thank my family and friends, especially my husband Quentin and my son David, who read, listened to, and discussed areas of my translation that were problematical.

Teri F. Chalmers
June 15, 2012
New Orleans

Gallery 1

Pages from Marc-Antoine Caillot, *Relation du Voyage de la
Louisianne . . .*, drafted between 1729 and 1758; The Historic
New Orleans Collection, *2005.0011*

PLATE 1

RELATION

DU

VOYAGE

de la

Louisianne

ou

N.lle France.

fait par le S.r CAILLOT en l'anneé

1730.

PLATE 2

VOYAGE

de

L'Amerique

M'étant proposé de vous faire part d'une petite relation en abregé des particularitez de mon voyage à La N.^{lle} France, je suis bien aise avant que de le mettre au jour de vous prevenir sur le mauvais stile de l'Auteur. et sur les deffaux que j'y ay pus commettre par mon peu de Capacité; mais d'un autre costé ceux qui en feront la Lecture. me feront l'honneur d'y ajouter foy, ny ayant

PLATE 3

demeuroit cet homme; enfin apres avoir bien fait des tours nous
arrivames chez luy, il nous pria assez legerement a diner, mais
voyant que nous nous en estions aucunement deffendu et que nous
l'avions librement accepté et aussy que nous partions de faire
apporter chacuns notre Bagage chez luy, cela luy fit peur
et apprehenda si fort que nous ne demeurassions quelque jour
dans Sa maison que pour cet Effet il prevint a nous Loger ailleurs.

je fit avertir de notre arrivée un nommé Jarry, traiteur chez
lequel dés le Soir même nous fumes coucher;

Le landemain nous nous habillames pour aller voir Mr.
de Berrier. qui est Commandant General de la Province de
la Louisianne ou nous fumes tres bien receus, il nous promit
que de tout ce qui dependroit de luy pour nous rendre Service
qu'il le feroit de bon fœur, nous prumes congé de luy, et du
gouvernement nous fumes a la direction ou Mr de la fraise directeur
general et Mlles ses filles nous resurent tres bien, je leurs
remis des lettres de leurs parents et ensuitte ou nous presenta
le Caffé apres avoir causé pend 2 heures nous nous retirames
Et le Landemain nous primes Seance dans les Bureaux

Voila la relation de mon voyage depuis paris jusqu'a la
Louisianne; je vais maintenant vous donner celle de ce pays
Des peuples qui l'habitent et de quelle maniere ils se gouvernent
ou a la Suitte d'icelle je reprendray tout ce qui c'est passé pend
le tems de ma résidance en ce pays;

PLATE 4

RELATION

du

MISSISSIPY

et

des Sauvages qui habitent cette Contrée.

Ie Commanceray par la principalle ville nommé la Nouvelle Orleance
Ou se tiennent les Conseils, Superieur, et de regie. composez des cy apres

Sçavoir. Conseil Superieur

M.
de Pezieu General de toutte la Province de la Louisianne;

Mou de la Chaise cy devant directeur general, et Commissaire deputé par le roy

Mac Mahon presentement directeur General et P.^er Conseiller,

Brulé Commissaire Extraordinaire des troupes et Second Con.^er

Dausseville Commissaire de la marine et troisieme cou.

Prat medecin Botaniste payé du roy et quatrieme Cou.

Le Baron astrologue, et Cinquieme conseiller

Fleuriau Procureur General, et juge de Police

PLATE 5

Chez les Jesuistes qui sont assez bien fortifiez ;

Le 23 dud nous fumes avertis que les Sauvages Biloxis avoient été chassez de leurs village par les chactas qui en avoient tués deux pour avoir pris le party des françois, et qu'ils venoient se refugier au pres de nous les Chactas leurs avoient dit aussy que dans peu ils viendroient nous sacager.

Le 10 Avril, Landemain de Pagues on brula une Sauvagesse Natchere que les thonicas avoient pris et qu'ils nous amenerent pour nous vanger sur elle des tourments que sa nation et elle même avoient exercé Contre les françois, Voicy Comme on la fit mourir.

M. de Perrier ne voulant point que les françois s'en mellassent pour cet Effet abandonna cette malheureuse aux Thonicas qui l'avoient amené pour en faire ce qu'ils voudroient, dabord qu'ils Sceurent qu'elle étoit a leur disposition ils se preparerent la ville à dancer les dances et le Calumet de mort qu'ils ne chante que lors qu'ils veulent tuer quelquuns ou se declarer la guerre entre Eux, ce calumet est mataché en noir.

Lors qu'ils eurent faits leur preparatif, le Landemain Sur le midy ils furent une partie dans le Bois chercher les cannes les plus seiches et les autres accommoderent deux perches de cette maniere qu'ils nomment en fait de Bruler Cadre, pour y attacher cette miserable ;

Lors qu'ils Eurent finy ils se matacherent, apres firent le cris de mort autour de ce cadre et se mirent a courir comme s'ils eussent été possedez du diable et toujours en Criant (c'est leur coutume) ils S'en furent au corps de garde ou elle étoit aux fers qui ajustoit un ruban pour tresser ses Cheveux qu'elles

PLATE 6

An American Journey

It having been proposed to me to share with you, in an abridged form, a brief account of the particulars of my journey to New France, I feel I must warn you about the bad style of the author before carrying this to fruition. I must also advise you about faults that I may have committed here due to my lack of ability. But, on the other hand, those who will read this account will do me honor to give credence to it, since to my [2] knowledge I have not said anything untrue. Indeed, I am a long way off from using certain exaggerated digressions, as many historians have done in their works for the purpose of ornamentation and to attract to themselves the applause of a few people who are infatuated with their fable.

Thus I will begin my story in Paris, which I left on February 19, 1729, the day that I set out on my route. My first stop was at Palaiseau, and from there to Bonnelles, where I slept. That first day seemed very rough to me because of the weariness of the horse and because of the countless number of thoughts and regrets in having to leave a family who had only shown me manifestations of kindness.[1] Added to the fact that I was leaving several friends, all these things united together upset me so much that I lost both my rest and my appetite. Nonetheless, the night having passed, I had to get back on my horse, which was another source of sorrow, because the farther away I went, the more I was afflicted. In brief, when I arrived at the Lauray ford, which was the second stop, I did not feel any hungrier than usual. On the contrary, I went from bad to worse. When two gentlemen with whom I had left Paris saw me in this state, they did all they could to lift my spirits. They examined me intensely and realized that if I continued on in my sadness, far from making it to the end of my voyage, I would run a great risk of making

---

1. For a recent exploration of the concept of familial "kindness" in the early modern period, see Linda A. Pollock, "The Practice of Kindness in Early Modern Elite Society," *Past and Present* 211 (2011): 121–58.

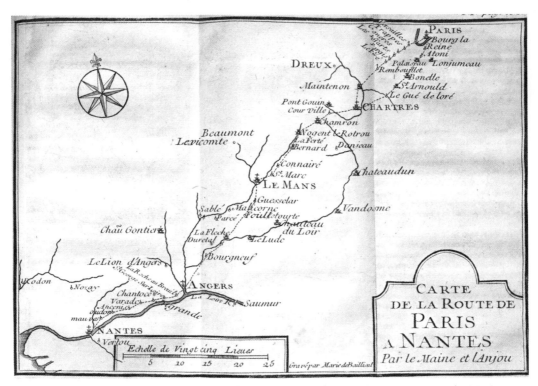

Figure 6. Route taken by Caillot and his traveling companions from Paris to Nantes; map by Marie de Baillard, from Jean-Aymar Piganiol de La Force's *Nouveau voyage de France*. Paris: T. Le Gras, 1724 (Courtesy of Special Collections Research Center, University of Chicago Library)

it only a quarter of the way. Thus, from that point I began to change [3] my mood by erasing for a while thoughts about my parents and friends, which was no small undertaking and which I would never have accomplished if I had not availed myself of some Bacchic liqueur. It was for me a very charming strategy, for, when I had taken a certain dose, I forgot not only my parents and friends but myself as well. After I had rested a few hours, we got back on the horses in order to reach our lodgings in Chartres [see fig. 6]. But before we got there, the eagerness I had to leave the place where I thought I had left all my sorrow made me urge my horse forward with such violence that one of its front feet slipped, causing me to fly over his head, harnessed pretty much like Don Quixote, except, instead of a lance, I had my musket at hand leaning against the saddlebow and my hunting horn around me.[2] They both were quite mistreated, for as a result my musket was broken in half from the blow. That is how I left Beauce.

---

2. The *trompe*, or *corps de chasse* (hunting horn), is better known in English as a "French horn," a term dating to the seventeenth century. The French horn first appeared as a hunting horn in the mid-seventeenth century and quickly evolved into an orchestral instrument. The French horn played by Caillot would not have included pitch-altering valves, as valves did not appear on brass wind instruments until the early nineteenth century.

I arrived in Chartres, a town situated on a knoll whose approaches are very bad, chiefly in the winter. It is necessary to go down appalling paths and then go up again before entering the town. The streets are paved quite badly and are very narrow. Except for that, they are for the most part very rapid. Thus, having arrived next to the mill, the first person who appeared before my eyes was Mademoiselle Jutos. At that moment I felt a certain joy, which was soon dissipated by the memory of the time I had spent with her so agreeably in Meudon.[3] [4] First she invited me to come have supper at her house, where she received me most graciously. I was charmed to see her, but this pleasure cost me dearly, for it again plunged me into my former sorrows, especially when we had to take leave of each other. Since I had to get back on the horse very early the next day, I said goodbye to her in the most tender way that I could and left her around midnight. From there I went to rejoin my traveling companions. I went to bed, but it was quite impossible for me to get the least bit of rest, since my thoughts were as muddled as they were before. As soon as day broke, we continued on our route, and by dinner we were at Champeron,[4] and by bedtime we arrived at Nogent le Rotrou, which is in Perche.

The next day we arrived at La Ferté Bernard for dinner and at St. Marc for supper.[5] Both are little villages, and the latter is quite pretty. At the inn where we dismounted we found a plump, jolly girl who took us to a room, where she made sure we were lacking in nothing and took very good care of me. She was the innkeeper's daughter. I received her attentions with pleasure and I showed her my gratitude for this.

While waiting for supper, I went for a walk with my hunting horn, since this house was situated on the edge of a beautiful wood with clusters of tall trees where there were very beautiful avenues. I found some magnificent echoes there, which provided me with much more pleasure than I might have expected, for I was not long without company.

When I had not gone too far from the [5] château of Monsieur de St. Marc, I saw two young ladies coming toward me. I did not remain long without talking to them and without finding out who they were as well. While conversing with them, I was entranced by their beauty and I found myself between them, like a piece of iron between two magnets, not knowing which of the two had more merit. Nevertheless, Mademoiselle

---

3. Located approximately midway between central Paris and the Château de Versailles, Meudon was home to the Château de Meudon. The château was one of several households in the network of royal châteaux served by the Maison du Roi, the term used to refer collectively to the religious, military, and domestic personnel who served France's royal family. Caillot's father and uncle were both members of the Maison du Roi at Meudon, and Caillot spent his childhood in the eponymous town.

4. Probably Champrond rather than Champeron, as Caillot transcribed.

5. Dinner, taken in the early afternoon, was often the main meal of the day; supper, a lighter meal, was taken in the evening.

de St. Marc, although with an attitude of great disregard, allowed me to see, by means of a headdress half fallen down, the most beautiful eyes and the most beautiful mouth that nature has ever formed, the loveliest and most perfect under heaven. Delighted by my fortunate encounter, I was already beginning to feel the effect of so many delights upon my heart, which had already begun to feel the regret and suffering that their absence was going to cause me.

At that moment I saw a very good-looking young man approaching us. He resembled his sister so much that, if she were back where he was, I would have sworn that it was she, disguised as a boy. He begged me on behalf of his father to come to the château, for his father wished to see me. Even though I was not at all as clean as I would have wished, but only as clean as a horseman who had just set foot upon the ground, with my riding boots still on, I nonetheless could not refrain from the honor of giving my hand to Mademoiselle de St. Marc, who accepted it with kindness and a completely charming naiveté, and I saw that this did not cause her any grief at all. On the contrary, she listened with pleasure to what I had the privilege of telling her. Then, when I was at the door of the apartment, I entered and made my excuses to Monsieur and Madame de St. Marc for presuming to appear before them in my riding boots and in the state I was in. They [6] showed me the utmost hospitality and insisted that I put myself at ease. After questioning me about Paris and where I was going, they most kindly asked me to have supper with them, which I dared not refuse due to the honor they showed me.

We sat down at the dinner table, where we were attended to not like in the countryside but in the Parisian fashion—that is, very properly. After supper, the lady of the house asked me to play the horn, which I did well enough, although I had eaten quite a bit. The echoes were charming in that wood; all I was lacking was the opportunity to be able to get back to the same point where I had been before with the lady's daughter, but, on the other hand, my eyes gave me the satisfaction of making her understand the straits I found myself in. Since it was already getting late, I wanted to take my leave of them and thank them for the honor they had willingly shown me, but I found it quite impossible. They made me come back inside to drink various liqueurs, and Monsieur de St. Marc said that he had business at the Saillard ford very early in the morning and that he would take me there. He said that we would get there before the courier and that he would tell one of his servants to go to the courier service to tell them not to wait.[6]

---

6. While on land, Caillot and his traveling companions usually followed the *grands chemins*, or royal roads, that radiated out of Paris to the Atlantic and Mediterranean coasts and to France's land borders to the north, west, and south. For added protection against potential roadside attacks, the trio often traveled with the mail couriers from one *relais de poste* (postal exchange) to the next, stopping when necessary for lodging, food, horse care, and even religious services. For more on the role of *grands chemins*, *postes*, and messengers in ancien régime France, see Erin

I lay, in fact, in a very nice bed, even though if I said that I slept I would be lying, if I were to dare to say it. For combined with thousands of pleasant ideas that came to my mind that night, I was in a room close to Mademoiselle de St. Marc's, unable to say even one word to her, which made me feel like someone who has a piece of bread but cannot get to the roast, and has to be satisfied with the smoke from the roast.

[7] **When day** broke I got up to try to get ready to go to the inn, but was quite astonished to see Monsieur de St. Marc come into my room all ready to leave. We passed through his room, where he had a table set for breakfast, consisting of a soup and a selection of cold meats. Madame de St. Marc was in her bed. What grieved me was that before leaving I had the misfortune of not seeing the object of my attentions one more time, because it was too early. Nonetheless, we had breakfast, and then I took leave of the lady of the house by thanking her for the kindness that she had shown me. I was very touched by the signs of friendship she had shown me. She said farewell to me, saying to me that I would perhaps lose France forever, since I was going to a very dangerous environment. I thanked her once again for all that she had done for me, and that is how I left her. Monsieur de St. Marc and I then climbed into a carriage, and we were at the coach stop before the courier even arrived. Since he had business at a distance of a league and a half from the Saillard ford, he took leave of me with all the tenderness of a real father, and I of him with more regret than you can imagine.

I lit myself a big fire while waiting for the courier to arrive, and I had time to abandon myself to my daydreams and the encounter that I had had and then lost almost immediately. While I was daydreaming in this way I saw my traveling companions coming. They were rather upset with me for [8] my habit of leaving them at almost all the places we stopped to rest. I defended myself, saying that I had found myself so honored and urged with such charm that I had not been able to avoid responding to the polite requests that had been addressed to me, which were of the sort that would rejuvenate me. We then dined, and being as usual very well attended to, I drank more than I normally did in order to chase away a sadness that asked for nothing better than to take root again in my thoughts. Then we got back on the horses in order to get to La Flèche [see fig. 7], a very pretty town where we would be staying that night.

M. Greenwald, "Company Towns and Tropical Baptisms: From Lorient to Louisiana on a French Atlantic Circuit" (PhD diss., The Ohio State University, 2011), 65–69; Georges Livet, "La route royale et la civilisation française de la fin du XVe au milieu du XVIIIe siècle," in *Les Routes de France depuis les origines jusqu'à nos jours*, ed. Guy Michaud (Paris: L'Association pour la diffusion de la pensée française, 1959), 57–100; René Héron de Villefosse, *Histoire des grandes routes de France* (Paris: Librairie Académique Perrin, 1975), 17–22; and Eugène Vaillé, *Histoire générale des Postes françaises*, 6 vols. (Paris: Presses Universitaires de France, 1947–53).

Before we arrived there, as I was not very well mounted, I fell into a hole that had at least five to six feet of water in it, my nag at times on top of me and at others underneath me, which made me drink more than I would have liked. Eventually, by struggling hard, I got myself untangled and got out of the hole, half-drowned, and my horse as well. I left one of my pistols behind, then climbed back up on my beast, both of us staggering off in a very bad state of affairs, to try to catch up with the courier, who was already very far away. Well, I still had five leagues to cover in very cold weather, so that by the time I arrived I was frozen in my boots. The one named De Troyes, who was my traveling companion, had made fun of our recent tumble and was still taunting us about it.[7] So then he insisted on making his horse prance about, since his horse looked a bit better than the rest of ours. But he was just as tired and maybe more so, and this horse threw him quite hard into a dense quagmire right underneath him, and the horse ended up on top of De Troyes. In short order we saw a man who found himself very much in a predicament, and who no longer had any desire to make fun of us at all. After he had [9] remained there a moment, we whipped his horse, which, with tremendous difficulty, got back up, and then Sieur De Troyes followed. But it was all that he and we were able to do, for he couldn't manage to get out of the muck with his boots on and was thus obliged to get out bare-legged. Nevertheless, he tried to get his boot out with a rope that he attached to the bootstrap, but it did not work, and the boot went to pieces. He took it like a gallant man and mounted his horse barefoot. Luckily for us it was dark when we got into town, for we would have been greeted with catcalls by the children because we were so dreadfully covered in mud.

This town is quite pretty and filled with young people, so after we had changed from head to foot and rested a little, we went to see a comedy, which was performed as well as could be expected. They presented *The Imaginary Invalid* that day.[8] Above the theater where we were, we made the acquaintance of a very well-dressed young man, who came to our inn with us when the play had finished. After our simple entreaties, he agreed to stay for supper and ordered a huge quantity of extraordinary fare, both desserts as well

---

7. A Sieur De Troyes traveled with Caillot from Paris to Louisiana, where both had been commissioned to serve as clerks in the New Orleans offices of the French Company of the Indies. The third companion traveling with Caillot from Paris to the coast was probably Sieur De Bussy, another company employee who had received a commission to serve as bookkeeper in New Orleans. "Etat des passagers embarqués sur le vaisseau la *Durance*," 15 March 1729, Archives nationales d'outre-mer (ANOM); Ship Register for the *Durance*, ANOM, F5B 49, fo. 38; and "Commission, Teneur de Livres à la Louisianne [*sic*] pour le Sr. de Bussy," 27 January 1729, ANOM, B43b, fo. 845.

8. *The Imaginary Invalid* (*Le Malade imaginaire*), first performed in 1673, was the last play written by French actor and dramatist Molière (Jean-Baptiste Poquelin). The lead role in this three-act play, Argan, was originally performed by the playwright. Given the story line—Argan is a miserly hypochondriac preyed upon by greedy doctors—it is ironic that Molière himself collapsed on stage during the fourth performance. He died later that same evening with doctors at his side.

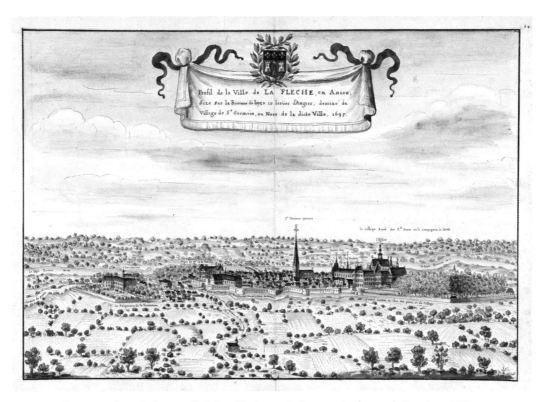

Figure 7. The town of La Flèche; *Profil de la Ville de La Flèche en Aniou* by Louis Boudan, 1695
(Courtesy of the Bibliothèque nationale de France)

as wines and liqueurs. Since I certainly did not want to be played for a fool, I took the
host aside, seeing that the extraordinary expense was climbing very high. I inquired of
him who the young man was, and if he knew him. The host responded yes, that he was
a young man related to him, but that he was a brawler and a gambler, and he felt like he
should warn us about him, but until then he had not found an opportunity to do so.[9]
Since we were alone, he said [10] not to trust the young man, for he would try his best
to lay traps for us in order to get at our money. I thanked him for his timely warning,
of which I took notice. He also told me that until he had gambled, he had the silly idea
of wanting to pay for everything. I was delighted to have been thus informed, and then
I went back to the table and took it upon myself to make him play, not at cards, but

---

9. Games of chance were outlawed in France during the last years of Louis XIV's reign, but they remained a
popular diversion, especially among the elite. Games ranged from billiards to roulette to card games with hundreds
of variations; taverns, inns, and private homes served as the primary gambling sites. See Francis Freundlich, *Le
Monde du jeu à Paris: 1715–1800* (Paris: A. Michel, 1995); Olivier Grussi, *La Vie quotidienne des joueurs sous l'Ancien
Régime à Paris et à la Cour* (Paris: Hachette, 1985); René Favier, "Jouer dans les villes de province en France au
XVIII siècle," *Histoire Urbaine* 1 (2000): 65–85; and Thomas Kavanagh, "The Libertine's Bluff: Cards and Culture in
Eighteenth-Century France," *Eighteenth-Century Studies* 33 (2000): 505–21.

the role of the dupe. In order to make this happen, I inspired in him a great deal of cheerfulness about his money, and I was not at all bothered to do so anymore, because anything that I wanted to drink and eat, I had only to barely suggest something, and I was sure to have it right away.

At the end of the meal I wanted to know how much was owed, but our man refused to let us have any idea at all. I had advised De Troyes about what was going on, as well as how I intended to have some liqueurs put on my bill, but he refused to let me do it. After conversing a moment, he proposed for us to go masking to pass the time. I refused to accept and argued that we were very tired. When he saw that I was not taking the bait at all, he offered us coffee. I accepted it, not to make him pay, but in order to at least give him some liqueurs. We offered, but he absolutely insisted on paying for everything and went to talk to the wife of the host of the said place.

During this time I took advantage of the opportunity to tell Monsieur De Troyes that we should go, for it was time, but he would not listen to me at all. [11] Having thought it over quite well, he insisted on staying, telling me some nonsense, and I answered him that he would do much better to sleep it off and that he really needed to. Yet he still continued to tell me off and then got up. Having stung me to the quick, he asked me to go outside, and I was barely out the door when he drew his sword and immediately tried to strike me. Luckily for me, I blocked him with my hand, and, by jumping back two steps, I had time to pull out my sword and to place myself *en garde*. In the meantime, our adventurer came out, and a few other people who separated us. They got us to go back inside, which I did, though with little desire to do so, but I refused to leave De Troyes, who had some gold on him that he would have undoubtedly lost, except for me, since he wanted to play at all costs. I took the action of intoxicating him completely, so when he finally reached that state, he left us at peace and just wanted to sleep.

There was nothing left for me to do except be bothered, what with the other one, who did not let off trying to get me to play cards with him. When at the end I had been pushed to my limits, I told him that, as far as games went, I did not know any at all, except for *brusquembille*, which I played a bit.[10] We played it until three thirty in the morning. Not only that, he lost about twenty écus to me, even though I let him get away

---

10. *Brusquembille* can be played with two to five players, with two-on-two play in effect for groups of four. Each player receives three cards from the dealer. The next card from the deck is placed face up; its suit acts as the trump suit for the round. The remaining cards are placed face down as the draw pile. Each round of play is called a trick, with the winner of a trick determined by the value of his or her card in relation to the trump suit and trump cards (usually aces and tens). Play continues with the winner of a trick leading the next hand. After all hands are played, players add up points accumulated at each trick. The player with the most points wins the game. For wager-based games, wagers are typically made prior to the initial card distribution.

with many subtle tricks that he thought that I didn't see at all.[11] He nevertheless paid for the liqueurs we drank, which added up to twenty-five or thirty livres. In this way we retired as much friends as enemies, on the condition that I owed him another game before leaving. [12] I myself, being easy and not at all unreasonable, told the courier to prepare for our departure at the end—I mean, at the break of day—and to get him to do so, I gave him an écu. He did not fail to do so, because at daybreak he woke us for breakfast, and then we mounted our horses. Monsieur De Troyes asked me to forgive everything he had done and said to me the night before, of which he remembered not a thing. So, instead of our having been the dupes of our player, he remained totally ours. We reached Durtal, where, since it was Sunday, we found the priest was waiting on us to say Mass because the courier service sent word to tell him to wait until we arrived to say Mass.

The women of this village, as well as those of Suette, where we slept, are attired handsomely enough. The former wear sorts of mantillas, some of them blue in color and others red, full of folds. They are very backward there, even the priest, who did not know a thing about wickedness. He would have needed a schoolteacher to teach him how to read, for he didn't know how to at all.

After we passed through Suette, we arrived the next morning at the city of Angers, which is a little second Paris, where there is a thriving high society and where people are attended to very well. It gave me extreme pleasure to imagine myself to still be back home.

I forgot to tell you that before arriving in town you can see some fine quarries where they excavate slate. Since I didn't stay long [13] in that city, I can't tell you anything about it, except that it is very mercantile, and that the Loire passes through it. We left there the next morning and boarded a small covered boat they called a *cabane*,[12] since, being cabinlike, when you are inside, no matter how bad the weather, you don't get wet at all. We found ourselves inside with quite good company, which meant that we were not bored for a single moment. That evening we set foot on land at the point, and from there we spent the night in Ingrande [see fig. 8]. That place is not very nice, even though the Loire, which passes in front of it, gives it a certain cheerfulness that makes

---

11. An écu, also known as a silver Louis, was a French coin, usually minted from silver but sometimes gold. The écu originated during the reign of Louis XIII (1601–43) and remained in circulation in various forms into the late nineteenth century. Unlike écus, livres tournois (the predecessor of French francs) were never issued as coins but were instead used as money of account. In 1726 the value of an écu was six livres.

12. According to William Falconer's *Universal Dictionary of the Marine*, a *cabane* is "a flat-bottomed passage-boat, with a deck, navigated on the river Loire" (London: T. Cadell, 1776), n.p.

Figure 8. The village of Ingrande; *Veüe de la Ville d'Ingrande* by Louis Boudan, 1695 (Courtesy of the Bibliothèque nationale de France)

it agreeable, and it would be even more so if it were well constructed. We lodged at Les trois morts,[13] where we were attended to by very pretty girls. After supper, since there were some violins outside our windows, we went to look out. I was as surprised to see that there were gentlemen and ladies there as I was to see that there were only Breton

_____

13. Les trois morts (the three dead men) was an inn.

dances being danced. These are dances with the most bizarre steps that one could ever see, and by the end we were in a heated argument over it, all because of Monsieur De Troyes, who is quite easily intoxicated by wine. Then, while he is in that state, he says impertinent things, thinking them to be courteous. There was such an uproar that, once the dance was over, there was total chaos. I was quite mortified because of the acquaintance that I had just made of three lovely young ladies, who, on my behalf, helped calm the tumult, which would have been the cause of our group's getting a very bad deal. We continued after [14] they went out, for I myself was invited to stay by the young ladies who overpowered me with their compliments. While conversing with them, I found out that they had been in Ingrande for eight days with their mothers for a holiday and that they were counting on finishing up the last four days of Carnival there. We had many other conversations in which I began to take extreme pleasure, but unfortunately for me, when day broke, I had to take leave of them and of the whole assemblage so I could then go get myself on board and reach Ancenis. We stopped there with a gentleman from that town who had come from Angers with us, and he very kindly hosted us. We got back on the road in order to arrive at Nantes, where we stayed for five or six days.

I spoke about Angers because of the similarity between that place and Parisian ways, but Nantes [see fig. 9] surpasses it because of the great quantity of merchants and the fashionable young people who live there, following the same styles as in Paris, and besides that, you see numerous vessels there in the port, which make the city even more attractive.[14] In short, it is most pretty. I will not forget, however, to speak about La Fosse, which is a place where the people of Nantes go walking along the Loire.[15] When I passed by there, they were finishing construction of the stock exchange, which is magnificent, and a bridge too, which was no less well constructed. While I stayed there, time did not last a day for me. It is a place where people invent new pleasures every day.

---

14. Nantes was home to the Company of the Indies' warehouses until 1734. Company ships arrived from the Americas, Africa, China, and the East Indies in Lorient, where their cargoes were unloaded and shipped overland to Nantes. Company sales of trade goods took place annually, attracting hundreds of merchants from across France and Europe. Their numbers swelled the city's population of roughly forty-five hundred; their need for food, lodging, entertainment, and business services during their stay accelerated the development of Nantes's hospitality sector. Greenwald, "Company Towns and Tropical Baptisms," 84–92, 221; Léon Vignols and Henri Sée, "Les Ventes de la Compagnie des Indes à Nantes, 1723–1733," *Revue de l'histoire des colonies françaises* 13 (1925), 489–534; Philippe Haudrère, "Les ventes," in *Les Compagnies des Indes* (Rennes: Editions Ouest-France, 2005), 77–93; Olivier Pétré-Grenouilleau, *Nantes au temps de la traite des Noirs* (Paris: Hachette, 1998); Liliane Crété, *La traite des nègres sous l'Ancien Régime: Le nègre, le sucre, et la toile* (Paris: Perrin, 1989); and Jean-Michel Deveau, *La France au temps des négriers* (Paris: France-Empire, 1994).

15. La Fosse, the most fashionable of Nantes's four *faubourgs* (suburbs), was home to the city's leading merchants. See figure 9.

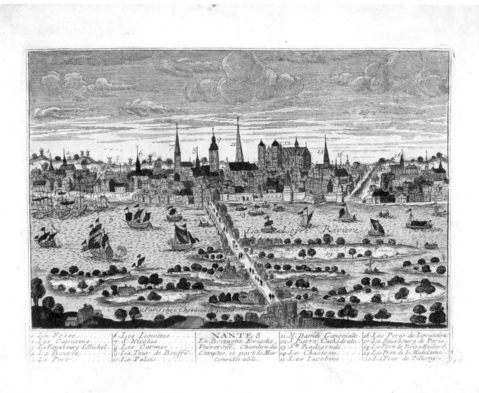

Figure 9. In this map of Nantes, faubourg La Fosse can be seen along the Loire, at left. *Nantes en Bretagne*, by Pierre Aveline, late seventeenth or early eighteenth century. (© Château des ducs de Bretagne-Musée d'histoire de Nantes, Alain Guillard)

The money I won in La Flèche by playing the fool [15] helped me spend my time well. I went to the theater, where they were playing for the first time *The Feast of the Statue*, which was not badly acted.[16] But the next day *The Married Philosopher* was in general well received by everyone.[17] I also went to the concert that was given two times a week at the home of Monsieur Montaudoin, an important merchant of that city.[18] In

---

16. *Don Juan, or the Feast of the Statue* (*Dom Juan, ou le festin de Pierre*) is a five-act comedy by Molière, first performed in Paris in 1685.

17. Philippe Néricault, known by the pseudonym Destouches, is credited with introducing elements of English Restoration theater to the established genre of classical French comedy. Destouches's *The Married Philosopher* (*Le Philosophe marié*) debuted in Paris in 1727.

18. Nantes served as France's largest and most lucrative slaving port, outfitting more than 50 percent of all slavers sent from France to Africa in the eighteenth century. In the early eighteenth century, René Montaudoin helped establish Nantes as the nexus of the French slave trade. He was the largest outfitter of slaving ships in France, sending out an estimated forty-five ships between 1706 and 1731. A 1726 tax audit of 230 Nantais merchants shows that Montaudoin was the wealthiest merchant in Nantes, with a personal fortune that topped 600,000 livres (3.2 percent of the total wealth reflected in the 1726 survey). André Perret, "René Montaudoin, armateur et négrier nantais (1673–1731)," *Bulletin de la Société Archéologique et Historique de Nantes et de la Loire-Inférieur* 88 (1949): 86–94.

short, I never would have planned on leaving if I had had the means of leading the life I was living the rest of my life. But since I had only just what was necessary to complete my voyage and no more, I thought to do what was needed to leave that place.

I left with great regret with the courier in order to get to La Rochefoucault, of which the Duke de La Rochefoucault is the lord. We dined there. His château is very ancient, and it is necessary to climb very high to go out on the terrace, which is magnificent because of the panorama of the countryside that can be seen from up there. I had the pleasure of playing the hunting horn and rousing a pack of dogs numbering eighty. I got them so excited that they broke their collars so they could come to me. I think that, if I had continued, I would have led them to Pont-Château, where we went to have supper.

The place itself is very ugly; it's a shame that it should contain within it such beautiful specimens of the fair sex. We had just barely arrived there when Madame La Chenechal,[19] who, finding out that some gentlemen had just arrived, discreetly notified us that she was having a ball that night at her home. I had no great desire to go out that evening, because I had argued that it would make us have a very meager [16] meal on one of the last days of Carnival, which had happened to us only in that place. Nonetheless, being a bit refreshed, I proposed to De Troyes that we both go, and then we got ourselves ready. Since we had met an abbot while on our way, we didn't want to leave him alone. We urged him to come with us, which was quite difficult for our part, but eventually he let himself be enticed away and came with us. Assuredly I would have been worse off if I had not gone there, for I was welcomed in a most gracious manner and had the pleasure of conversing with some very lovely young ladies, who formed the centerpiece of the assembled people. They asked me for news about Paris; I told them about everything I knew and also about the court from where, I told them, I had left. Finally, it was time for the day to start, for I began to feel like I would soon lose my liberty. If it was with regret that I left those places I had passed through, I had every reason to put this one in that number. We remounted our horses after taking some refreshments. As far as the amount of aversion I felt when we arrived at this place, I had the same amount of difficulty in leaving it. There were three of us who rued it differently—the abbot rued the sleep he had lost, for he could barely keep himself on his horse; De Troyes rued the great quantity of wine he was obliged to leave there, since he was not able to take it with him; and I rued what I told you just now. Thus you see that our regrets were all three very different from each other's.

---

19. "Madame La Chenechal" refers to the wife of the estate's seneschal, or steward.

[17] **From Pont-Château** we next stopped to rest and eat at La Roche-Bernard, then we reached Vannes, a very pretty town, well-built but small. We left there the next day at daybreak in order to reach Auray and from there to Hennebon, where we parted from the courier. We got there so early that, if we had wanted to, we would have been able to make it all the way to L'Orient.[20] We rested a bit. We were only at the harbor, where we chartered a ship's boat[21] in order to go out there the next day. I had the pleasure of renewing the acquaintance with our hostess. I had never seen her, but she took me for someone that she had seen a few months before. That gave me pleasure, because she did not treat me as a stranger in the least bit. Since she was quite pretty, I let her go on in her mistake as long as possible and kept silent in order to take advantage of it. The fear of missing the *Durance* [see plate 13] made me find out if it was still in the roadstead,[22] and I was told yes.[23]

Upon hearing that, I calmed myself until the next day at ten in the morning. We did not hurry ourselves at all; we went to the port where we found our boat all ready to leave. Monsieur De Troyes and I got on board, and, as I was pushing off, I saw two most agreeable girls coming up. At least I thought so, but I was mistaken, because there was one who was married, but that didn't take away anything from her merit—quite the opposite. They came to ask us to give them passage, which they did not have too much difficulty in obtaining from me, since by my nature I am always ready to do a favor for the fair sex as much as it is within my power. I got back to the shore and gave them a hand so [18] they could get in, and then we left. I was charmed by their conversation. I asked them where they were staying in L'Orient, and they informed me. I expressed my pleasure at learning the whereabouts of their lodging, but also sorrow at the same time for not being able to enjoy this happiness for very long. They

---

20. The home port of the Company of the Indies was established just across from Port-Louis along the Brittany coast in 1666. The port quickly became known as L'Orient, a name synonymous with the geographic location of the company's primary trading hubs in the Far East. The evolution of the town name from "L'Orient" to "Lorient" occurred through the eighteenth century, with both versions being in use for much of that time. In the 1730s Lorient was home to approximately fourteen thousand people. Claude Nières, *Histoire de Lorient* (Toulouse: Privat, 1988), 79.

21. The ship's boat (sometimes called a jolly boat, though not all ship's boats were jolly boats) is the small, usually oar-propelled vessel that a sailing ship lowers into the water once anchored. Ship's boats usually shuttle people and goods from ship to shore.

22. "Roadstead" refers to a site offshore where ships anchor while waiting for repairs, sailing orders, or provisions.

23. The 1729 sailing was one of eight undertaken by the *Durance* between 1721 and 1734. Though the majority of the ship's sailings left from Lorient bound for Louisiana, the *Durance* also sailed to Saint Domingue and Senegal for the Company of the Indies. The *Durance* was a five-hundred-ton ship—the largest of eleven vessels bound for Louisiana in 1729—and in that year had a crew of forty-eight men, headed by Captain Louis-Laurent Aubin, Sieur Du Plessis, known as Aubin Du Plessis in company records, of Le Havre (see plate 9). Armament of the *Durance*, 16 March 1729, Fonds de la Marine à Lorient, Service historique de la Défense (FML), 1P168-244; 2P2-23, no. 624.

said to me, "Apparently monsieur is embarking on one of the ships." And I answered yes, that it was on the *Durance*. I was never more astonished than when they told me that they were also embarking on it for Caye Saint Louis.[24] I was charmed by our encounter.

While in transit on the course the boatmen were taking us on, these boatmen, who heard our whole discussion, correctly judged that it was the first time we were passing through those places, and also from the fact that we asked them the name of many woods and houses that appeared before us. They did not say anything, but when we arrived at a place called the Petit Bonhomme and the Petite Bonne Femme, they wanted to baptize us, but we preferred to give them a coin rather than to let them dunk us. We arrived at L'Orient [see fig. 10]. The young ladies went to their homes, and we were lodged with the Count of Toulouse[25] at Bachelier's, which is one of L'Orient's best inns, but also very expensive, for each day cost us one écu, worth six livres per head.[26]

After staying in L'Orient about ten to twelve days, I could stay put no longer, even though I was surely in very good company every day. But the anxiety of knowing the day of our departure, the sorrow of being away from my parents, and also the sorrow of seeing my wallet get thinner [19] right before my eyes without being able to do anything about it, all of these things made me feel an unparalleled commotion in my soul.[27] Nevertheless, I concluded that all I had to do, and the best approach for me to take, was to go relegate myself to staying on board our ship. I had my small amount of baggage carted off, and I did not go out anymore, except to go walking once in a while.

---

24. The Company of the Indies had a trade outpost and ship provisioning port at Caye Saint Louis, a small settlement on Saint Domingue's southern coast.

25. It is unclear whether Caillot was referring to Louis-Alexandre de Bourbon, Count of Toulouse—who as admiral in the French navy may have had reason to visit one of France's fastest-growing Atlantic ports—or the officers of the company ship *Comte de Toulouse*.

26. The inn run by gentleman-proprietor André Bachelier was popular among company officials and maritime officers. At six livres per night, Bachelier's was expensive for a lodger on a clerk's salary of just six hundred livres per year. Upon arrival in Lorient, Caillot received a two-month salary advance from the outfitting office, totaling one hundred livres. He spent at least 70 percent of it at Bachelier's. "Etat général des Dépenses qui doivent se faire à la Louisianne pendant l'année 1728," 15 March 1729, ANOM, B43b, fo. 770; "Etat général . . . 1729," 15 March 1729, ANOM, B43b, fo. 821; and "Etat des passagers embarquées sur le vaisseau la *Durance*," 15 March 1729, ANOM, F5 B49, fo. 38.

27. Individuals awaiting passage on outbound trade vessels often had to wait weeks or even months to depart. The process of loading trade ships was tedious, with small boats ferrying goods from shore to ship, where goods were then loaded through the ship's hatch via a system of ropes and pulleys. Aside from loading, crewmembers had to organize the goods on board so that the cargo's weight was evenly balanced throughout the hold. In 1726 Louisiana-bound Jesuit Father Nicole-Ignace de Beaubois complained to a company secretary in Paris that each day he remained in port wreaked havoc on his "modest purse" and made "the blood boil in [his] veins at every quarter hour." Father Nicole-Ignace de Beaubois to Monsieur de la Loë, 2 November 1726, in *The Jesuit Relations and Allied Documents: Travels and Relations of the Jesuit Missionaries in New France, 1610–1791*, ed. Reuben Gold Thwaites (Cleveland: Burrows Brothers, 1900), 67:264.

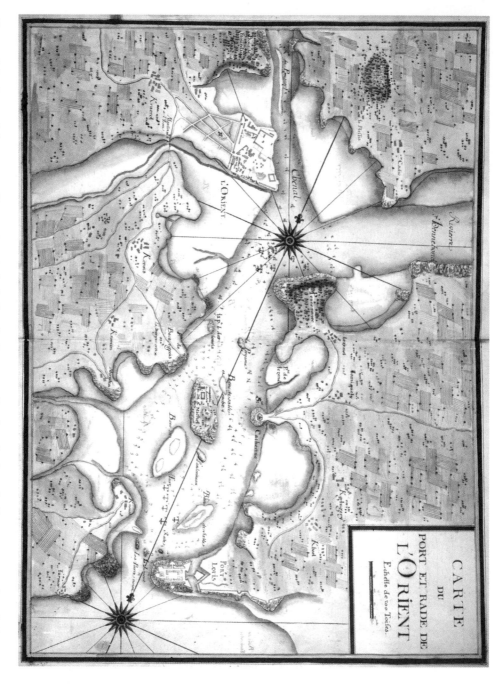

Figure 10. Lorient and the surrounding roadsteads, including the Penmanec Roadstead, where the *Durance* was anchored; *Carte du port et rade de l'Orient*, ca. 1725 (Courtesy of the Newberry Library, Chicago, Ayer MS map 30, sheet 113)

In addition, since we were a quarter of a league from L'Orient, in a roadstead that was called the Penmanec Roadstead, it was not at all easy to find a ship's boat unless it was the one from our own ship, but it was not at all readily available to go here and there. When I arrived, I found some very polite officers with great aplomb, and it gave me pleasure to be with such pleasant people. I thought it would be the same thing at sea as in a roadstead, but later on I saw it was just the opposite.

One day, when we were all assembled on board, not knowing what to do, the weather being quite nice and a fresh breeze blowing, we took off to go for an outing on the sea off the coast of Belle-Isle so we could try out a ship's boat. When we had been out for about three-quarters of an hour, at a distance of two leagues from land, we were surprised by a squall that made the seas very heavy and, being in a ship's boat, quite frightening. We had time only to tie off our sails, and then let ourselves go where the wind wished to take us. Nevertheless, we still took great care to head into the waves. In spite of our precautions, the wind and rain [20] continued to increase in strength and made us take on more water in our boat than we would have liked.

At that time I did not say what I was thinking, and up to that point I had been holding up well and had hidden my fright, taking solace in the fact that I was with three good sailors. But when I saw them so confused, in short, I became very frightened, but I only let it show as much as they did. Since we were at the mercy of the wind, all of the sudden, without expecting it, a wave came and hit us broadside, knocking overboard both an officer of the *Duc de Chartres* and me too. Luckily for us, another wave threw us back close to the boat, where we climbed back on more dead than alive. There was only one sailor of the three who had jumped into the sea after us who was not able to get back on board. We threw him the small foremast, which he rested upon while waiting for the squall to end and for us to rescue him.

After an hour of torment, we began to get over our fears. The winds died down and we were able to rejoin our ship, looking like poor wretches who had been shipwrecked. To console us they made fun of us. The next day they went on another excursion at sea, and they asked me to come along. However, I just thanked them and told them I was to join a hunting party on land. I had no desire to go back out after the assault I had just endured the first time I had been out to sea, which sorely put me off of that element.

Two days later I fell into the water again but I didn't suffer any ill effect, because it was on board a longboat while baggage was being loaded, when the plank, as it swung around, [21] plunged me into the water for a second time. I didn't have too much trouble getting out because everything was calm. Finally the wind became favorable for setting sail, and we said farewell to the officers of the ship *Duc de Chartres*, who were going to the Indies.[28] They sailed on March 15 and we departed on the 16th with a northeast wind and started on our way to Saint Domingue and Louisiana.[29]

We left the port with favorable winds. I began to take pleasure in finding myself on board a ship that sailed quite well, and also in seeing most of the passengers sad and pale and subject to unending dizziness. I was feeling overjoyed not to have their deplorable luck, when, as I lost sight of land and the ship started to move in a more agitated manner, I began to feel certain sensations that made my delight turn to dolefulness. Nevertheless, this passed, while all the others with whom I was traveling just got sicker and sicker. I would have preferred to be in the same predicament as my fellow passengers because of the vexation I suffered from not being able to talk to them and seeing them continuously vomiting in the most awful manner. A few days passed in that way, then a few passengers regained their appetite; the others vomited only rarely and recuperated with the passing of each day. Unfortunately for me, there came a wind that was stronger than ordinary, which put us all in a sorry state, especially me, who had not yet had a bad time of it. For seven days I was unable to drink or eat or sleep and I always had dizzy spells and awful disgorgements. I was assuredly unable to restrain myself from laughing, no matter what [22] state I was in, when I would look alongside of me and observe a line of people all making the same music, which, while we were looking at each other at length, would cause us to renew our efforts until we had entirely paid the tribute that is due to the sea. Thus, each of us having our body new again, we consoled each other, in spite of what we could hear the officers and sailors say. They, far from being sorry for us, behaved as if we were anything but beaten down and very sick. It took me only three whole days to get completely back to my usual self, since my appetite came back again as much as it had been lacking, which allowed me to quickly regain the weight I had lost, and I was squared away as far as that was concerned. It was not the same for everyone, especially for some of the ladies, who had all the trouble in the world to recuperate and remained sick for more than half the crossing.

---

28. The *Duc de Chartres* was one of the largest ships in the company's fleet, with a carrying capacity of 800 tons and a crew of 180 men. Ships of this class were most often employed on the East Indian circuit, the company's lengthiest and most profitable. *Duc de Chartres* armament, 1729, FML, 1P 168-116, 2P 2-III.3.

29. The average journey between Lorient and Louisiana for direct-trade or passenger vessels ranged from three to six months, depending on a variety of factors including sailing conditions; whether the ship stopped on the Canary, Cape Verde, or Madeira Islands or in the West Indies for provisions; and whether passengers were deposited at the mouth of the Mississippi River or the port of New Orleans. This estimate is based on a survey of eighteen voyages between Lorient and Louisiana between 1723 and 1729. René Estienne, ed., *Les armements au long cours de la deuxième Compagnie des Indes, 1717–1773* (Service historique de la Marine, Archives du port de Lorient, 1996), 21–30.

Figure 11. Speaking trumpets, like this ca. 1738 French example by Jacques Vincent, were used as a means of intership communication. (© Victoria and Albert Museum, London)

Two days later we sighted two ships around six in the morning, one coming from the south making headway toward us and flying a white flag, which we recognized at four and one-half leagues with the spyglass. Since we were not going at all straight toward it, we adjusted our route a bit and ended up more to port in order to head more directly toward it, still taking care to keep ourselves at the ready in case of surprise.

We allowed it to approach as close as the range of the speaking trumpet [see fig. 11], wherein our captain, Monsieur Aubin Du Plessis of Le Havre, shouted with his speaking trumpet to bring the ship abreast.[30] [23] At the same time he asked who they were, where they were going, and where they were coming from. They responded that they were French, that the ship was called the *Vénus* from Bordeaux, and that it was coming from the "Queue" quarter of Saint Domingue.[31] Then they asked us questions in turn; we also told them where we were going, and afterward we separated and we wished each other a safe voyage. I was sad to see them go, but the desire I had to know who was sailing behind us made it pass more easily than the regret I had in leaving the *Vénus*. We were sailing with only the foresail while waiting for the ship that was behind us. It followed us a half day, and when we finally recognized that it was English and that it

---

30. Aubin Du Plessis was a member of a well-connected family from Le Havre. His father, Jean-Baptiste Aubin, Sieur Duchesne, was Le Havre's artillery and citadel commander. His uncle Gilles Cambry was commander of the company's shipbuilding facilities in Lorient from 1730 to 1739. The 1729 sailing of the *Durance* was the twenty-eight-year-old's first as captain, though he had sailed the Lorient-Louisiana circuit as a junior lieutenant on the *Dromadaire* in 1727. Du Plessis made five voyages as captain of company ships from 1729 to 1744. After helming the *Durance* in 1729–30, he served as captain on the more lucrative triangular route between Lorient, Senegal, and Saint Domingue in 1731–32, and then on ships bound for Southeast Asia in 1737–39 and 1742–43. *Dromadaire* armament, 1727, FML, 1P 167–89; *Durance* armament and crew register, 1729, FML, 1P 168–117, 2 P 23–III.14, 2 P 2–III.4.

31. This *Vénus* was a privately owned merchant ship, unlike the ship by the same name owned by the Company of the Indies. The company-owned *Vénus*, based in Lorient, not Bordeaux, was anchored off the coast of Senegal at this time. David Eltis, Stephen Behrendt, David Richardson, Herbert S. Klein, eds., *The Trans-Atlantic Slave Trade: A Database on CD-ROM*, hereafter *TASTDB* (Cambridge: Cambridge University Press, 1999), s.v. "*Vénus*" (32909).

was staying its course, we too got back underway and let all the sails out and soon lost it from view. From all indications, it seemed to be coming from England and going toward Cadiz.[32]

The following day we had foul weather, which began around eight to nine o'clock in the morning. At eleven thirty we were assaulted by a blast of wind. It was then for the first time in my life that I truly gave thought to a great many moral questions about myself, thoughts that were capable, in the way I was thinking them, of bringing back the most lost soul. I was sinking deeper and deeper into these thoughts when I was pulled back from them by the sight of a large school of dolphins, which made us hope for a change of weather, and a more favorable one at that.

I had just recovered from the fear that [24] I had just been feeling when I was plunged again into another one resulting from the totally opposite situation. A completely flat calm came upon us, and that made me more anxious than the storm we had just gotten through. For not seeing a breath of wind, and because a ship at sea without movement is a sorry sight, plus seeing that it was unlikely we would have any wind anytime soon, I fell even more deeply into my thoughts than I had before. Besides this, I heard the seamen swearing they were mortal enemies of the calm because, ordinarily, as long as it endures, their rations are cut back in order to make sure they will last.[33] In the end I was deploring my sad fate when, in the meantime, without anyone noticing, our captain, who had been observing the stars, abruptly left his cabin and had all the sailors go on deck so that they would be ready to lash the sails to prepare us for a frightful storm coming our way. I went into his cabin with the others to see it approach but could not suffer the dark and somber air without a sense of horror.

Seeing a furious sea not far from us, and one which was going to surround us, I was not at all as afraid as I had been of the first storm. But I had no sooner heard the confused cries of the sailors trying to carry out their orders than I imagined it to be much worse than it was, which made me totter about just like a child who is learning to walk. It was nonetheless violent despite appearances, but then, since it seemed to be calming down, dinner was served. We went below to [25] take our places at the table, but we were there not two minutes when a second blast of wind struck us broadside and made the ship lean so much that it made us fall down upon one another.

---

32. Located on Spain's Atlantic coast, northwest of the Strait of Gibraltar, Cadiz was the principal port for the shipping trade between Spain and the Americas.

33. Multiple ration levels existed onboard company ships. Each was based on passenger and crew rank, with those at the top of the ration hierarchy, including company administrators, sharing the same type and quantity of food found at the officers' table. Soldiers and criminals being transported at company expense typically stood at the bottom of the ration hierarchy. Typical water rations for all passengers and crew stood at three pints per person, per day, with one reserved for drinking and the other two for cooking and food preparation.

Not a single dish stayed on the table, even though they had been secured. Everyone got up as best they could, one with two broken teeth, another completely covered in sauce, and they came to tell us that we had almost lost our mast because of the shock of the wave. That cruelly gave me pause to think about the rest of the voyage and what might be in store for us, since we had barely left the roadstead and were having such bad weather.

The next day, after everyone had passed the day quite peacefully, we had, as a reward, a very bad night—not because of heavy seas, but because we found out that we had to pass by way of Cape Finisterre along the coast of Portugal, a cape that is very dangerous when approached too closely. The next day they told us we had passed it, at a distance of seven leagues, around two o'clock in the morning, which reassured us entirely. That day we encountered a ship that was heading north, but we were not able to recognize it because it was too far from us. At dusk the wind picked up a bit, and while we were walking along the deck, I was very astonished to see the ocean all sparkling. Nonetheless I dared not call this to anyone else's attention for fear that it was an ordinary occurrence. In fact, I found out that it was the salt that [26] caused this effect when the sea was agitated, and we recognized the veracity later, because after a great calm took hold of us, the waters ceased to be agitated, and the sea became quite smooth. Seeing that we were not moving anymore, our captain suggested that we dance, and he led the dance himself. After we had danced in a circle, since we had three violins, a viol, and two flutes, we had them play and spent the rest of the night dancing and also played many other games that provided us much entertainment.[34]

Never did I go to bed with more pleasure and go to sleep more quickly than that night. I was even beginning to enjoy the charms of sleep when piercing cries and sounds of chaos coming from the deck soon woke me. I listened very carefully, but, not hearing anything but an increase in the chaotic noise, I promptly jumped down from my bed and ran to the deck. I was not long there when I saw a little drama between some sailors to whom a goose had been given that had immediately fallen into the sea. They jumped in after it. They not only had trouble catching it but also had to fight off sharks, which were out to get both the game and the hunters. In spite of the danger these people risked, we could not keep from laughing, because they themselves were tumbling about with these animals. It is a pleasure to see sailors in the sea, knife clenched between their teeth, because they never jump in without one so that they will always be able to defend themselves [27] from sharks and other dangerous sea creatures.

---

34. Dancing, singing, and playing music, along with games of cards and dominoes, were standard forms of entertainment at sea.

We sailed very peacefully for two days. The wind astern made us run seven and one-half knots per hour* for those two days as well. But the wind increased the following day with such violence that we thought it was going to blow down our mizzenmast. That very same morning we saw a ship that we took for a pirate or rover, which is about the same thing. It was coming from the east and was bearing down on us with all of its sails filled. When they were about two leagues' distance from us, they rolled up part of the sails, and they changed their plans and headed north, either because they thought we were stronger than we actually were, because of the spacing of the masts and because they were seeing us from the side, or else because they took us for a ship of the king or something.[35] The wind, having increased a great deal around noon, made us furl, or, as it is also said, shorten, the mainsail and the mizzen topsail. That day we saw a huge number of flying fish, some of which got caught up in our sails and fell on the deck. This was the first fish I ate while at sea. It has a very good flavor and is very delicate. The next day we did not make ten leagues because the sea was so turbulent that it made us roll about a great deal, the waves hitting us on the side. The winds lining up in the west caused us to stay on course, but in the end we did not cover such a great distance as all that, for the winds soon reversed direction. They stayed like that the whole night. It was quite impossible to sleep, seeing the sea in its fury with waves that seemed like [28] they could swallow up fifty ships like our flute at any moment.[36]

The next day we sighted a bird, which made us estimate that we were about one hundred or one hundred fifty leagues from land. Sunday we had a storm that overtook us during Mass. The priest was barely able to finish. Luckily, he did finally finish, because as he was disrobing there came a second one so frightful that we thought we would sink, combined with the rolling of the ship that caused the ship to heel over on its side. Otherwise, there was no harm done, except that many of our hens, geese,

---

*   The expression "run a certain number of knots" in sailing terminology is when a cord of a certain length, with knots to mark the leagues, is thrown in the sea and allowed to pay out. The number of leagues per hour is calculated using a sandglass. This is what is called heaving the log.

---

35. Because the *Durance* was a merchant ship, intended to maximize cargo space for trade goods rather than cannon, powder, shot, or extra crewmembers to man the guns, its 12-cannon capacity and 48-man crew made the ship relatively poorly equipped to handle attacks at sea. In contrast, the *Duc de Chartres*, which was normally employed on the East Indian circuit, could carry 230 crewmembers and up to 50 cannon.

36. A flute, or *fluitschip*, was a triple-masted Dutch vessel used primarily in the transatlantic and Pacific carrying trades. On the development of the flute, see Robert Parthesius, *Dutch Ships in Tropical Waters: The Development of the Dutch East India Company (VOC) Shipping Network in Asia, 1595–1660* (Amsterdam: Amsterdam University Press, 2010), 83–86.

turkeys, two pigs, and a donkey were swept away by the wave, which broke over the deck.[37] We were obliged to haul up all the sails except the foresail and the fore-topsail. What struck me as the saddest was that we could dine only on stale biscuits, just to help us sustain ourselves.

Seeing that the wind would continue on with the same force, they did not put out any sails until about four o'clock. A quarter of an hour had not yet passed from the time when they had finally finished hoisting them when all of the sudden there came a gale. They wanted to lower the sails but it was impossible to carry out the slightest maneuver. Our topsail and foresails were blown away into the sea. To think I was just beginning to get used to the sea! On that occasion I could not help showing some signs of fear, but it was quite understandable, since it was true that we were near the brink of disaster. The sailors themselves did not say what they were thinking, but after the storm I heard them say that they really thought they were going to be forced [29] to bring down the masts. Even the chaplain was all prepared to give us our passport to the next world. That was all I needed to toughen me and to fear no more except with good reason.

I thought myself to be well reinforced, having seen the terrible sea and our ship plunged into abysses that were surrounded by waves like mountains. I thought this was the worst that one might see without actually perishing. But I was sorely mistaken. I remained in my mistake no longer than I did the previous night, when, even though the stormy weather continued, sleep overcame me. In spite of the storm, I had been able to throw myself onto my bed, when at about one thirty in the morning, being in a deep sleep, I was woken with a start. My mouth full of salt water and my body completely drenched, I began to lose all sense of where I was, what I was doing, what I was saying. Upon hearing it said to the chaplain, "We are lost, Lord have mercy on us," I then truly believed it was my last hour. With that, I heard the ladies crying too, and it did not take anything else to make me believe that we would surely sink. I entrusted myself to God and all his saints. The chaplain gave us the sacrament at that point and I used what little time I thought I had left to ask God to forgive me my sins. There is nothing that can inspire more devotion in you than those types of occasions.

---

37. Violent storms at sea often resulted in livestock's being drowned or washed overboard, depleting stores. In a letter to her father written two years before Caillot's journey on board the *Durance*, Ursuline novitiate Marie-Madeleine Hachard reported "the death of forty-nine sheep and a number of chickens" that had "suffocated" in a strong storm en route to Louisiana. Marie-Madeleine Hachard to Jacques Hachard, 27 October 1727, in *Voices from an Early American Convent: Marie Madeleine Hachard and the New Orleans Ursulines, 1727–1760*, ed. Emily Clark (Baton Rouge: Louisiana State University Press, 2007), 49.

Then, seeing that the chaplain had gone up to the deck, I did not delay at all to go find him. I left our ladies on their beds in a faint, for on [30] that occasion there was not a bit of gallantry left in me; at least, I wasn't able to conjure any, thinking only of my own skin and how I was going to save it.

Then, while I was on deck, I saw the most ghastly spectacle that could be seen by one's eyes. First, the sea was extraordinarily agitated and all on fire. The rain and the lightning seemed to throw their light for the sole purpose of showing us the chasm. The wind and darkness of the heavens were horrible. In the end I accepted my lot until it pleased God to decide our fate. I asked what had been broken on the ship. I was told that nothing had been broken, that a wave had broken over the deck and had fallen into the officers' eating hall, which had alarmed the priest, who swore to us that, in the twelve years he had been sailing, he had never seen such frightful things as these. Not wanting to believe it was that same wave that had left me with my mouth full of water, I went down into the room, where, after looking around carefully, I discovered that the little windows on the portholes had been smashed in, and that there were still some pieces on my bed. I got off with just being frightened and having to search around my bed. I then went to the ladies, whom I revived with the help of the first lieutenant as quickly as we could. The weather continued the same for three whole days. If it had continued like that any longer, we were ready to put into port in the Canary Islands, having gone no farther than 117 leagues from them.[38]

After [31] that day the sea calmed down a bit, which allowed us to cease our labors. I leave it to you to imagine what three days and three nights of rain on one's body is like, working the whole time. For everyone right down to the chaplain was involved in working. I had to perform my duty if I wanted to eat well and sleep.

After good weather returned and I was well rested, I had an urge one day, upon seeing the sailors climb to the crow's nest, to do the same. To make sure the sailors did not say anything to me, I spoke to the captain about it and told him that I was going to climb up to it at least as quickly as they. He pretended to be ignorant of the events that were about to take place. To the contrary, he said to me, "Let us see if you will climb up to it even as quickly as I."

Right away I took on the task of taking the chainwales and climbing, but when I was close to the crow's nest, instead of seeing Monsieur Aubin, I saw a dozen sailors climbing

---

38. The Canary Islands, a Spanish-controlled archipelago located approximately seventy miles from the northwest African mainland, sometimes served as a provisioning port or protective harbor for ships on transatlantic crossings.

after me, some to starboard and others to port. Well, when I saw them pressing upward, I thought, without really considering it, that they were coming to help me climb into the crow's nest on behalf of the captain. I wore myself out from shouting to them that they had only to stay put; I would climb up there all by myself. They told me that it was their duty to help me; otherwise I might too easily fall into the sea. I was grateful to them, for I was beginning to feel like I no longer had the strength I needed. They put me up through the lubber's hole. When I was in the crow's nest, one of them began to grab one of my legs, another fellow my other leg, and they bound me fast with a rope. Well, I understood quite well what was going on after I had gotten a bit angry, which did no good except to make the ropes tighter and make the officers who were below laugh. It was not too long before I had promised them a flagon [32] of brandy holding five pints.

First they untied me and helped me climb down, where I had to give them what I had promised. Afterward they told me that the first time someone climbs into the crow's nest, he has to pay the tribute, and then they drank to my health. A few days later they did the same to a young lady whom they only bound at the bottom of the stays, although the only thing she had done was to simply say that she was going to climb up. I loaned her a flagon of brandy. One-half to three-fourths of the passengers succumbed to that marine ordinance.[39]

We passed that day among reefs—these are rocks, some hidden under water and others just at the surface. Having very good weather, we went by them very easily. The next day we entered the trade winds in a calm sea. When you are in that sea you almost always have quite good weather.

We were enjoying some tranquility and were passing our time quite well when the cry of "Ship ho" was heard. Right away our captain took his spyglass, and because of the people he observed and their manner of maneuvering, he gave us notice to stop playing, because he believed the ship was a pirate ship. These words seized us; nothing else was required to make us stop right away. Nevertheless, I was hoping that we could find ourselves in a skirmish with them. At once the order was given to stow all the hammocks and clear the decks, and all the bedrolls were brought up to the deck to barricade the ship as a precaution. The gunner prepared his cannon, the master-at-arms his muskets, buccaneers, blunderbusses, pistols, sabers, [33] halberds, pikes, half-pikes, and battle axes. These aforementioned arms were distributed to each of the male

---

39. Ritual bribery and extortion under the guise of maritime initiation was a common and accepted practice on board eighteenth-century sailing vessels. Initiations usually resulted in the payment of money or spirits by passengers and first-time sailors to more seasoned crewmembers. See Greenwald, "Company Towns and Tropical Baptisms," 135–39.

volunteers, and the honor of bearing these arms was given to us on the poop deck. Then the captain took roll and put each man at his own post. There had never been any knights errant from the time of Don Quixote better armed than we were, for, first of all, we each had a buccaneer in our hand, on the right side a battle axe attached to our belts and a saber on the other side, with two pistols on the same belt. That is how we were armed. Believing them to be out of cannon range and that they were undoubtedly waiting for night, when it would be more favorable, some of us stayed on deck in this posture. Others threw themselves on their bunks to rest while completely armed, waiting for the moment the conflict would begin. What troubled me was to see our chaplain, dressed in his surplice, crucifix in hand, all ready to give us the sacrament. We spent the night in this state, and the next day we did not see them anymore.

We took an incorrect bearing the next day because of our compass, which resembled new wine when it starts to ferment and goes sour—this happens when someone who is not in order comes near and ruins the whole vat.[40] Likewise with the compass, a young lady who found herself sitting next to it was the reason the needle did not function correctly, and immediately we had stiff breeze stirring to fore [34] from aft. It was apparent to all that there was something surprising in this affair. They studied the situation, and, noticing that this young lady was seated near the binnacle, they asked her to move, which she did. The needle went back to normal, and the wind again returned to our stern like it was before.[41] Nevertheless, it did not last for long, because about midday the wind blew from the opposite direction, which was the reason we could sail only by tacking.

We had been having good weather for quite some time when we were hit with a small gale. Instead of worrying me, it made me rejoice, because it reanimated the crew and gave them something to do. It also made me understand that, in all things, there is nothing like habit to make one no longer feel the need to fear anything.

That very day a sailor was made fast by tying his two thumbs to the breech of a cannon. He was given eighty lashes with a braided cord called a sennit* for having

---

* It is actually three pieces of rope braided together to make one. These serve not only for lashing but also for maneuvering and for the sails.

40. It is difficult to determine the exact nature of this reference, though Caillot may be alluding to superstitions surrounding menstruating women. The notion that a menstruating woman could ruin a vat of wine with her presence echoes the early modern belief that a menstruating woman entering a sugar refinery would cause sugar to blacken. Similarly, the idea that compass functions could be disrupted by a woman's proximity recalls the taboo against menstruating women coming near a warrior, for fear that his sword would be dulled. See Laura Fingerson, *Girls in Power: Gender, Body, and Menstruation in Adolescence* (Albany: State University of New York Press, 2006), 43–44.
41. A binnacle houses a ship's lamp and compass. A person sitting too close could in fact affect the proper functioning of the compass through interference with the instrument's magnetic field.

stolen two shirts. It was the greatest mercy one could obtain, for without us he would have been plunged from the yard. This is done two ways. The first is the one they call the wet way, and it is for petty thefts or other such things. One is plunged three, five, seven times more or less from the end of the mainmast's yard, which is easily fifty or sixty feet in height. The dry way is also done at the end of the yard, but the difference is that, instead of falling into the water, you fall within two feet of the deck suspended in the air. They make you jump in this way more or less according to your crime, and many die from the jolt that they receive when they are kept from hitting the deck.[42]

[35] **The seamen** have another type of punishment for the ship's boys, which is used when a ship's boy has caused some kind of mischief.[43] They do not normally strike him and are content just to menace him. They wait until there are several who deserve punishment. When there are five or six of them, they tie them to the bars of the capstan by the middle of their bodies or, for those who are too little, by an arm. Then they give each one a whip so that they can lash each other themselves. Right from the beginning it doesn't go very well, for there may be one who has hit his comrade with a strong blow. When this one feels himself hit sharply, he becomes animated and does not go easy on the one who is in front of him, so when they really get going, you see them running one after the other, twisting and turning and all crying out like they are possessed. They more or less go through the same paces as those who run at the ring.[44] When it is decided that they have had enough, they are told to stop, but since the one who has felt himself hit last is angry, he still continues to hit his neighbor, so that if they were not untied from each other quickly, they would continue forever. What I find bad for these hapless wretches is that, when wind is lacking, the officers, in order to amuse themselves, say that the wind is closed up in their breeches, and on these simple apprehensions they are forced to pull their breeches down, and they tie them to the capstan where they do the same go-round as above. Sometimes it happens that these poor creatures end up with bloody buttocks from the force that is used on them.

---

42. A variation on keelhauling (*la grande cale*), which involved being dropped into the sea and dragged under the ship's keel, being dropped from the yardarm either into the sea (*la cale mouillée*) or just above the deck (*la petite cale*) were common forms of punishment onboard military and merchant vessels in the eighteenth century. Violent instances of maritime discipline in general were common at that time. Shipboard torture occurred under the guise of maintaining a strict social hierarchy. Captain-sanctioned violence against crewmembers ranged from whippings to dunking the individual in seawater to bludgeoning him to death. See Marcus Rediker, *Between the Devil and the Deep Blue Sea: Merchant Seamen, Pirates, and the Anglo-American Maritime World, 1700–1750* (Cambridge: Cambridge University Press, 1987), 212–22.

43. The five ship's boys on board the *Durance* ranged in age from thirteen to sixteen. Crew Register for the *Durance*, 1729, FML, 2 P 2–III.4.

44. To run at the ring, or *courrir la bague*, is to engage in a jousting game in which the horseman uses a lance to capture a metal ring.

April 6 at four o'clock in the morning, having jumped out of my [36] bed and climbed up to the deck half asleep, I believed, with great pleasure, that I saw a number of mountains in front of the ship. I had already proposed to myself to go for a walk when we anchored at our next port, since it had been twenty-two days since I had seen land. I was sitting beside the gunwale with my legs stretched out in front of me, rubbing my eyes a bit, when I soon awoke from the sweet error of my daydream. My sleepiness, having entirely dissipated, forced me to see that those mountains were made of liquid and that it was a storm approaching us. We weathered it rather well. When it had passed, around two in the afternoon, we saw a ship on the same course as we were, ahead of us at a distance of about two and a half leagues. I thought we would be able to approach it, but, since it handled the rolling waves of the sea better than we did, we lost sight of it.

The next morning we saw lots of flying fish and dolphins [see plate 15]. Shortly after dinnertime we saw a large quantity of seaweed, which made us decide that there must have been some strong wind along the closest coast, because if we had not been in the middle of the ocean, we would have suspected that we were close to land. That seaweed I was just talking about is ordinarily yellow and sometimes black, composed of little clumps as big as pumpkins. Its leaves are rather rapier-like, and attached to its branches are little berries the size of peas, clumped together more or less like grapes.[45] Furthermore, growing in the seaweed [37] is a certain little seashell (quite a surprising thing) that opens when it has reached the size of an egg. It is called a barnacle when it is little, and, when it attains the size indicated above, after opening itself a little animal comes out, which, to tell the truth, does not look like anything at all unless you see it move. Nevertheless, upon examining it you can see something like wings on it. When this animal has remained floating on the water in the middle of the ocean for three or four weeks without leaving its clump of seaweed, and when it has finally taken its form, it takes flight and always goes alongside marshy shorelines. It is what is called a scoter.[46] This is how it begins its life.

About five o'clock of the same day we made ready harpoons and gigs with two trolling lines that were put behind the ship in the water. Just seeing so many fish I had what I needed to satisfy the passion I had for fishing, and I was the one who caught the first fish. It was a sea bream, which we ate in many types of stews. This animal is very good; it is very dry and has the taste of fresh mackerel. To see its tail you would think you

---

45. The seaweed described here was likely sargassum, a free-floating seaweed commonly found in the Sargasso Sea, a portion of the North Atlantic defined not by land, but by the Gulf Stream and North Atlantic, Canary, and North Atlantic Equatorial Currents. Large mats of sargassum provide a habitat for a variety of wildlife, including fish, seabirds, turtles, and eels.

46. A scoter is a type of diving sea duck that breeds in lakes and winters in the coastal waters of the Atlantic and Pacific Oceans. Though Caillot calls it a scoter, the true identity of the creature he describes here is unclear.

were eating herring. Its eggs taste just like calf's liver. Its illustration is drawn on the attached page [see plate 15].

After passing several days fishing as much by line and gig as by harpoon, we finally found ourselves near the Tropic of Cancer. I should tell you that we were advised of this a day in advance by one of Tropicus's messengers,* who appeared [38] after supper at the top of the maintop gallant sail. He told us where we were and how far we were from the tropic. He told us that the next day, around two in the afternoon, we would cross it. He also told us that Tropicus, his master, having been advised that it was Monsieur Aubin who commanded the flute *Durance*, sent him to welcome Monsieur Aubin to his kingdom and to express on his behalf the pleasure he felt about his arrival. He also asked to duly prepare for baptism those who had never been there, and, in order to accomplish this, he asked that everything should be made ready.[47]

Our captain came up to the deck of the forecastle and took his speaking trumpet, in order to tell the messenger to pay his respects to his master and that he would execute his orders punctually. The messenger immediately disappeared or, rather, waited a moment to come down without anyone seeing him.

Beginning that evening, without any of the passengers noticing, they began to fill the ship's boat full of water, and below, a half dozen half tubs. The half tub to be used for the baptism-by-water ceremony was on the starboard side, with a small plank across it upon which you are made to sit. On each side next to this tub were two more to be used for wetting in case they ran out of water.

They had already spoken to me a few days before the baptism, and I had imagined it to be worse than it was, which was the reason I was fearful right up to the moment it happened.

---

* This is a seaman who represents the messenger. The most agile and least stupid is chosen. He has a voice that thunders and trembles, which represents a strong and extremely old man.

---

47. The baptism of the tropics ceremony is a variation on the more common "crossing the line" rituals practiced by seamen crossing the equator. The baptism, or initiation, of first-time crossers into the Tropic of Cancer was practiced largely on board French ships and offered a rare opportunity for sailors and seamen to subvert the ship's normally rigid hierarchy. The composite sea god Tropicus, who shares traits with the Greek Poseidon and Roman Neptune, presides over the ceremony. Greenwald, "Company Towns and Tropical Baptisms," 135–39; Kenneth Banks, *Chasing Empire Across the Sea: Communications and the State in the French Atlantic, 1713–1763* (Montreal: McGill-Queen's University Press, 2002), 77; Robert Harms, *The Diligent: A Voyage Through the Worlds of the Slave Trade* (New York: Basic Books, 2002), 105–8; and Rediker, *Between the Devil and the Deep Blue Sea*, 186–89. For additional contemporary accounts of the baptism of the tropics ritual, see Robert Challe, *Journal d'un voyage fait aux Indes orientales (Du 24 février 1690 au 10 août 1691)*, ed. Frédéric Deloffre and Jacques Popin (Paris: Mercure de France, 2002), 303–9; Jean-Baptiste Labat, *Nouveau voyage aux isles de l'Amérique* (The Hague: P. Husson, T. Johnson, P. Gosse, J. Van Duren, R. Alberts et C. Le Vier, 1724), 1:12–13; and Jean-François Benjamin Dumont de Montigny, *Regards sur le monde atlantique, 1715–1747*, ed. Carla Zecher, Gordon Sayre, and Shannon Lee Dawdy (Quebec: Septentrion, 2008), 87–90.

That particular day having arrived, and as we had just about finished our meal, we heard a lot of noise up on the deck. Since I was extremely desirous of seeing old [39] Tropicus, I was not the last one to arrive on deck, and immediately after me everyone left the table. Monsieur Aubin entered his cabin to wait for that fine old fellow, who had arrived just then on the main topgallant sail. We were looking very attentively at this ancient figure when we saw appear from the cutwater, at starboard and port, a troupe of people, or rather a troupe of demons, because of their clothing and their faces all daubed with different colors. These well-armed guards approached as far as the shrouds, which they climbed up in order to escort their king.

When they had climbed up, they helped their master climb down as far as the main-mast crosstrees. He had the most difficult time in the world climbing down because of his decrepitude, making the shrouds shake at each ratline* of the shrouds as he climbed down. After he reached the main crosstree, he rested there from the long trip he had just made on foot, since he was accustomed to traveling only in a chariot pulled by six dragons, flying in the air and on the sea, and even sometimes pulled through the sea by six creatures that were half horse and half fish. Then, when he had caught his breath and all of his retinue was assembled, he asked for our captain, in order to give him notice of his arrival and also to greet him. Monsieur Aubin came out of his cabin immediately, came to greet him very respectfully, and asked him if he wouldn't climb all the way down, which he undertook as best he could, with those of his people who were lower down than him placing his feet in the ratlines. Not having enough strength himself, two angels who more resembled two devils were on each side of him and were holding him from above the rungs. The rest came down afterward.

[40] When he got to the deck, two seamen served him as a horse, on which they had placed a beautiful embroidered rug. So, when he was down on deck, they got him up on this conveyance in order to take the path that led to our captain's cabin, where we were with him in body only, for our eyes and our thoughts were singularly riveted on this king and his frightful entourage. Before continuing any further, it is a good idea to explain their marching arrangement to you. First of all, at the head of the procession were four black men daubed with flour.[48] One had a drum and another an old broken

---

*   Ratline is like what you would call a step of a staircase or the rung of a rope ladder.

---

48. There were no crewmembers of African origin on board the *Durance*, suggesting that the men described by Caillot were smeared with tar, soot, or another black substance. Crew Register for the *Durance*, 1729, FML, 2 P 2–III.4.

pot with a fingerboard composed of a stick that had some strings, which created a Guinea-style fiddle, the third had my hunting horn, and the fourth had a tambourine. That is what made up the symphony, which was as extraordinary and bizarre as the troupe that followed them. Then, two by two, marching to the music, numbering ten in all, came soldiers, completely painted from head to foot, frightening to look at. They were also armed with halberds, pikes, swords, and battle-axes. Following these men came two seamen dressed as pilgrims, with shells and tall pointed staffs.

Then, riding on his nag, came Tropicus, who assuredly had a very reverent air about him because of his age. His hair was white, and he had a rosary, whose beads were as large as two fists put together, wrapped around him like a bandoleer. Next to him, both to starboard and port, marched his two angels, each completely nude except for a sheepskin, the tail of which flapped between their thighs. Likewise their king was all covered in fur so that he wouldn't be cold. After him there followed ten more soldiers, [41] still two by two but much more frightful than the first ones. This is what his procession was like.

When he arrived, with great difficulty, at the door of the room where we were, our captain got up and went to the king to help him off his horse, and then had him come into the room. Then he offered him some refreshments, composed of a light meal and some good wine. Before he had gotten off his horse, Monsieur Aubin paid him a compliment and expressed the pleasure and honor this visit bestowed upon him, to have a person of such rank on his ship. He also said that it certainly had been quite a while that he had been hoping for this good fortune, and that since Tropicus had come he hoped he would accept a little refreshment. Even though he was extremely old, the offer suited this fellow to a tee. He accepted everything most graciously and then performed his duties better than any of the rest of us.

While he was drinking and eating, his people, who were at the door, genuflected deeply to him from time to time as a mark of submission. In order to show us that he was all-powerful and omnipresent without being visible unless he so wished it, he told us everything we had done during the voyage and assured us that we had always been under his protection. As for our captain, whom he loved without bounds, he also told us that we would see a ship* at twilight, a ship on which he had been before, paying us a visit.

For a person of his age, he performed his duty with as much wisdom, prudence, and measure as possible, with the exception of his teeth, which were going a bit too quickly and without repose. When the meal ended, he asked to wash his hands, and they brought him a basin, whereupon after he had rinsed out his mouth [42] and washed his hands, he got his horse and mounted it with a bit more force than before. They led him,

---

* Unbeknownst to us, this ship had been discovered with the spyglass just an hour earlier.

with as much pomp as when he had arrived, to the longboat and ship's boat, where all the paraphernalia and preparations were ready for the baptism.

When he got there, he was put in an armchair in front of the baptismal font (that is to say, in front of the half tub where the baptism for those who had not yet been baptized was supposed to take place). With the basin on his knees, ready to receive his entitlements, he next asked that all the people who were to be baptized be brought to him, one by one. When our ladies heard that he had asked for the people who were to be baptized, they wanted to go hide, but Monsieur Aubin informed them that they would be drowned if they did not obey all that the old fellow ordered them to do, for he himself was no longer their master. In brief, they accepted their plight with much chagrin and had to put on corsets and white petticoats. Thus, when they had returned, the old fellow sent his two angels to assemble the men and women who were to be baptized.

As we were filed in like herrings, in a line one after another, we were attached to a rope that was stretched from the mainmast to the mizzenmast. It was one of these ladies who was first, and the other ladies afterward. The two angels came to get her to lead her to be baptized. When she was in front of the old man, he interrogated her about whatever came to mind, and then he made her swear with her hand on the Bible, which was actually just a big old book that one of the angels held open. She had to swear that she would be faithful in everything he commanded her to do, and then, doing what we had been advised was necessary, she threw a six-livre écu [43] in Tropicus's basin and seated herself over the half tub, which was full of water. One of the angels dribbled some water in the form of a cross on her forehead, and the other dripped three drops of water between her chemise and the skin along her arms. Afterward she curtsied deeply to King Tropicus, asked for his protection, and believed herself to have settled her debt.

None of the seamen actually threw a single drop of water on her. However, the captain and the officers, who had climbed into the ship's boat when she was getting ready to leave, hit her with more than fifty buckets full of water just when the angels were going to lead her back, so that she ended up like the proverbial wet hen. The first thing she did was to promptly go and change, and then she returned to the deck half angry, where she had the pleasure and consolation of seeing the same thing she had experienced done to the other young ladies.[49]

---

49. Kenneth Banks writes, "it is not clear if women were subjected to this ceremony," but Caillot's description, as well as the account written by Ursuline novitiate Marie-Madeleine Hachard, makes clear that both sexes endured the baptism of the tropics. Banks, *Chasing Empire Across the Sea*, 77; Hachard, *Voices from an Early American Convent*, 54.

As soon as they had all been baptized, it was my turn to slide over. The two angels came to get me, untied me, and led me like a criminal. When I was brought before Tropicus, he asked me if I felt committed to following his commands. I told him yes. Then I put an écu and a flask of brandy in his basin.

The two angels made me sit on the tub, and then they tied me up. Even though I promised to give them something, they told me that it was necessary for them to observe the rules or else they would be punished. Afterward they brought me the Bible, on which they made me place my hand and swear [44] that I would not kiss any of the sailors' wives, which I promised.[50] Then they made a cross on my forehead as they had done to the others. They would have smeared me as black as they were while making that cross,[51] if I had not paid well. Next, they held up my left arm and poured a half goblet of water along it. I was preparing to soon be done with it, when the captain gave them a signal to pull away the plank on which I was seated, which they did, and I was plunged into the tub. The angels and Tropicus pretended to be angry, but I was no less soaked. They untied me and then thanked me. As I was going away, pleased enough that nothing worse than that had happened to me, I suddenly felt myself drowning, unable to see because of the water that blinded me on the side from where the wave came.

Nevertheless, when I was a bit farther away, I understood quite well that it was only the officers, who had just washed me in that fashion. After that, I no longer worried about getting wet, since I was already soaked to the bone. I climbed up, like them, into the ship's boat, where I exerted my arms as much on the captain as on those poor young ladies who no longer knew where to stand, since Monsieur Aubin had posted a sentinel at the door of the great cabin's stairway and had had all the hatchways locked. Because of this, they were forced to remain soaking wet or else defend themselves. We had to laugh once we had all been baptized. Next they baptized the soldiers, who had not yet participated.[52] These poor wretches were soaked, especially those who had no money. [45] Instead of the half goblet of water that should have been poured along their arm, they threw a full bucket on them. The baptism began at one o'clock and ended at five.

Tropicus took his leave of Monsieur Aubin and went to steerage with his retinue to divide up their money, which was found to be 146 livres and 11 flagons of brandy, with

---

50. The pledge to refrain from sexual relations with crewmembers' wives was the most commonly extracted from initiates. In-port philandering had the potential to seriously undermine shipboard solidarity.

51. Those deemed to have paid an insufficient tribute to Tropicus were sometimes smeared with tar or soot.

52. Between 1724 and 1730, the Company of the Indies sent more than 250 soldiers to Louisiana from Plantin's company, a military unit initially charged with protection of the company's port at Lorient. Twenty soldiers from Plantin's company accompanied Caillot onboard the *Durance*. Most were skilled laborers; metal workers, carpenters, toolmakers, millers, and tanners were among those bound for service in Louisiana. "Liste de soldats détachés de la Compagnie de Plantin, embarqués sur la flutte la *Durance* pour servir à la Louisianne," 14 March 1729, ANOM, D2C 51, fo. 71.

which they amused themselves for the rest of the day. Fortunately the day passed in good weather, for if by misfortune stormy weather had come, we would have been in an awkward position since there was not a seaman on board who was not drunk. And in this way the baptism ended.

The days that followed were very unpredictable. The wind at times blew from the south, from the west, and at times from the northeast. Finally, after varying like this for many days, it stayed to the south, which was against us. It stayed there a half day and afterward became a wind right aft again. We spent that night conversing and playing various games. At daybreak we saw two marlinspikes, a bird so named because, in fact, one might say it has a marlinspike one and a half feet in length stuck in its bottom. These are actually just two feathers that form its tail.[53]

We figured we were no more than two hundred leagues from land. The next day, two whales passed us on the port side. Our first lieutenant insisted on firing a cannon at them, but as they were aiming it they disappeared.

One thing that surprised me was that for half a quarter of an hour it rained on the forward part of the ship up to the middle section, [46] without a drop of rain falling astern. At nightfall we had horrible weather, with lightning, thunder, and rain mixed with wind, which made us change course because the tiller would not steer anymore. After the wind died down, it became dead calm. We had the pleasure of seeing a huge number of fish passing alongside the ship. Their scales glittered like they were made of fire.

When Easter arrived, we celebrated that day in a very holy manner, for there is no one more devout than a sailor at sea, especially when danger is near.[54] We began the day with a High Mass, which was said with great ceremony. Three charges were fired. With the banner and flags flying, the first charge, consisting of fifty muskets and eleven cannon, was made at the beginning of the Mass, the next at the elevation of the Host, and the last at the end of Mass. When the service was finished, we broke our fast and ate really splendidly. Our captain had taken care to give his orders the night before so that nothing was lacking. At dessert, when the spirits of the liqueurs that we drank had heated our brains, we began to sing, and each one sang his own song, thinking only to

---

53. Caillot uses the term "*paille en cul*," or "straw-in-bottom," which derives from the bird's appearance of having two wisps of straw stuck to its bottom. The English equivalent, "marlinspike," evokes similar imagery, except, in place of straw, seamen reference a marlinspike, the long, needle-shaped tool used in ropework. Numerous seabirds possess streaming central tail feathers. They are known collectively as tropic birds.

54. In 1729 Easter fell on April 17.

amuse ourselves and pass the time. For myself, I decided that I felt not at all embarrassed that I should find myself passing the time quite agreeably.

On this point, our chaplain, who was a waggish Irish rogue, knew there was a young lady whom I was courting (who was one of the ones I had met in Hennebon).[55] He knew she was receiving [47] my attentions, without letting anyone see anything in the least. On the other hand, there was another young lady for whom I professed, completely as a joke, to have some affection, and who took much pleasure from it. He therefore took it upon himself to put on a comedy for us by wanting to marry me with the latter, who was head over heels in love with me, and who, far from hiding this, announced it foolishly to all who would listen to her. I should tell you that this young lady was going to Louisiana to see a Monsieur de Périer, commander of said country, to whom she said she was related.[56] She actually was too, but very distantly.[57] Notwithstanding this, she was going to the Mississippi region under the auspices of our captain in order to establish herself there.

This is her portrait: she was not pretty at all. She was very stupid and mean and bad tempered as well. She was a very small specimen, with a very badly formed figure, golden blond hair, a long and sun-burnt face, a pushed-in nose, four teeth in her mouth, which ran one after the other, and was twenty-five years of age. I was the lucky mortal who possessed her heart, so much so that she was saying that as soon as she arrived in New Orleans she would ask monsieur her cousin to not give her any other spouse but me. She also told me that, the moment she laid eyes on me, she had recognized such perfection and merit in me that she had planned from that point on to have no other husband but me and that she had been well persuaded that I would not refute her. "Assuredly not, mademoiselle," I answered her, "I give thanks to God for the happiness

---

55. The chaplain was Reverend Father Dennis O'Kelly (spelled "Denys Oquely" in company documents), a twenty-eight-year-old Irish Jacobin. *Durance* armament, 16 March 1729, FML, 1P168–117, 2P 23–III.4.

56. According to the outbound passenger list issued in Lorient, there were only two women on the *Durance*, Margueritte-Françoise Le Coq and Marie Lamy de Camaret, the wife of surgeon Jean-Robert Chierdel. Yet both Caillot's account and the list of passengers disembarked in Louisiana indicate that there were additional women on the ship. Why their names were left off the official register of departed passengers is unclear. Le Coq, daughter of François Le Coq and Suzanne Demous, was a native of Le Havre de Grace and is listed on the register of the *Durance* with 270 livres of expenses "tant pour son troussel que pour nourriture" (enough for her trousseau and rations). In an effort to balance the gender ratio between male and female white colonists in Louisiana, the company financed passage, and sometimes provided modest dowries, for marriageable white women onboard company ships sailing from France. *Durance* passenger register, 16 March 1729, ANOM, F5b, 49 fo. 38; *Durance* disarmament, FML, 2P23 III, no. 14.

57. Le Coq's connection to Louisiana Governor Etienne Périer was indirect. Her sister Marie-Louise Le Coq had traveled to Louisiana in 1726 as Madame Périer's lady's maid. Marie-Louise left the Périer household soon after her arrival in New Orleans to wed Joseph Chaperon, a Montreal native, who became a landholder in Louisiana and developed a reputation as a brutal slaveholder. Marriage of Joseph Chaperon and Marie-Louise Le Coq, 20 May 1727, Saint Louis Cathedral (SLC), M1, 128. On Chaperon, see Jennifer M. Spear, *Race, Sex, and Social Order in Early New Orleans* (Baltimore: Johns Hopkins University Press, 2009), 52–53.

he desires to procure for me. You [48] pay me more honor than I should hope for in my life, and, if I have delayed up until now in declaring my love for you, it has not been at all for lack of love but only the respect for a person of your station and merit that made me keep silent, and also that I could never imagine that you had felt the slightest spark for me." But since it was thus, I was going to try in the future to merit, by my efforts, the good things she wanted to have for me because of my attentions.

We stayed a good quarter of an hour paying compliments to each other, and I think we would still be there if I had not finished first, since I was beginning to get bored. Later I truly repented the time spent in this conversation telling her about the love that in appearance I was saying I felt for her, because for the rest of the crossing I could neither speak nor go anywhere without her getting involved in the conversation, or without her following me. Worse yet, when she saw me speaking to the other young ladies, she would reproach me and get jealous, and with reason, for there was someone else who was agreeable to the same degree as this one was disagreeable, not because of great beauty but because of an appearance that, from head to toe, had not one feature that could be ridiculed. On the contrary, one could easily notice innumerable things to ridicule in my charming sweetheart, who did not cease to bore me by repeating to me at each and every occasion that this young lady took great joy in pleasing me, and that if one were to measure her merit to [49] the other's, they would most certainly be the same.

I did my best to assure her that she always had the advantage over her everywhere, and that she alone had a place in my heart without any exception. Anyone else but she would have easily realized how little truth there was in what I swore to her, for when love does not come into play at all, you have to admit that it is the same as a body without a soul. Nonetheless, I did the best I could, like a man with little experience in that language. In the meantime I did just enough so that she believed I not only loved her, but even worshipped her.

Many days having already gone by in this apparent cleverness, I was already beginning to grow quite weary of the whole thing. When I thought I noticed that this farce was not at all amusing to Monsieur Aubin, it gave me great pleasure, and I used that as a pretext to speak to the chaplain about it, so that he would dissuade the poor girl from the error she was committing. I then told him that I thought I had noticed that this diversion was not at all amusing to our captain. The chaplain told me that it must end, but only when our part was played. In order to do that, it would be necessary for me to urge her to get married and for me to engage him to speak to her about it. Since she had money, he would ask her for one hundred livres to marry us on board. Thus it was concluded.

The next day when we were going to bed, the abbot, the first lieutenant, the clerk, these ladies, and I were in the great cabin, and my bed was very close to my sweetheart's bed. I woke her, since I couldn't [50] sleep, and set myself to courting her, so I did not have any difficulty in convincing her to marry, and if I had insisted she even would have paid me some favor in advance as a pledge, but I didn't want to go up against Monsieur Aubin. In short, I told her it was time for us to get married since that was her plan, because for me the delay would seem too long if we were obliged to wait until New Orleans, for I could not wait anymore. I also told her that I had informed the chaplain, and he had told me he would be delighted and all we had to do was choose the first beautiful day so that the celebration might not suffer trouble from any quarter. She was in agreement with all I desired.

I told her there was one thing troubling me and causing me sorrow. She urged me to tell her what it was, and after many entreaties I let her know what state I was in, and I declared to her that I had no money with which to pay the abbot. She scolded me severely and told me that she had a purse of money in the amount of fifty *pistoles*[58] that was at my service and that as soon as she got up she wanted me to accept it. Indeed, as soon as day broke, she got up, transported with joy about all I had told her during the night, and went to pull out from her coffer that purse, which she brought to my bed. I told her that I needed only ten pistoles and that I was indebted to her for that amount. As for the other forty pistoles, I asked her to keep them, which she did only after I gave her many reasons why she should do so.

In addition, I told her [51] that we needed to join ourselves in marriage that very day, without putting it off any longer, and that all she had to do was put on her finery, not on my behalf, since I found her charming at all times, but on behalf of the others, who would be delighted to honor us with their presence. I was not saying this without reason, for she herself was very unkempt, with her stockings always down to her ankles and her shoes worn down at the heels. She did everything I told her, and from five o'clock to eleven in the morning she fussed and primped. Because of our jesting, she entirely ruined a very beautiful Persian dressing gown, which she covered with gadroons.[59]

When she had put on her beauty marks and fixed herself up, everyone was assembled in Monsieur Aubin's room, waiting for us. Before going there, I gave her back her ten pistoles and told her it would be better for her to give them to the chaplain herself. She took them and promised me she would give them to him. Then I took her by the hand,

---

58. The Spanish *pistole* circulated widely throughout Europe from the sixteenth through eighteenth centuries. One pistole equaled approximately ten livres tournois.

59. In its eighteenth-century context, "gadroons" could mean elaborate folds, gathers, or tucks, similar to what one might find on a bustle.

with beautiful white gloves, and escorted her to the captain's cabin, where they were unable to watch us come in with our serious attitudes, especially her, without stifling their laughter. There was no one in a more awkward position than I was, because I would have burst out laughing with all my heart, seeing them make fun of her, if I hadn't feared ruining everything, but I played my role quite well.

When I entered, I presented her to Monsieur Aubin so she could wish him good day. He received her quite coldly, but she wasn't at all troubled. Then she greeted the whole assemblage and afterward sat near where our abbot was sitting. When she was seated, she spoke to him, and imperceptibly she [52] slipped him the money we had agreed to for the marriage, thinking no one had seen her.

The young ladies could not take it anymore, so they went out and led everyone who was in the room away, closing us in with the chaplain and remaining at the door to listen, holding their sides in laughter, as much for the remonstrances that the priest made to us as for the extravagant discourses she made to him. After he had finished exhorting us to love one another, he ordered us to embrace, which we did not delay doing. He was exhorting us again when a little Moorish boy[60] came on behalf of the captain, informing me that his master was asking for me to come down to the great cabin. As soon as I left the room, everyone came in to congratulate Mademoiselle Le Coq (that was her name) on our marriage. She received these congratulations as if things had actually been done, and with an unequaled joy.

During that period of time I went down to speak with Monsieur Aubin, and no sooner was I before him than he burst out laughing at me. He did not have to urge me much at all to do the same, since I believed I understood the reason why he was doing it. But by chance I turned around and was astonished to see my alleged bride behind me, and I redoubled my laughter seeing her still as a statue, which we laughed about a great deal. Not knowing the reason, and being beside herself, she pretended that she needed to search for something in the chests, and after a while, seeing that we were going to continue to stay there just looking at her without saying a thing, she decided to go back up.

[53] When she was no longer there, he told me that, since she believed that things were in a very advanced state, it was necessary to come up with some sort of inconvenience in order to be able to create an impediment to the marriage so that it would have to be broken off. After thinking a moment or two about that subject and how best to do it, he used his authority and said to me, "You must tell her that I have forbidden you

---

60. There is no record of this "Moorish boy" on the ship's register. It is possible that he was the captain's personal servant or slave.

to communicate with her anymore, and moreover, if I notice even the slightest wink, I will know exactly how to remedy that, which would not be pleasant for you and which each of you will be certain to repent."

I followed this advice, which suited both him and me to a tee, but for quite different reasons. He was pleased because he had not been able to enjoy her company like he had previously, since she, being attached to me alone, had not been going to see him in the evenings anymore in his cabin. I was pleased for the opposite reason, because she had been going everywhere I went, which tired me greatly, for I was no longer able to freely converse with the other young ladies.

When we had finally agreed upon what I should say, we went back up, but he did not go into the cabin and instead kept himself hidden behind the door so he could listen to what she might say. As for myself, I went in with a very sad countenance, and I sat in one of the corners of the cabin. She did not hesitate at all to come over to me and ask me the reason for my sorrow, and why I was so lost in thought, and whether I should not be overcome with joy, since we were destined for one another. At these words I let out a long sigh that almost [54] turned into a huge burst of laughter, but miraculously I kept it in. She kept at me so much, seeing that I would not give her any answer, so that I had to let her in on the secret. I told her that I was the most unfortunate of all men, that assuredly I had sometimes suffered reverses of fortune, but never had I had such a one as this, which undoubtedly was going to wrest my unlucky life from me, which after this blow would be forever hateful to me.

She remained in a trance at this discourse, and a moment later she came to her senses and asked me with a trembling voice what the misfortune was that had just befallen me. I refused to tell her at first, but only after many supplications. The whole assembly—who were talking among themselves in order to leave us more at liberty, and also so they could laugh at their ease about her extravagances, which they observed very attentively—heard everything she said. On the other hand, I was quite comfortable letting the captain, who was still watching from behind the door, see that he was not the only one who was loved. I told her everything that Monsieur Aubin and I had agreed. She believed me, and no sooner had I finished speaking than she fell into a reverie again, even deeper than the preceding one. Afterward she rose like a desperate person against the captain, gesturing and saying things that caused the people who were in the room to leave (she really knew how to swear to perfection). I myself pretended to be very deeply touched by her fate and mine, and withdrew to join the chaplain and the young ladies, [55] whom I found sitting on their beds, where they were laughing their hearts out. I did the same, and gave free reign to the laughter I had been obliged to hold back.

Meanwhile, Monsieur Aubin, who had come into the cabin just as she was ranting against him, surprised her and spoke to her in a very severe tone. He threatened to lock her up if he saw her give me even the slightest glance. All his threats had little effect on her spirit and did not prevent her from speaking to me. But, actually, it was only by accident, when she found the opportunity to do so. She told me that a time would come when neither she nor I would be under his power any longer, and that for the time being we could peacefully enjoy more perfect pleasures together than the god of love had ever accorded his children. And that is how, little by little, our love ended, a love that afterward turned into hate.[61]

That very same day, alongside the deck around dusk, we saw a *mort*. It is a perfect bird. Its body is all white, and it is the size of a pigeon. Its beak and feet are very bright red and it has big black eyes. Its wings and tail are sea green in color. This animal gave us reason to believe that we were no more than twenty leagues from land, for this bird does not travel far from land.

It had been only eight days since our last scene had come to an end when another one came to pass, but much more serious than the preceding one. It started over the subject of food, [56] since we were very malnourished. For a very long time we were continually served the same things, and we were unable to restrain ourselves from letting our captain know how we felt about it, for we were tired of being so bad off. The occasion presented itself to us one day when he insisted on cutting back our water, no matter how foul, telling us there were only so many barrels left. Since we already did not have very much, and since the heat was unbearable, which in turn made us unbearably thirsty, we all flew into a rage and told him that he was giving us too much salted meat to eat.

We told him that those were not at all what the company's intentions were, and that they had intended and maintained that they had loaded good provisions, like ham, tongue, andouille,[62] cheeses, and so forth. And furthermore, as far as the water was concerned, if he had not used so much of it to water his orange trees, we would not have been in such short supply. Instead, we had been forced to eat sauce thickened with peas infested by aphids, yellow lard, salted beef, and rice that had been very poorly stored. This food disgusted us a great deal, even more so because all of us knew, in fact,

---

61. Once in Louisiana, Margueritte Le Coq married Joseph Larcheveque, native of Quebec, son of Jean and Catherine Delonay. The couple lived upriver from New Orleans until Larcheveque's death, in September 1732. Marriage of Joseph Larcheveque and Margueritte-Françoise Le Coq, November 7, 1729, SLC, M1, 183, and Interment of Joseph Larcheveque, 7 September 1732, SLC, B1, 78.

62. The andouille loaded aboard the *Durance* was likely a chitterling- or tripe-stuffed sausage (like its modern continental French equivalent) rather than the Cajun-style pork sausage better known in the present-day United States.

that every day he and the other officers were dining on the fresh food that had been intended for us as well as them, and we were going to tell him as much right away. But on that point he got extremely angry and told us that, if we were not content, we could go play cards.[63] We threatened him, saying that we would draw up a memorandum that we would all sign, in which we would state to the company all the bad things we had suffered at his hands, and that we would send these grievances off [57] at the first opportunity.

He was determined to use his absolute power and called for a sergeant, to whom he gave the command to go look for some armed soldiers to put us all in irons until we arrived at Caye Saint Louis, where his point of view would prevail upon us. No sooner had we heard that, being in the large cabin that was used as the gun room,[64] than each one of us grabbed a weapon with which to defend ourselves. One of the group was a young man full of courage, named Reytet, who had fought in numerous battles where he had been well liked and recognized as a courageous man, mainly at Belgrade, where he had carried out many remarkable deeds.[65] When he saw our captain putting his hand to his sword, he pulled out his saber and was ready to strike him. Fortunately, I was quite close to him and was able to counter the blow with the barrel of my musket, upon which he made a cut. We told Monsieur Aubin that even though he was the master of his ship, if he continued to treat us like we were being treated, we would certainly know how to get ourselves treated in a different fashion, and if he or anyone else did not think it a good thing, they could just go play cards, and if they still wanted to dispute this, we would throw them overboard.

We were speaking to him in these terms because we had twenty soldiers on our side who were very unhappy with him and had already grumbled.[66] Thus we did not fear either him or his crew in the least bit. He understood this, and little by little he calmed down, but in the bottom of his heart he was no less enraged about it than before. [58] The thing that made him realize everyone was unhappy was that the sergeant he had sent to fetch the soldiers did, in fact, go, but then also stayed there and did not come

63. "Go play cards" was the contemporary French equivalent of the modern-day English expressions "go fly a kite" or "go jump in a lake."

64. "*La Sainte-Barbe*" was the term used to describe the gun/artillery room onboard French ships. St. Barbara, patron of artillerymen, was invoked to prevent explosions.

65. Jean de Reytet was one of two company surgeons traveling to Louisiana, where he had been commissioned as surgeon major of the company troops. *Durance* armament and disarmament, FML, 1P244 liasse 21 and 2P23 III, no. 14; and "Etat des passagers embarqués sur le vau la Durance," 15 March 1729, ANOM, F5B 49, fo. 38.

66. The twenty soldiers from Plantin's company stood at the lowest end of the ration hierarchy. The cost of the rations they received was deducted from their already meager pay. The only other passengers at the same ration level as the soldiers were two tobacco cheaters, exiled to Louisiana as punishment for selling or buying tobacco in violation of the company's state-sanctioned tobacco monopoly.

back. This man did well to desert after arriving at the caye, for he was not going to be let off easy. The day following our dispute, we ate a bit better. He was (like a very prudent man, being a cunning and miserly Norman) pleasant to all of us; otherwise he risked that the soldiers, and perhaps some of us other passengers, would side with the enemy at the first attack. I confess that a captain finds himself in quite a fix when he has many passengers who want to be treated well, and who prevent him in this way from profiting as much as he would like to at their expense.[67]

We calmed the soldiers, who were still grumbling, as best we could, for in truth I held our captain in great esteem, and he deserved it too. However, his involvement in this affair made him unbearable to those of us who suffered from it.

The next day, while taking a walk on deck, I saw many Portuguese man-of-wars on the water. They are groups of sea lemons[68] shaped like the pastries known as Swiss ears. The middle is like the fine skin of an onion, and the edges are bordered in pale pink. I captured one, but no sooner did I have it in my hand than I thought I had lost my hand. It was completely on fire, like it was being cooked. I threw it back immediately and asked some seamen what had burned me and what it was called. They started laughing about what I had caught. They told me it was a Portuguese man-of-war, and that I could easily get [59] scabies if I scratched at myself. But fortunately I did not get anything.

I went down into the cabin, where I started to play cards with the young ladies. No sooner had I got started than someone came to tell us they had caught a fish of a frightful size on the parbuckle (which is a type of hook attached to an iron chain, which is kept on cordage as thick in diameter as a thumb). We climbed up, where they proceeded to haul up the sails in the brails, except for the mainsail.[69] The sailors went on deck, some to hoist this animal and others to look. All the rest of us looked too, and, after they had pulled about thirty fathoms of cordage out of the water, we thought we saw at the end of this parbuckle a black animal of prodigious size, for in the sea objects can attain an infinitely large size. In the end, after everyone had spoken their mind as to what it could be, it turned out to be a barrel of pitch that had been caught in the parbuckle.

Shortly afterward, we saw a school of fish to starboard. You could see them from very far away. They resemble platoons of one to two leagues in length. This school was

---

67. Surplus provisions, when available, were often sold by the captain once a ship reached its destination. By withholding or reducing rations at sea, Aubin Du Plessis stood to increase personal profits in New Orleans. Captains were also known to switch out tainted provisions in the officers' supply with fresher stores from the general provision pool.

68. Caillot used the terms "*galleres*" and "*limons de mer*" to describe man-of-wars.

69. Brails are small ropes fastened to the edges of sails to truss them up before furling.

composed of bonitos, sea bream, and others, which jump after flying fish, and in the air there were frigate birds, boobies, and seagulls, which were diving at the little fishes. It was an animated war between the birds and the fish. A quite strange thing is that the booby, as soon as it sees a flying fish, plunges down on it, but when by chance it doesn't catch it by the tail, it doesn't swallow it and soars very high, then lets it fall so it can [60] catch it by the head and then swallow it. It is amazing to see the agility with which this is done.

While speaking about this and that, Monsieur Aubin heard that my name day was the next day, and gave a little party for me that very evening with the instruments that were on the ship.[70] He presented me a flagon of liqueur as a gift, and the following day gave me a fine breakfast. I do not doubt at all that what he did was for friendship, for in fact I was not hated, but politics played a small part in it. That evening we saw a ship three leagues away and west by south that was on our bearing, which we quit in order to head west-southwest to intercept it. In the meantime, we looked at it with the spyglass and saw that they had hoisted the English flag.

In order to go more quickly toward them, we unfurled the mizzen topsail and the mizzen topgallant, having the rest out already. When they saw that we were bearing directly on them with all sails full, they brought to in order to wait for us, with their sails hauled up. When we got closer, we saw that they were lowering the English flag and raising the Flag of No Quarter. This is a flag that sometimes has three skulls with tears and two crossed sabers in red, all on a black cloth; others have three crescents, etc.[71] Our captain, upon seeing that it was a pirate ship, changed his mind, since the orders of the company were to avoid combat, even though he wanted to head for them as much as we did.[72]

[61] As we had ceased following them and were going to return to our heading, we saw them, in turn, set all their sails, right to their staysails, and head straight for us. Since there was no time to lose and they were sailing faster than we were, we decided to bring to, as they had done, and we hauled up all our sails. When they saw that we were

---

70. Individuals were often named after Roman Catholic saints, whose feast days took on special significance for those sharing their names. Caillot celebrated his name day during the feast of St. Mark, on April 25.

71. The Flag of No Quarter is also known as the Jolly Roger. Marcus Rediker gives a useful overview of the types of flags flown on pirate ships in *Villains of All Nations: Atlantic Pirates in the Golden Age* (Boston: Beacon Press, 2004), 98, 201n41, 202n42. See also Raymond Firth, *Symbols: Public and Private* (Ithaca: Cornell University Press, 1973).

72. Aubin Du Plessis received explicit instructions from the company not to engage with pirates or ships from nations at war with France. In the event that combat seemed unavoidable, company directors recommended that, if possible, the captain throw overboard, in a bag weighted down with a cannonball, all official correspondence intended for administrators in Saint Domingue and Louisiana. "Mémoire de la Compie des Indes servant d'instruction pour le Sr. Aubin Du Plessis Commandant le Navire la Durance destinée pour la Louisianne," 19 February 1729, ANOM, B43b, fo. 840v.

resolved to wait for them, and when they examined the distance between our masts, they resolved to ply windward, either because they thought we were one of the king's ships, or else because they thought we were stronger than they, and so sometimes they were in front of us and sometimes behind. They always took great care to keep themselves out of range of our cannon. They continued this exercise until it was completely dark, when we were expecting them to come surprise us. In the event we might be attacked, we prepared everything in readiness. We also took grenades and powder horns up to the tops of the crosstrees, in the event that we might be assaulted and boarded. Afterward, we were all posted to suitable positions. In the meantime, seeing that we would not be discovering anything new, some of us went below to throw ourselves on our bunks with our weapons in order to rest a few hours and then relieve the others.

About two o'clock, while we were chatting on deck and not thinking anymore about anything, a soldier who had gone to the chainwales to take care of his needs perceived that ship at a distance of half a cannon shot, and they intended to board us all at once. Well, whether it was because he did not have the strength to finish his business or because he had deposited half of it in his breeches, he came back [62] scared to death, stinking like a cesspool, to tell us that we were lost. His air of alarm and his trembling voice worried us at first. We kept on asking him what he meant by that, but we couldn't find out anything else. Our captain sent a seaman to find out what it was, but as soon as he left the cabin, many others came to warn us that the pirate ship was upon us. Instantly everyone went to their positions, we kept close to the wind and hove to without them noticing, because it was very dark and we didn't make any noise. We fired off a blast of our cannon. Then, without giving them time to get their bearings, we came about and fired off another round of cannon at them and promptly recharged. They decided that they were not going to be able to achieve what they had begun well enough, and promptly pulled away without their row of cannon doing us any harm. We spent the rest of the night on alert, but they did not come back again.

Toward eight o'clock in the morning we caught about thirty boobies that had come to perch on the yards. These birds are very stupid, for they allow themselves to be picked up by hand, and, when they are put on deck, they do not fly away, even though they have large wings. About nine thirty, the sailor who was up top on lookout cried out that he saw land. He came down and was given a double ration that day in recognition. We climbed up the main topgallant, where we in fact saw land at about ten leagues' distance, according to our pilot's estimation.

[63] **The island** of Dominica was the first one we saw to starboard; to port was Martinique. We passed between the two islands, which are separated from one another

by a distance of twelve leagues. The next day we passed by Guadeloupe to starboard and the island of Barbuda. The rest of the day we ran at eleven knots. That same day we caught a porpoise. What is strange about this animal is that, no matter how many pieces it is chopped into, it continues to move. It has teeth right to its neck and has a stone in its head, which people allege to be a very useful aid to women who are in labor. If you give them a broth made from this ground-up stone, it works as well as turtle and is suitable for all sorts of remedies. It is warm blooded, and for my sense of taste it is not very good to eat, notwithstanding that its flesh is very white, rather like sea pike. However, I was put off of it because it seemed like one was eating human flesh.

The *Driade*—an English frigate—(having run out of provisions, and having decided to put in at the closest port in order to get water at the same time) told us that, upon seeing a huge shark passing alongside the ship, they harpooned it and were barely able to hoist it on deck with two relieving tackles. Notwithstanding its condition, this animal thrashed its tail around so forcefully that it struck an unfortunate pig, which was instantly killed from the blow it received. They were eventually constrained to set six men with axes upon it, in order to cut off its tail, where its life and strength are; afterward they cut it open. As they were getting ready to open its stomach, which was very fat, [64] it split open at the first cut of the knife, enough to allow them to see a hammock in which there was an entire man, whom they recognized as someone they had just thrown into the sea about eight hours previously. They very quickly threw him back in the sea. We gave them the assistance they asked for to help them reach the closest port.

That day our captain announced to us at supper that we had lost ten barrels of water, which had been bitten through by rats, and therefore we would get no more than a pint per day. We did not say anything, and it was necessary to endure this. It was a pity to see the ship's crew worn out because of the lack of water. As for myself, I could not take it anymore. When I drank wine, it made me feel much thirstier, and brandy even more so. In the end, by luck, I remembered I had four full flagons that I had filled with water in Lorient in order to keep them from getting tossed around in my little wine chest. Up to that point I had a very great disdain for that water, but, finding myself in a hotter climate and this unforeseen cutback in water having occurred, I did not know what to do.

So, I was offering my wine for half as much water, without being able to find anyone who would accommodate me. I believed in the end that I had found a secret, which was to lie down on my bunk to sleep and try in this way to dissipate the extraordinary urge I had to drink. But I was never able to stop thinking about water. In fact, precisely during those moments I pictured streams and beautiful fountains of clear, fresh water, which only increased my misery.

While thus overcome, I luckily remembered that I had four flagons full. Transported, I jumped up [65] to look under my bed and went to my wine coffer, where I partook of one of them, which seemed to me as good to the same degree as it had seemed horrible before. I closed it back up and took care that no one saw me, because these flagons would have been stolen from me. From that shortage, twenty-two of the ship's crew fell ill with scurvy.[73] The pint of water we received had little worms wriggling in it and was stinking and greenish besides. Moreover, it was very hot, but nonetheless, we drank this nectar with pleasure.

All sorts of troubles plagued us, for we were only two leagues from Puerto Rico without being able to sail around it because the tide was against us and pushed us out to sea, just at the very moment when we had no more water at all. We saw a ship that was about one and one-half leagues' distance from us and was on the same course as we were. We immediately hoisted the ensign with a waft to signal distress, and shot a cannon leeward to ask them for assistance. But, unfortunately for us, they did not hear us and continued to stay their course. Two hours later we saw land, which was for us a cause for public rejoicing, and it reanimated the ship's crew. All the sails were used, and, although we had been sailing large and then were almost close-hauled,[74] our efforts were still in vain, for we had only the satisfaction of recognizing the island of Saint Domingue [see fig. 12].

We plied windward for three days. By day we would stay our course, and by night we would heave to and bring the ship about for fear of running aground. Finally, after much effort, we passed the point that was causing us the problem, but we [66] were not ten leagues away when the wind died. I thought we were going to suffocate that day, for there was not the slightest breath of air.

---

73. Scurvy has long been associated with those who made their living onboard ships during the Age of Sail. The nutritional disorder first appeared as "red spots in the *Arms* and *Legs*" that soon turned "*black* and then *blue*." In its more advanced stages, the vitamin C deficiency was characterized by "an extraordinary *Weakness*, a *Redness*, *Itching* and *Rottenness* of the *Gums*, and a *Looseness* of the *Teeth*." William Cockburn, *Sea Diseases; or, A Treatise of Their Nature, Causes, and Cure* (London: G. Strahan, 1736), 11. Scurvy's causes were poorly understood, although there was general agreement that nutrition played a role, perhaps because the malady's most prominent manifestations occurred in the mouth. It was not until the decades following James Lind's 1754 publication of *A Treatise on Scurvy* that the addition of citrus fruits to seamen's diets became a recognized method of prevention.

74. Sailing large means to sail before the wind, with the wind blowing from aft to fore. When the sails are close-hauled, they are drawn in close to the ship's sides, allowing the ship to sail as close into the wind as possible, with the wind blowing nearly from fore to aft.

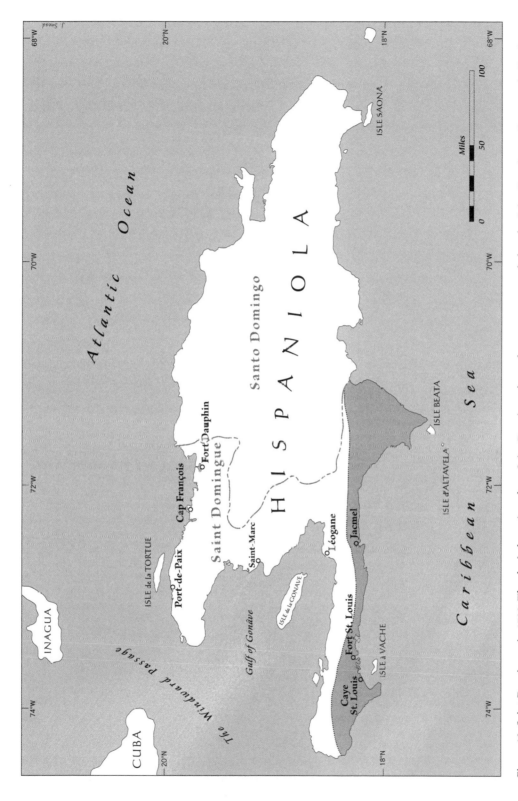

Figure 12. Saint Domingue in 1729. The shaded portion along Saint Domingue's southern coast was ceded to the Saint-Domingue Company by Louis XIV in 1698 and was transfered to the Company of the Indies in 1720. (Map by John Snead)

About two o'clock in the afternoon, we saw a small island called Artavelle.[75] We decided we were only twenty-five leagues from Caye Saint Louis.[76] Every morning we had the good fortune of being enveloped by a fresh breeze that was coming from the land. It was filled with an assortment of diverse aromatic odors that completely delighted our sense of smell. My impatience was without bounds, to see land without being able to get there and eat as many oranges as I desired, as well as many other exquisite fruits that are found there. But since I could not help but do otherwise, I took the course of a gentleman and amused myself by fishing through one of the artillery room's portholes, where I caught eight hundred little fish that were good for frying.

About four o'clock of said day, we saw a ship windward to us, to port, which seemed to be sailing straight for us, which in fact it was. It made three leagues in less than an hour. In the meantime, having raised the English flag, and we the French flag, they approached us to within speaking-trumpet distance. We called out to find out where the ship was coming from. They answered us and asked where we were going and where we had been. We answered that we were from Brest, and that we were privateering.[77] As we were speaking, we put them leeward of us little by little. We were each at our positions in the event that it became necessary to fire on them, which we truly believed, because with their ship having come broadside to us, the only thing we were waiting for was to be boarded. All of us, eager to join the fray, were ready to respond to them, when we saw their ship's boat at the prow of their vessel. [67] We did not waver from our

---

75. This is Caillot's first reference to the "small island called Artavelle." Here he claims the island is twenty-five French leagues (twenty standard nautical leagues, or sixty-nine miles) from Caye Saint Louis, but he later calls the island Aztavelle and claims it is nine French leagues from Caye Saint Louis. Based on contemporary maps of the coast of Hispaniola, it is likely that Caillot first referred to the island of Altavela, a small island southwest of the border between Spanish Santo Domingo and French Saint Domingue that is roughly forty-two leagues from Caye Saint Louis. The second reference is likely to Cape Altavela, which was significantly closer to Caye St. Louis.

76. In 1698 Louis XIV granted the southern portion of French Saint Domingue to the Saint-Domingue Company, which based its operations in Saint Louis, a small settlement along the island's southwestern coast. The king's concession allowed the company full control over trade, immigration, and land grants. By 1715 the Saint-Domingue Company had been absorbed by the Senegal Company, which was itself acquired by John Law's Company of the West in 1718. When the Company of the West became the Company of the Indies in 1720, the company retained all privileges granted to its predecessors and located its operational base just southwest of Saint Louis at Caye Saint Louis, or Les Cayes. The outpost served primarily as a provisioning port for company ships en route to the Gulf Coast, with livestock, produce, and other foodstuffs supplied from the company plantation, but also served as a trade entrepôt for surrounding plantations. On Saint Domingue's history prior to 1763, see John D. Garrigus, *Before Haiti: Race and Citizenship in French Saint-Domingue* (New York: Palgrave Macmillan, 2006), 21–50; James E. McClellan III, *Colonialism and Science: Saint Domingue in the Old Regime* (Baltimore: Johns Hopkins University Press, 1992); and Doris Garraway, *The Libertine Colony: Creolization in the Early French Caribbean* (Durham: Duke University Press, 2005).

77. The *Durance*'s crewmembers likely led the unfamiliar English crew to believe they were Brest-based privateers in an effort to conceal the ship's status as a company vessel. Company ships laden with trade goods and sometimes coinage en route to and from the colonies were frequently preyed upon by pirates.

positions, and we let them come on board. What had made them take so long to put their boat in the sea was that they were waiting for us to put ours in, for otherwise they would have launched it more quickly, since it had been suspended between two tackles.

So, when the one who had been sent as a representative came on board, he told us he was the first lieutenant of that vessel. Monsieur Aubin received him and, in his customary fashion, was extremely polite to him. He then had him come into his cabin, where he gave him a bite to eat. This envoy told us that the ship was a privateer, the *St. Fort*, commanded by a Monsieur Scemithe.[78] He also told us that, about six hours before, they had attacked a pirate ship without being able to capture it. They had followed it quite a long time, but, since it was lighter than they were, they had lost sight of it. When they saw us, they had believed it was the other ship again, which, having made preparations, was coming back to attack. While he was telling us this, the crew of his boat had come on board and inquired of ours how many of them there were. But they fell into the hands of some sailors who were as clever as they were, who told them that there were three hundred men in the crew and thirty passengers. We saw that on board their ship they were also all ready to fire. I noticed two English ladies, who seemed very pretty to me, at the windows of the captain's quarters. It is quite customary for the English to bring their wives with them when they are privateering.[79]

When the privateer's first lieutenant had taken as much food and drink as he wished, he told us he was going back to his ship to try [68] to interest his captain in coming with his ladies to amuse themselves and pass the rest of the day together. He took a couple of bottles of wine and told Monsieur Aubin that he would bring back some beer in its place. He was no sooner returned to his ship than he had the ship's boat hoisted. We realized then that he was the captain and everything he had told us was only a ruse to probe us in order to understand our forces and who we were. We truly believed he was going to fire on us, because of the silence that reigned, and, since we were almost certain in these beliefs, we had already cocked our muskets and had the match almost on the touchhole of the cannon. We were very surprised when, after a quarter of an hour that they apparently spent holding council as to whether or not they should attack us, they let the sails fill, wished us a safe journey, and left.

---

78. Smith

79. On women at sea in the Age of Sail, see Margaret S. Creighton and Lisa Norling, eds., *Iron Men, Wooden Women: Gender and Seafaring in the Atlantic World, 1700–1920* (Baltimore: Johns Hopkins University Press, 1996); Joan Druett, *Hen Frigates: Wives of Merchant Captains Under Sail* (New York: Simon and Schuster, 1998); and David Cordingly, *Seafaring Women: Adventures of Pirate Queens, Female Stowaways, and Sailors' Wives* (New York: Random House, 2007).

The next day we doubled the little island of Aztavelle,[80] which is only nine leagues from Caye Saint Louis. After dinner, while the caulkers were caulking the ship's boat, the pitch kettles caught on fire and burned some of our cordage. It was with great difficulty that we extinguished it. If, by misfortune, it had been in the gunpowder magazine, where there were six thousand pounds for the cannon, we would have sunk near the port without any possibility of rescue, but luckily this did not happen.

About four o'clock we saw Caye Saint Louis's fort [see plate 16]. We fired a cannon to let the harbor pilot know of our arrival, and to have him come on board to bring us into the port. He came, and we entered into the port about six o'clock. At seven we were anchored and moored by the head.

Monsieur Aubin got in his ship's boat right away [69] to go greet the commander, and then, following that, to bring the company's packages to the director.[81] The next day we also went to greet the above-mentioned gentlemen.[82] We found the commander, but we did not see the director. Instead, at his house, we saw Monsieur Siroux and Monsieur Girard, agents of the company, who, in his absence, were most hospitable. We had not yet been waiting an hour when Monsieur Chalon, who is the director of this place, arrived.[83] Since it was dinnertime, he invited us to eat, and not just that one time but for the whole time we would be staying on the island of Saint Domingue. We thanked him for his kindness and did not want to inconvenience him to that degree. During dinner we spoke about Paris and about what had been happening there that was most interesting. We were very pleased with Monsieur Chalon's sincere manners. Good wine and good food were never lacking whenever we were at his house.

Finally, after dinner, some went to take a siesta (that's the word used in hot countries, which means "to sleep"), but as for myself and two others, delighted to feel land under our feet, we went to hike up and down in the mountains, which are filled for the most

---

80. In navigation, "doubling" refers to the act of passing or going around a cape or promontory.

81. Before leaving Lorient, Aubin Du Plessis received detailed instructions from company directors regarding his voyage. In the section dealing with the captain's time in Caye Saint Louis, the directors advised him to go directly to the offices of Messieurs Chalon and Marlot to deliver company correspondence. Once there, he was also instructed to submit a list of his provisioning needs, including specific requests for orange juice and *guildive* (a sugar-based distillation more commonly known as *taffia*). "Mémoire de la Compie des Indes servant d'instruction pour le Sr. Aubin Du Plessis Commandant le Navire la Durance destinée pour la Louisianne," 19 February 1729, ANOM, B43b, fo. 840v. On guildive, see Labat, *Nouveau voyage*, 1:321–24.

82. Given that the company explicitly forbade Aubin Du Plessis from letting any of his passengers off the ship while in port at Saint Domingue, it is interesting to note that company employees, including the bookkeeper and three clerks, were permitted to disembark. "Mémoire de la Compie des Indes servant d'instruction pour le Sr. Aubin Du Plessis Commandant le Navire la Durance destinée pour la Louisianne," 19 February 1729, ANOM, B43b, fo. 840v.

83. Unlike in Louisiana, where the company director oversaw operations throughout the entire Louisiana colony and the Illinois country, Sieur Chalon, as the company's director at Caye Saint Louis, had jurisdiction only over the southern portion of Saint Domingue.

part with orange trees, lemons, Spanish jasmine, and a great number of other fruits and flowers that create an incomparable fragrance. To me, it seemed like I was in an earthly paradise, seeing so many different fruits made just for eating. Among others, there were cashew, pomegranate, coconut, and banana trees, fig bananas,[84] guavas, pineapples, and many others with which I am not familiar. In short, these places were enchanting. The orange trees bear [70] oranges four times as big as those of Portugal. As for the lemon tree, it is very small; that is to say, the lemon is, but it has much more juice than other, bigger ones, and they are delicious candied. The other kind of lemon there also produces a very large amount of juice. I will not forget to talk about the pineapple as an excellent fruit. It is the size and shape of a melon and is very pernicious. When you eat it, you must only suck the juice from it, in order to prevent it from doing harm, because it is very acidic. Nevertheless, I ate a great quantity of it, which did not bother me at all. It is so harmful that if you stick the blade of a knife into it, up to the handle, leave it there three or four hours, and then pull your knife out, you will find only the handle left, and the blade will have dissolved. There is nothing with a better flavor and aroma than this fruit. It is also very good candied, but it is better fresh. It is usually eaten cut up into small pieces in some good wine with some sugar. The banana is as long as a large gherkin, and the fig banana as well. This fruit is very sugary and a bit mushy.

Guava is a fruit that looks like the Reinette apple and is the same size.[85] The inside is red and filled with seeds. It is eaten when soft. There are watermelons that are the same size as a pumpkin. They are very refreshing, and they never make you sick, even when you eat some when you are very hot. Coconut is also quite excellent. To refresh oneself, it is broken open to obtain a milky water, which is very sweet and quite refreshing. The cashew apple [see fig. 13] is filled only with juice, which is very good at quenching thirst. At the bottom of said apple, which is very yellow when ripe, you find the cashew nut hanging there.

[71] **Finally,** after we had walked quite a bit, we went to see the town (it is more a village than a town), where there are nevertheless quite a number of very pretty Creole women there. Their clothes are a dazzling white, whereas they are not, though they would seem to be.[86] Instead of a coif, they wear a muslin kerchief neatly knotted around their head,

---

84. The fig banana, also known as the lady finger, is a small banana variety common throughout Latin America and the Caribbean.

85. The Reinette was a popular apple variety in seventeenth- and eighteenth-century France.

86. A 1713 general census of Saint Domingue recorded 5,648 whites; 1,117 free mulattos, blacks, and Indians; and 24,156 slaves. A more geographically focused census, taken in 1720 of Saint Louis and the surrounding areas of Isle à Vache, Cavaillon, and Aquin, shows 797 free men, women, and children and 4,818 slaves. In the 1720 census, free blacks and people of mixed racial ancestry were counted under the more general categories of men, women, and

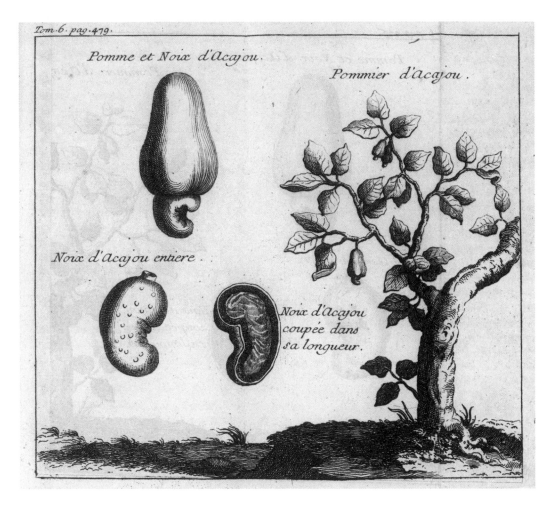

Figure 13. Cashew tree with cashew fruit and nut; from Jean-Baptiste Labat's *Nouveau voyage aux isles de l'Amérique*, vol. 6, 1742 (Courtesy of the John Carter Brown Library at Brown University)

and they have corsets of dimity[87] with muslin skirts, everything well pressed and white. Clothed like this, they have the appearance of goddesses, capable of ravishing all of the proudest of hearts (judge if mine was free). There are some who wear panniers.[88] The

---

children and were not enumerated by race. Caillot's use of "Creole" in this instance suggests he applied the term to women born in the colony, regardless of race. Though the definition of "Creole" has been contested since at least the nineteenth century, there were contemporary precedents for the use of "Creole" to describe people of both European and African ancestry born in the colonies. See especially the writings of Dominican priest Jean-Baptiste Labat, who visited Saint Louis in 1701, *Nouveau voyage aux isles de l'Amérique*, vol. 5 (Paris: Guillaume Cavelier, fils, 1722), 245–46, 256; 1713 and 1720 censuses, ANOM, G1 509, no. 12 and 17.

87. Dimity, or *bazin*, is a cotton-based fabric similar to fustian (a type of twill), but finer and stronger.

88. Panniers were hoops made of cane, metal, or whalebone, hung from straps at the waist to expand the sides of women's dresses. On the role of panniers in eighteenth-century dress, see the *Heilbrunn Timeline of Art History* (New York: Metropolitan Museum of Art, 2000–), www.metmuseum.org/toah/works-of-art/1973.65.2; Harold

only thing displeasing about them is their manner of walking with their arms hanging at their sides. Nevertheless, there are some who can carry this off, and it gives them a childlike and playful air. These Creole women have many slaves, and this is the reason they are so lazy, even to the point that if they drop something on the ground, they have the patience to call a slave five or six times to come pick up what is just at their feet.

The men, for the most part, also dress in jackets made of dimity from the Indies, breeches, and white stockings. Nonetheless, there are some who have suits made of very lightweight fabric. This is the first place where I saw male and female Negroes going about naked. At first view, this seemed to me the most ridiculous thing I had ever seen, but I was not there but eight days when I became accustomed to seeing them like that, and even to going about almost like them because of how terribly hot it is in that place.

The houses there are covered with fan-palm leaves, some with banana leaves, or with sugarcane from which the sugar has been extracted. But the most important people in the village or town, like the company headquarters and the church, have their houses covered in clapboard. [72] There are also huts for the Negroes, which are more or less made like tents, and they are covered with banana leaves.

The church is at one end of the town, and for a bell tower there is a large oak tree to which a little bell is attached. This is the only bell that can be found there. It is a pleasure to see all the inhabitants on the occasion of their feast days and Sundays. There one sees beautiful women shining like so many suns in the shade of innumerable parasols. The streets are not wide enough for the panniers. Even the slaves themselves are just as magnificent in linen, but it is only on these days that they dress, for the rest of the week they usually go about completely naked.

If I had followed the inclination that drew me toward these Creoles, I would have been able to satisfy my desires, but the warnings I received—and also the predicament in which I would have found myself if I had the misfortune to be among the number of so many young men who were very afflicted because of the lack of help—stopped me and bridled my passion.[89]

Koda and Andrew Bolton, *Dangerous Liaisons: Fashion and Furniture in the Eighteenth Century* (New Haven: Yale University Press, 2006); and Norah Waugh, *Corsets and Crinolines* (London: Batsford, 1987).

89. By "afflicted" Caillot most certainly means infected with a sexually transmitted disease. *Les maladies de Vénus*, or venereal diseases, were poorly understood and rarely treated effectively in the eighteenth century. Two of the most commonly contracted sexually transmitted diseases were gonorrhea and syphilis. See Linda Evi Merians, *The Secret Malady: Venereal Disease in Eighteenth-Century Britain and France* (Lexington: University Press of Kentucky, 1996); Mary Lindemann, *Medicine and Society in Early Modern Europe* (New York: Cambridge University Press, 2010), 66–70; and Karen A. Weyler, "'The Fruit of Unlawful Embraces': Sexual Transgression and Madness in Early American Sentimental Fiction," in *Sex and Sexuality in Early America*, ed. Merril D. Smith (New York: New York University Press, 1998), 283–314.

Getting back to what took place after our walk, nightfall had surprised us, and since none of us had much desire at all to go close ourselves up on board our ship, we found, in fact, just the place, a place where tobacco was sold. We went in to buy some, even though none of us had any money. Nevertheless, we fixed the price for a few carrots of tobacco.[90] While speaking about this and that, the hostess—who was very refined, knew how to manage her business well, and was very pretty besides—offered us a pineapple to refresh ourselves. We accepted her gracious offer, and, not only did we eat the pineapple, we stayed there three days without [73] worrying about a thing, always eating well and enjoying ourselves a great deal. Nevertheless, I myself, who knew that I did not possess any coins with a king's portrait, did not want to stay in that place any longer without knowing what I owed and who would pay the expense. I pulled the host to the side and asked him to tell me how much he was charging per meal. He told me that he did not charge less than a piastre, or six livres.

At these words I trembled and did not say a word. I ran off to find a certain Monsieur De Bussy, who was one of our party and who was the reason that we found ourselves in this fix with regard to the tobacconist. Since I knew that he had no more money than the rest of us, but that he was well equipped with household goods and furniture and would not worry about selling some of them in order to abandon himself to his pleasure, I proposed to him to pay for what I had spent, and that I would give him a promissory note payable from the first salary I received in Louisiana. He refused my offer to pay him back and told me not to worry about anything except having a good time. Upon hearing that, I was reassured and returned to enjoying myself like the others. We had the good fortune to stumble upon a good tavern, where we had a great time.

Tired of always being at the table, I was taken with a desire to go hunting. Since hunting was permitted there, I went to kill some parrots, turtledoves, wood pigeons, and others, for they have them in very great numbers there. Two of my friends also came with me. We had gone only one quarter of a league when I had already killed nine parrots and two turtledoves on my own. I would have gotten many others, but the extreme heat prevented us from going any farther. We stretched out under some lemon trees (which formed an arbor), and we even removed our clothes right to our shirts, which were completely soaked. [74] And, to avoid getting sick, we scrubbed ourselves with lemons, which cost us only the effort of picking them, likewise with oranges. I had every reason to remember this part, for, among other things, my face had completely

---

90. Tobacco in carrots (*en carotte*) refers to a certain quantity of rolled-style tobacco commonly produced by French growers. Unlike Chesapeake-style tobacco, which was fully dried, rolled tobacco was wet-cured, heavier, and better suited to sniffing or chewing than smoking. A remnant of the *en carotte* classification can be seen in the orange or red carrot-shaped signs that still designate tobacco shops in modern-day France.

peeled. After I had relaxed a while, I got dressed again, and, seeing that the others were relaxing and eating oranges, I went hunting. While going back toward the house, I saw a smooth-billed ani, known there as a *bout de tabac*,*[91] perched on a branch. Since it is very difficult to shoot this animal, I took pleasure in taking aim at it, and I killed it. Its death precipitated a bad state of affairs for me, for I had no sooner recharged my musket and gathered up this game than I saw two soldiers coming toward me to make me give up my musket, having fired it against the injunctions of that government's ordinances, of which I knew nothing, since no one had advised me about them.

These soldiers came to within musket range, took aim, and shouted at me to put my arm down or else I would get three balls in my body. Not knowing what that meant, I nevertheless lost no time and I took aim at them, yelling at them to shoot, that I did not have an arm to give them, but if by their misfortune they were to miss me, I would not miss them, and I would blast their brains out. They shouted at me to stop and said that, even if it were the king himself, they would disarm him, and that there was no need for me to get so worked up. Preferring to kill the devil rather than have the devil kill me, I fired and dropped one of them to the ground. Then I threw down my musket and took my sword in hand to run down the other one, but, since he did not have the nerve to shoot, he ran off and escaped into the woods. Having no enemy to fear anymore, I went to the one who was down, quite upset to see him in that state, believing him to be dead. Despairing that I had killed him, I drew close to him, [75] but then, moving him a little, I saw that he was not dead at all. I set myself to the task of giving him aid. I undressed him and saw with relief that he was only wounded in the arm, but that the large quantity of blood he had lost was the reason he had fainted. I bound his wound with my shirt, which I tore apart, and then made him sniff some Queen of Hungary's Water.[92] In the meantime, my friends had just arrived, and I told them what had happened. When the wounded fellow had recovered a bit, we left him and spent the rest of the day in our lodgings without speaking to anyone about what had happened to me.

The next morning, when we were not thinking anymore about a thing, and while we were still resting in our beds, we heard a great fracas between our hostess and some other people. Right away I decided it was some of the fusiliers, who were coming to get me and my friend who had followed the one who had run away into the woods. I promptly

---

* It is a black bird the size of a blackbird.

91. Tobacco butt

92. Named for fifteenth-century royal Queen Elizabeth of Hungary, Hungary Water is an alcohol-based perfume infused with rosemary and other essential oils that was thought to have healing or restorative qualities.

jumped out of my bed and took off running through a back door for the woods, which were at most forty to fifty steps away. My companion did not have enough time to leave, and he hid himself between two mattresses. When the eight fusiliers entered our room and did not find what they were looking for, they decided to look for us in town, where our hostess told them we had gone. I was immediately called back. I returned and got dressed, and we set about having breakfast as if nothing had happened.

Some of the officers from the *Dromadaire* came to offer their assistance to us after they heard about our affair.[93] They spent [76] the rest of the day with us enjoying themselves. After we had supper, around midnight, and not feeling like sleeping on land for fear of getting caught, we decided to go back on board. These gentlemen came along to conduct us as far as the shore, where we embarked on their ship's boat, which took us to our ship. They spent the night with Monsieur De Bussy and someone else from our ship. After day broke and Monsieur Aubin had gotten up, I went to see him to get his advice about what I should do concerning the juncture where I found myself.

As I had the honor of being in his good graces, he told me that he had been angry about what had happened to me and my companion, but he advised me to go to the fort to turn myself in without delay. He told me that, furthermore, Monsieur D'Esquerac (who is governor and commander of the fort) had written to him that two gentlemen of such and such a description must turn themselves in at the fort.[94] He showed me the letter. After I had read this letter, I became afraid, not knowing at all how the fellow I had wounded was doing. I begged Monsieur Aubin to let me be brought back to shore, so no one would know I had come on board, and, as far as he was concerned, he had only to continue to claim ignorance of where I might be. He allowed me to do this and ordered the coxswain to make ready his boat, in which, after taking leave of him, I took off like a bolt of lightning.

When I got back to shore, I went to find my friends again and enjoyed their company until noon. However, when we were only halfway through dinner, a ship's boy came, bringing me a letter on behalf of my captain, in which he indicated to me that to prevent my situation from becoming more serious, I would do well to surrender myself at the fort, and that he had just [77] received some new orders for me to go there. It was absolutely necessary for me to settle the matter. I was all alone on the shore, for

---

93. The *Dromadaire* was a three-hundred-ton Company of the Indies ship used in the carrying trade. From 1728 to 1730, it traveled on the Lorient–Saint Domingue–Louisiana circuit under the direction of Captain Guillaume Pinchon. *Dromadaire* armament, FML, 1 P 167, no. 108.

94. Sieur D'Esquerac (D'Escairac) was commissioned as commander of La Caye's Fort Saint Louis in March 1728. Personnel Colonial Ancien, d'Escairac, ANOM, COL, E 171; and D'Escairac to Directors of the Company of the Indies, 20 September 1729, ANOM, C9 30.

my companion in misery refused to come there with me. Fortunately for me, I did not encounter any of the soldiers who were looking for me and who would have been pleased to get ahold of me so they could take me to the fort like a despicable wretch. Only a half quarter of an hour had passed since I had arrived on the shore when fortune decided to favor me. As I was settling on a price with a boatswain to take me to the fort, a woman and a young lady arrived at that very moment and heard me saying to the man that all he had to do was take me straight to the fort. They offered me a place in their pirogue. I left the man and with great pleasure accepted what had been offered me with such good grace by some very charming persons. I gave them my hand in order to come aboard. Thus I was enchanted with my encounter and with being with them.

This pleasure, for them as well, was on the point of costing us dearly, for no sooner were we offshore than a wave tried to overturn this conveyance, which was quite small. For the short time it was in motion, it rocked back and forth to a great degree, being very fickle. While we were on the water, we spoke about this and that. I learned that she was the wife of a certain Monsieur Sicardy, a captain at the fort.[95] This worked out very well as far as my affair was concerned, for she asked me (since women are quite curious by nature) what my business was at the fort and why I seemed so dejected. I then profited from this opportunity to tell her about my affair, and I asked her at the same time for the honor of her protection concerning the governor. She [78] promised, as did her daughter, to be of service to me in every way they could. This completely reassured me.

When we arrived at the fort, I offered my hand to Madame Sicardy, to help her ashore, and then to her daughter, when I became aware from certain furtive glances that I was, in fact, at that moment, not uninteresting to her. That appeased the frightful ideas of the prison where I was going to be locked up for the first time in my life. Indeed, I was imagining something completely different from what happened to me, because instead of bearing the fetters of Themis, I bore the chains of the beautiful Sicardy.[96] But, alas, had I not lost my whole life, my freedom, for that charming person whom I would have served as the most faithful slave?

I was counting on conducting them to their house when, to my misfortune, the comrade of the one I had wounded showed up. He came and asked me for my sword, having easily recognized me, and even told me that I was going to be locked up right away. These last words got me fired up and made me be stubborn about not giving in to him in the least bit. I told him, in quite a lofty tone, to bring me to speak to the duty

---

95. Sieur Sicardy (Saccardy) was a lieutenant, not a captain, at Fort Saint Louis. Chevalier de la Rochelar to Maurepas, 1 May 1729, ANOM, C9 30.

96. Themis, the Greek goddess of wisdom and good council, is often associated with justice and order. Modern-day representations of Lady Justice incorporate elements associated with Themis, including a pair of scales.

officer on guard, to whom I would surrender, but, as for him, it was quite useless for him to ask me again, unless he wanted me to do to him what I had done to his comrade with my musket. He finally came to a decision and went to look for the duty officer in charge for me. In the meantime, Madame Sicardy and her daughter expressed their best wishes for me and left for their house. As for myself, just thinking about my new chains gave me [79] so much pleasure that, not only did I have little concern about my present situation, I was even delighted that this affair had happened to me.

The officer whom the soldier had been looking for, and whose memory he had just refreshed concerning the details of my affair, arrived. Approaching me, he said in a surly voice, "So, you, sir, are the one who had the audacity of firing on a soldier who was wearing the uniform of the king, which you ought to recognize." I responded yes, that soldier had come to me with his musket cocked and even took aim at me, while telling me with absurdities to lay my arms down. I then said that he was more to blame than I was, and that if he had asked me differently I would have known what I was supposed to do, but since he had acted very badly in this, he had gotten what he deserved. "Well, then, sir," he said to me, "Follow that soldier and give me your sword." I gave it to him, and, as I went away, he said to me, "We are going to teach you what kind of person you are to fire on a man whom you owe respect for the uniform he wears."

I would have been much more worried at those words, and my affair would have cost me much more, if I had not had the protection of those ladies. So I followed this soldier, who led me into a sort of vaulted chamber, which was very dark. I shivered as I went into it, and even more so after they had locked some huge doors on me, of which the mere sound of the keys and bolts were capable of inspiring terror.

I was not there a half hour when I heard those terrifying doors reopen, but I was quite scared when I saw a Negro, whom I [80] took for the executioner, entering with the jailer, since it is ordinarily Negroes who perform this job in the colonies.[97] He told me to go with me—I mean, with him; it was at those words that I believed myself lost and that I was condemned to die.

I remained rooted there in a swoon; I paled to an extreme degree, so much so that I was unable to follow him, being stricken too keenly. I was overcome on that very

---

97. Throughout the French Caribbean, colonial officials introduced a twist on the long-standing ancien régime practice of commuting the death sentence of a condemned man in exchange for his service as the local *bourreau*, or executioner. On the islands, in Louisiana, and even in New France, Africans filled the post, meting out whippings, brandings, amputations, and hangings in exchange for freedom and sometimes rations or land allotments. On this practice in the circum-Caribbean, see Gene E. Ogle, "Slaves of Justice: Saint Domingue's Executioners and the Production of Shame," *Historical Reflections* 29 (2003): 275–93; and Shannon Lee Dawdy, "The Burden of Louis Congo and the Evolution of Savagery in Colonial Louisiana," in *Discipline and the Other Body: Correction, Corporeality, Colonialism*, ed. Steven Pierce and Anupama Rao (Durham: Duke University Press, 2006). On Quebec, see Daniel Gay, *Les Noirs du Québec, 1629–1900* (Quebec: Septentrion, 2004).

spot, and when the jailer saw me in that state, he promptly sent the Negro to go let his mistress know what had just happened to me. Both of the ladies were kind enough to immediately come to my rescue, and, with the help of Queen of Hungary's Water, they brought me back to consciousness. When I had regained some consciousness, they asked me why I had fainted. I confessed to them that the sight of that Negro, whom I had taken for the executioner, had overcome me all at once. They reassured me and assured me I had nothing to fear.

I could not cease admiring their kindness, especially that of the lovely girl, who reassured me with an air of unequaled tenderness. Madame Sicardy brought me to dine at her house, where I had the honor of meeting her husband, who asked me about my affair, even though he had been informed about it by my two patronesses. I told him everything, and he confessed that in my place he would perhaps have done no less, but he was going to speak about it to the commander, and nothing would happen to me. He also informed me that the soldier whom I had wounded had quickly healed. I thanked him for the trouble he was going to for me so willingly.

As we were finishing our meal, my comrade [81] arrived at the fort to turn himself in according to the summons that had been given to him. They led him to the same place where I had been at first. We finished dinner speaking about Paris and Versailles, where Madame Sicardy and her daughter had spent a year and a half, and after that we got up from the table to go to the governor's house, where Mademoiselle Sicardy ended up mortally wounding me by the manner with which she encouraged the governor to treat me, not as a criminal, but as a foreigner who deserved his protection and his deliverance from prison.

Monsieur D'Esquerac, the governor, said to me, "Sir, you are fortunate to have had such a patroness, to whom I can refuse nothing. I was counting on showing you the fort at your leisure, but these ladies here are opposed to it, thus you may leave when you wish." We thanked him and took our leave.

We returned to Monsieur Sicardy's house, where I professed to my beloved, not only all that indebtedness could dictate to me, but also all that those beautiful eyes were making me suffer. I would have liked to tell her even more, but I did not find another occasion to do so.

My friend, who had left his prison cell, came to find me, and we were taken afterward to a room where we had a light meal. Meanwhile, these ladies began again to ask us for news about Paris. We spoke about it for a very long time. Next we spoke about clothes and, by degrees, about panniers. I saw quite clearly that they wanted to get some, but knowing that no one on board had any, I told them that I had not brought any, for which I was very [82] mortified. In fact, I would have desired very much to show my indebtedness to them by means of these little presents. I found only some blond bobbin lace, which I offered to them, seeing that they were working on making themselves some panniers, without, however, succeeding in making them refined.[98] Since they had only one loop below and a little one above, I had the good fortune of having them agree with my advice, which was to give three rows to each pannier. This was a marvelous success and stood me in their favor more than ever, for the next day and even until we set sail.

Toward evening a soldier came, and he brought back our swords to my friend and me, and, since it was late, we took leave of the ladies and Monsieur Sicardy. Before leaving the fort, we went to thank the governor in particular. He told us he was very annoyed to have forced us to come to the fort, but he had been constrained to do it so no one would find anything to criticize. We took our leave, and then we were ready to leave the fort contented, even though the soldier I had wounded was coming on board for me to give him some things. But, as we were entering under the gate's arch, a sergeant approached and told us we had to pay our exit and entrance. We offered him a piastre, each of us believing that he would be happy, but he told us it was not enough. I realized this was a tyrant, and, in order to get out of his grip, I gave him three more, and my friend did the same, and thus we left the fort, thanks to my hostess, who had loaned me ten piastres so I could leave.

[83] We embarked on the first ship's boat and returned to our ship, where, when Monsieur Aubin saw us, he was very surprised and expressed his joy at our being released at such a good price. I recounted to him how in my misfortune I had had good fortune, and how I had passed my time, and how by chance Madame Sicardy had done us a favor. They were at table, and we sat down too. We stayed at the table with the officers of the *Diane* and the *Dromadaire* until eleven o'clock.[99] Then we went from ship to

---

98. Mercantile policies embodied by the company's right to complete control over imports and exports rendered any alternative trading systems illegal, but actual enforcement of those policies proved difficult. Not all the goods loaded onto the *Durance* (or any other trade ship) could be considered legitimate. Before setting foot in the colony, Louisiana-bound passengers (not to mention ships' officers) ranging from high-level administrators to soldiers destined for the lowest ranks of an outpost's workforce took every opportunity to fill their trunks with contraband trade items that might help them sustain or further themselves once they traversed the Atlantic. Demand for metropolitan fashion accessories was high in the colonies, though it seems that panniers, given their fragility and awkward size, were not suitable for smuggling onto company ships. On smuggling to Louisiana, see Marcel Giraud, *A History of French Louisiana*, vol. 5, *The Company of the Indies, 1723–1731*, trans. Brian Pearce (Baton Rouge: Louisiana State University Press, 1991), 148–51; Daniel H. Usner Jr., *Indians, Settlers, and Slaves in a Frontier Exchange Economy: The Lower Mississippi Valley Before 1783* (Chapel Hill: University of North Carolina Press, 1992), 42–43; and Shannon Lee Dawdy, *Building the Devil's Empire: French Colonial New Orleans* (Chicago: University of Chicago Press, 2008), 103–7, 115–28.

99. The three-hundred-ton *Diane* anchored in Caye Saint Louis to provision and pick up trade goods bound for France, after having delivered a cargo of 464 slaves to Louisiana. *TASTDB*, s.v. "*Diane*" (32902).

ship the rest of the night, with an orchestra consisting of four violins, bagpipes, a viol, two recorders, a transverse flute, a tromba marina, a tabor, and my hunting horn.[100] All these diverse instruments created quite a pleasant music because of the echoes, which, the further we went away from the harbor, the more they rang out. The sea, being very calm, favored us a great deal. We retired about four o'clock in the morning after making a circuit around the fort with all of our instruments.

After I had rested a few hours, I did not neglect to go to Madame Sicardy's, where, after conversing for a while, two tables of quadrille were set up.[101] They asked me to take part, but, seeing that both tables were full—that is, there were enough people without me—I urged those officers and ladies to feel free to begin and not to worry about me. They began, and I took advantage of this happy circumstance to converse with Mademoiselle Sicardy, who was not taking part in their games either. After we watched them play, I suggested to her that we go take [84] some air along the fort's ramparts on the side facing the open sea, and she accepted. The first thing I did when we got there was to reveal to her little by little what I felt in my heart and to show her that, if, on the one hand, she had revealed, I mean, if she had given me my freedom so generously, that, on the other, she held me very tightly in her fetters, yet that it would be an incomparable pleasure for me to wear such beautiful chains for the rest of my days. She answered that she was thrilled to have been of use to me in some way, and that she had done it willingly. As she continued to speak, we were interrupted by an officer who approached us. I was quite discouraged because I lost an opportunity, which, by all appearances, was proceeding along quite favorably for me. We returned to the house, where I fervently wished to be able to find the time to renew our conversation, but it was impossible for me to do so. It was necessary to stay put there against my wishes. When evening came, I took leave of the group and went back on board ship.

The next day I came ashore again to go pay my bill, which amounted to one hundred livres. The same day we had a supper (for fourteen officers) that lasted the whole night. The following day and night brought to a close my expenses on land, so that, including laundering and food for twelve days, we were charged 980 livres. Well, it was a veritable comedy to see such a large expense to be paid by us, not a single one of us having any

---

100. The tromba marina dates to the fifteenth century and remained popular through the eighteenth. A very tall and narrow string instrument, the tromba marina is played standing up with a bow and emits a deep, brassy sound very similar to a trumpet. A tabor is a small snare drum held in one hand and struck with a stick.

101. Popular in eighteenth-century Europe, especially in France, where it originated, quadrille was a four-person variation on the three-person card game ombre. Quadrille is played with a forty-card deck and is a precursor to many card games employing a fifty-two-card deck, including whist.

money. It was necessary for all of us to employ every contrivance to extract ourselves from this dire situation.

Meanwhile, I spoke about it to Monsieur De Bussy, thinking that he [85] would advance me what I needed to be able to pay, but I saw that he was in as much of a predicament as the rest of us. I told him only that I had always counted on him, and that he had shown very bad manners to have engaged me in this expense by telling me not to worry about a thing.

The only choice I made, albeit with regret, was to give up my watch in order to not be indebted to anyone. I found the fort's chaplain, who had already asked me about it, and to whom I delivered it over, having negotiated the price for the amount of 240 livres. I paid my bill, which was 160 livres for my share, and left these gentlemen who insisted on staying ashore there. For myself, I went aboard, where, with what remained of my money, I bought the surgeon's watch, which was a real relic.[102] So I found myself like this—not owing anything and possessor of another watch almost as good as the previous one—while the others were in the predicament of not knowing what to do. Meanwhile, Monsieur De Bussy, who was best off and who had lots of linen and furniture, had to face reality and made a decision, albeit unwillingly, to sell some of it. Then, after seeing that he was having no trouble selling what he had, he parted with enough of it to cover the amount they owed among them. In this way, he extricated himself from the affair and had promissory notes drawn up for each one, to be paid in Louisiana from the first salaries they would draw.

In the end, to my great regret, we made ready to sail May 27. Not so much did I regret the pleasures I had been able to partake of while on land, but rather my agreeable prison and that charming lady jailer, which were the reason for my sorrow.

[86] We left the port about five o'clock in the morning, and luckily we had a wind that allowed us to double all the points. The following days we sailed along the island of Jamaica, sixty leagues long, which was to port, and to starboard, the island of Cuba, which is two hundred fifty leagues long, with an undulating coastline of seven to eight hundred leagues. After passing these islands, we doubled Little Cayman and Grand Cayman the following day, around ten o'clock in the morning. We were hoping to see the Isle of Pines that day, but nightfall obliged us to drift with only the mainsail until the following morning in order to keep from running aground.[103]

---

102. The surgeon, the ship's lowest-paid commissioned officer with a monthly salary of thirty livres, was twenty-eight-year-old François Pardimene of Lorient. *Durance* crew register, FML, 1 P 68.

103. The Isle of Pines lies south of Havana. The largest of Cuba's outlying islands, it was renamed the Isle of Youth in 1978.

On Sunday we then doubled Cape St. Antoine around half past midnight, and we entered the Gulf of Mexico.[104] Cape St. Antoine is the end of the island of Cuba. That same day we had many squalls. At nightfall we saw a longboat, I mean a waterspout,[105] one end of which was descending to a point in front of the ship at a distance of two musket shots and the other to the side. It is very dangerous to be underneath one when they are about to burst, for they are capable of sinking a ship. For this reason we shot the cannon several times to try to make it break apart before we reached it. The fourth shot was the one that broke it; more than two hundred hogsheads of water fell from it.

The preceding day, we saw a ship that we were only able to recognize at eight o'clock in the evening, when it was about two leagues from us. Since night had fallen and we were able to see each other only by the light of the moon, we fired two cannon shots [87] leeward, as a signal. They answered us in conformance with the rules of the company, by firing one shot. They lowered their courses and we did likewise. We recognized it then as a company ship by its signals. They next lit three signal lights as follows, namely the one at the mizzenstaff, the second one at the halyard of the main topgallant of the mizzen topsail, and the third in the stays of the mizzen, and raised their flag. We did the same. With the assistance of our lights, one after the other we approached each other to within speaking-trumpet distance, where we observed yet another little ceremony. They asked us where the ship was from; we answered from Brest, even though we had set sail from Lorient, all toward hiding our course in the event that it was an enemy ship. We hailed them with our speaking trumpet and asked where they were from. They answered that they were from Rochefort, even though they were from Lorient, just as we were. Next we asked who commanded the ship. They told us it was Monsieur Laisné, and we told them that Monsieur Aubin commanded ours. It did not take long before they recognized each other perfectly, and they wished each other good evening and good-bye. We shortened all the sails and let the ship drift all night with only the mainsail, and they did too. Our captain had the ship's boat put into the water and went with the chaplain and the clerk to have supper on the other ship. They did not return until three o'clock in the morning.

Monsieur Aubin informed us that it was the *Galathée*, which was coming from Louisiana, where they had been left with very few provisions.[106] These were not sufficient

---

104. The ship entered the Gulf of Mexico on Sunday, June 5, or Monday, June 6, 1729.

105. This is one of a few instances when Caillot wrote the wrong word and corrected himself textually rather than marring the manuscript with crossed-out text.

106. The frigate *Galathée* sailed from Lorient for the west coast of Africa on May 25, 1728, under the stewardship of Captain Pierre Quinet de Préville. After stops in Senegal and Gorée Island, the *Galathée* left Africa with a cargo of 400 slaves. The ship's cargo and crew did not fare well on the Atlantic crossing. The *Galathée* took a lethal 127 days to reach New Orleans. Usually French ships bound for Louisiana stopped either in Martinique

to get them to the next port, and it was necessary for us to give them some. He immediately put the longboat in the water, and they loaded it with brandy, flour, wine, and lard. It was the [88] first lieutenant and I who went to bring it to them, and we were heartily welcomed. We had a bite to eat and then took leave of them. The officers of their ship who were on ours returned, after which we parted from one another by giving each other in turn a seven-cannon salute, and each crew shouting, "Long live the king," seven times. With pennants and flags flying, we thus lost sight of one another.

We had not yet gone ten leagues when the weather, which became completely overcast from one moment to the next, ended up forcing us to light the candle in the binnacle in order to be able to steer, even though it was noon. The thunder, the rain, the wind, and, in the end, a frightful sea appeared before our eyes by the fervor of the lightning. It was then that I made a thorough examination of my conscience and commended myself to all the saints in heaven, seeing the ship on the brink of disaster at every moment. At times it seemed like we were being lifted to the clouds and a moment later we saw ourselves plunged into the deep abysses. In brief, I would have risked anything in the world to get out of that terrifying place. Nevertheless, the wind's becoming calmer and the sky a little less overcast, refocused me little by little into my ordinary state of mind. Although no one had noticed my worries one bit— on the contrary, I still bravely faced my fate—some people had been left completely immobilized, others were about to cry. Some of our ladies had fainted, and others were sobbing out prayers, yet, out of all those people, I was perhaps the one who was the most afraid, although [89] I did not show it. A half hour after our greatest fears had passed, we had another one, which was due to a whirlwind, also known as a dragon, which rose up to our port side, but it lasted only a moment. Fortunately it drew farther and farther away from us. It is just as dangerous as a waterspout and pulls into the air an amount of water as big as a ship. Still, on that same day, we had a very violent tempest but of short duration. The seas were so heavy that it took us almost half a quarter of an hour to get to the top of a wave, and the ship was listing so hard that the port side was more than a foot in the water. After these storms, we had a perfect calm. Never had I seen so many fish as I did that day. The sea was covered, mostly with sharks and porpoises.

---

or, more commonly, in Saint Domingue to stock up on provisions, but the *Galathée* bypassed the West Indies. The lengthy voyage resulted in very high mortality rates among captives (32 percent) and crew (20 percent). The average mortality on company slavers during this period was 7 percent. Before the *Galathée* reached New Orleans, Quinet de Préville fell ill. A new captain, Thomas Laisné, replaced him. *Galathée* armament, 27 May 1728, FML, 1P167, 2P2-23, no. 599; *TASTDB*, s.v "*Galathée*," (32905); Robert Louis Stein, *The French Slave Trade in the Eighteenth Century: An Old Regime Business* (Madison: University of Wisconsin Press, 1979), 98.

Gallery 2

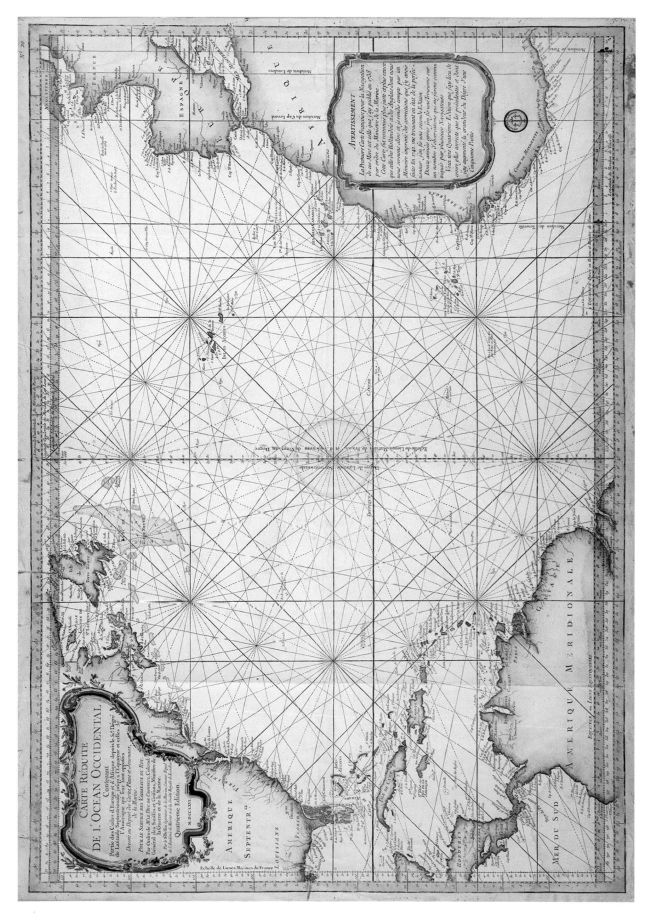

PLATE 8

La Durance
partie le 16. mars
1729.

N.º 87

Enregistré

1729.

Etat des passagers embarqués sur le V.^{eau} La Durance Capitaine
Le S.^r aubin du Plessy destiné pour la Louisianne, auxquels il a esté
payé les sommes Cy apres tant au havre et a Paris qu'à L'orient

Sçavoir

a La table Gratis	au havre	a Paris	a L'orient	Total
Les S.^{rs}				
De Bussy teneur de livre		500.ᵗᵗ	250.ᵗᵗ	750.ᵗᵗ
Goutier Commis aux ecritures			100.	100.
De Troyes Idem		300.	100.	400.
Caillot &.^c		300.	100.	400.
Reylet Chirurgien major			800.	800.
Chierdel dit maisonneuve Chirurgien			600.	600.
La femme dud.^t S.^r maisonneuve				

a L'office Gratis

| La dem.^{lle} Le Cocq a receu tant pour son trousseau que p.^r nourriture | 200.ᵗᵗ | | 70. 10 | 270. 10. |

a la station Gratis
pour le Caye S.^t louis

Le nommé Jean Baptiste Coffre
soldat des anglois

a la station pour
La Louisianne

| 20. soldats auxquels Il a esté donné en avis d'avance suivant l'etat Cy joint Cy | | | 450 | 450. |

Le nommé Joguet dit dailly
Dominique diturbide dit sanlette } fraudeurs de Tabac

| | 200.ᵗᵗ | 1100. | 2470. 10 | 3770.ᵗᵗ 10.ˢ |

a L'orient le 15. mars 1729.

sayu

Since the bad weather had pushed us off course, we did not know where we were going directly but saw three trees pass by, the largest of which was twenty-five to thirty feet in circumference and about two hundred to two hundred fifty feet in length.[107] This gave us reason to think that we were not far from land, and, consequently, by sounding we thought to find bottom that very hour. They sounded every quarter of an hour but grew weary of it. When they were sounding for the last time, they found bottom at twenty-seven fathoms, where, from the black sand at the bottom, they decided we were no more than thirteen leagues from land.

After heaving to the whole night, we saw the land of Mississippi at about eleven o'clock the next day while in about sixteen fathoms of water off the coast of Santa Rosa Island and Pensacola. We cruised along the coast, and at about five o'clock we saw [90] Dauphin Island and then Mobile.

The next day, which was the feast of Corpus Christi, at eight o'clock in the morning, I saw a frigate two leagues behind us.[108] I thought I was mistaken, but, to be more certain of the truth, right away I climbed the main topgallant, where, sure of my observation, I set about crying out, "Ship ho." The captain and his officers immediately looked with their spyglasses and saw that I was not mistaken. They began to try to guess who it might be. Monsieur Aubin thought it was Monsieur de La Renaudais, relative of Monsieur Landivisiau, who was returning from Guinea.[109] He indeed thought correctly, because upon closer inspection it turned out to be him. When he was with us, he was our commander, since he was the older captain and since his ship sailed better than ours.[110] He told us that he would go ahead, and that he would anchor that evening when they reached ten fathoms. We sailed until nine o'clock, when we saw their signal light. We steered toward it and then cast anchor leeward next to them.

---

107. Caillot may be referring to downed bald cypress trees that had drifted into the Gulf. Prior to massive deforestation in the late nineteenth and early twentieth centuries, old-growth cypress trees with circumferences up to fifty-five feet were commonplace in southeast Louisiana. Cypress remains the largest tree species in North America east of the Sierra Nevada mountain range, with the largest extant cypress in North America boasting a fifty-three-foot, eight-inch circumference, found in Louisiana's Cat Island Swamp. John V. Dennis, *The Great Cypress Swamps* (Baton Rouge: Louisiana State University Press, 1988), 115–16.

108. The feast of Corpus Christi, which occurs the Thursday following Trinity Sunday, honors the presence of the Body of Christ within the Eucharist. In 1729 the Feast of Corpus Christi was celebrated on June 16.

109. The ship was the *Vénus*, a slave ship operated by the Company of the Indies. The *Vénus* left Lorient February 4, 1729, and reached Senegal three weeks later. After trading along the coast from Gorée Island south along the West African coast to Rio Nunez (in present-day Guinea), the *Vénus*'s captain, Jean-Baptiste Gaultier de La Renaudais, set sail for Louisiana April 16 with a cargo of four hundred fifty slaves. The *Vénus* reached the Gulf Coast after a sixty-one-day Atlantic crossing and encountered the *Durance* off the coast of Louisiana on June 16, 1729. *Vénus* armament, 4 Feb 1729, FML, 1P168-244, 2P2-23, no. 622; *Vénus* logbook, Archives de la Marine, Archives Nationales (AN), B3 330, fo. 95 and 4JJ 16–17; and *TASTDB*, s.v. "*Vénus*" (32909).

110. The rules of naval hierarchy, which also applied on company ships, required that when more than one captain was present, as in instances when multiple ships traveled together as a fleet or squadron, the senior officer outranked the other captains and took on the role of commander.

Between Horn Island and the Chandeleur Islands we caught all sorts of fish, which are pictured in the print here on the side [see plate 17]. Among other things, we caught a kind of little monster, of which not a single sailor could tell us the name. This animal had a body brown in color, and the tail somewhat green. It had three black spines on its back, which it raises when it wants to prick. Its head and ears are more or less like those of a barbet,[111] with the exception of its lower jaw, which is very long with a kind of barb at the end, which is green [91] and which it is able to move quite easily. Its ears have green fur. Its eyes are black, and above all it is well endowed with teeth. Its two paws are scaly and green, made like those of a duck, except for the talons it has. It has one fin in front and two behind.

We stayed three days anchored in that spot, and the fourth day we raised anchor and got under sail with a wind from the south-one-fourth southwest. We had just come to within a league of the Balize when we were hit by a gale that forced us to go take refuge at Ship Island, which we had left a few days earlier.[112] While waiting for a favorable wind, we went hunting on this island, where there were many wild pigs and caymans, otherwise known as crocodiles.[113] I killed one that was nineteen feet long. There were some that were quite a bit bigger and were monstrous.

The next day we set sail, but it was not for long, because the wind quickly died down. We made ready to sail many times and many days in a row, without being able to advance more than one-fourth of a league because of this. One would have said that there was a jinx on the ship, for as soon as we would make ready to sail, we had to drop anchor. We had been going through the same drill for fifteen days, suffocating from the heat and with raging thirst because we were getting only a half bucket of very stinky water per day, when a little wind from the east-southeast took hold of us and let us advance one and a half leagues.

---

111. A Barbet is a breed of French water spaniel.

112. Before Louisiana's capital was moved from Biloxi to New Orleans, in 1722, French ships arriving on the Gulf Coast often anchored at either Ship or Dauphin Island. Beginning in 1724, arriving vessels began bypassing those islands, anchoring instead at the Balize, a swampy, semifortified island located at the Mississippi River's southeast pass. Mud lumps, tangles of dead trees, and sandbars at the river's mouth complicated navigation and posed serious threats to heavily loaded ships. To minimize risk, cargoes, passengers, and slaves were often unloaded or disembarked at the Balize. On obstacles at the mouth of the Mississippi and navigational difficulties for tall sailing ships, see Banks, *Chasing Empire*, 85–86. On the establishment of the Balize and an overview of working and living conditions there, see Pierre Leblond de Latour, "Plan [et profil] des ouvrages projettés à faire à l'isle de la Balise avec les logements necessaires," 1 September 1723, Dépot des Fortifications des Colonies, ANOM, 105C; Gwendolyn Midlo Hall, *Africans in Colonial Louisiana: The Development of Afro-Creole Culture in the Eighteenth Century* (Baton Rouge: Louisiana State University Press, 1992), 76; and Giraud, *History of French Louisiana*, 5:330–42.

113. Eighteenth-century French travelers to the Gulf Coast frequently remarked upon the presence of "*crocodilles*," a crocodilian reptile better known today as the American alligator.

Toward evening we saw a little sailing pirogue coming, which arrived at our ship about four o'clock. It carried an officer of the Balize with the harbor pilot, both of whom slept on board. Toward midnight the wind started to strengthen with such great violence that [92] with the foresail alone we were running three and a half knots. When the wind died down we unfurled the fore-topsail, the mainsail, the main-topsail, and the topgallant sails. No sooner were all these sails out than a gale came, which prevented us from being able to reef any sail. Nevertheless, with time and patience, we finished the job.

Day had just broken when, through the fault of our harbor pilot, who had become disoriented by the strong wind, we saw ourselves at a distance of just two musket shots from land. Immediately some officers and seamen cried out, "Luff!" and they put the ship about, for without that, we were going to sink in the port and break up on the riverbank. The currents of the river were also causing this to happen, having moved us half a league from the mouth of the river, which we were counting on sailing straight on up. So we had to return to anchor at a distance of two leagues to wait for the first good wind. Monsieur Aubin sent his ship's boat with the clerk to go get drinking water at the Balize. He returned just at noon, while we were at table. We treated ourselves to the fresh water he had just brought like it was the best of wines. It gave us much pleasure, but we rejoiced even more when he told Monsieur Aubin that they were coming to get all the passengers. I confess to you that however great the pleasure I had in drinking good water, it did not equal the pleasure this bit of news gave me. Just the mere thought that I would be able to go ashore gave me an inexpressible joy.

About three o'clock we saw two pirogues approaching, which were in fact for us. Since we were pressed for time, I brought only what [93] I deemed most necessary. While I was packing, Monsieur Aubin came to see me with a gracious and agreeable demeanor, offered to have some fresh food given to me, and also said to me that he hoped I would forget what had happened on the ship since our departure from France, just as he would. I promised him this and we parted our ways as very good friends. To reassure us of our perfect reconciliation, he said good-bye to us, along with his crew (after we had pushed off), shouting, "Long live the king," seven times. We returned the farewell and reached the Balize, where we arrived after nightfall, but the moonlight helped us greatly.

The first land that appeared before my eyes was a tiny speck of a half-submerged island, which was called Cannon Island. It gave me a very bad opinion of Mississippi, coupled with what I had heard our officers saying about it, as being land which sooner or later would perish by water. At that moment I would really have liked to get back to France, but, on the other hand, curiosity made me forget the past. We pushed ahead but saw ourselves get tangled in some big tree trunks, which carried us to the sea for a distance of more than two musket shots. By dint of rocking ourselves back and forth, we extracted ourselves from them and won back the time we had just lost, by means of the Negroes who were conveying us.[114] Since we were concerned only with defending ourselves from the trees that the river was carrying out to sea, we ran aground on a little sandbank. Even though we were not in great danger, it put us in a very awkward situation. After pushing first from one side and then from the other, and seeing that it was not budging, the Negroes, who were six in number, jumped into the water and carried us in the pirogue until we were floating. Then they got back in with us, and, at a distance of three musket shots, we landed at a small wooden bridge at the Balize, where the few inhabitants and the commander were [94] waiting for us [see fig. 14]. As soon as my friends and I were on land, we went to greet them. He gave orders for our trunks to be carried, and he led us to his house. It is a man by the name of Monsieur Duvergé who commands this post.[115] He is a man of great merit and a good engineer. We stayed with him for three days, taking a respite from the rigors of the sea and regaining our strength to go upriver to New Orleans.

Finally we had to embark again, though not for a long period of time, but the eight days it took us for that bit of navigation tired us more than the whole crossing from France to this place, as I will next describe for you.[116] So we then refreshed ourselves with good food because, as far as wine went, there wasn't any except what we had brought as a present for him. We would have given him all of it if my friends had been of the same mind as me, but we kept thirty-two of them for our voyage. The only

---

114. Much of the labor required to transfer cargo and passengers from arriving ships to smaller transports bound for either the Balize or New Orleans was performed by the more than three dozen company-owned slaves residing at the Balize. At least eight of these slaves were experienced seamen charged with navigating small craft between the Balize and New Orleans. These men likely carried out a labor role similar to that of canoe men along the west African coast. This must have seemed striking to arriving African captives, who found themselves shuttled to and from slave ships, on opposite sides of the Atlantic, by skilled African seamen. The eight sailors at the Balize were part of a larger group of company slaves tasked with working the colony's waterways. Enslaved sailors made up 20 percent of the company's slave holdings: thirteen men were assigned to half a dozen small boats based in New Orleans; eight to the Balize; seven to the Natchez post upriver from New Orleans; and nine to Governor Périer's plantation. "Etat general des Dépnses de la Comp. des Indes à la Louisiane pour l'année 1729," ANOM, B43; "Inventaire de l'habitation de la Comp. des Indes sur le fleuve St. Louis vis à vis la Nouvelle Orléans et de tous les Batiments marchandises, des ustensils, des nègres et bestiaux," 2 September 1731, ANOM, C2 24. On company slaves at the Balize and the use of company slaves as maritime laborers, see Greenwald, "Company Towns and Tropical Baptisms," 150–51, 179–82, 257–58.

115. Bernard Duvergé (sometimes spelled Duvergés) served technically as chief engineer, but his duties at the Balize extended to those of port director, or harbormaster, and general overseer.

116. Travelers often remarked upon the extreme difficulty of the journey from the Balize to New Orleans. In 1727 Ursuline novitiate Marie-Madeleine Hachard wrote to her father that "all the hardships of the *Gironde* were nothing compared to what" she suffered in the "little crossing, which is only thirty leagues upriver, from Belize [*sic*] to New Orleans." Hachard, *Voices from an Early American Convent*, 67. See also Banks, *Chasing Empire*, 85–86.

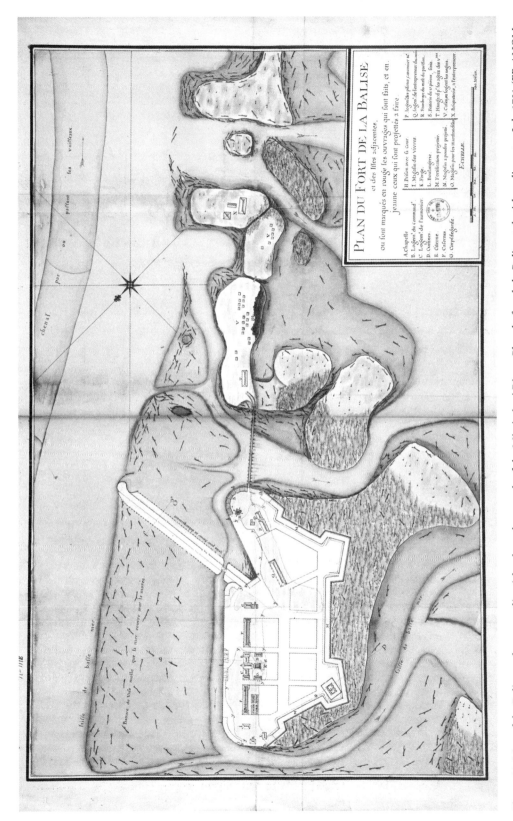

Figure 14. Map of the Balize and surrounding islands at the mouth of the Mississippi River; *Plan du fort de la Balise et des isles adjacentes*, July 1731 (FR.ANOM. Aix-en-Provence. 04DFC 111B)

thing that gave us any trouble during our stay at this place was with regard to sleeping, because we had all left our sleeping mats on board. However, he had a bed prepared for us on the floor, where eight of us slept. Never in my life have I spent nights like those and the ones that we spent on the river.

Finally, the day of our departure having arrived, we embarked in several pirogues and flatboats with Negroes that had arrived from Guinea, four hundred fifty in number, of which each of us had a certain number in our boats. When the boats were loaded, we took our leave of Monsieur Duvergé (since we were ready to push off), and we left. We had gone only three leagues when four Negroes died of scurvy, which ordinarily strikes most of them when they leave the ships to go on land. It was nevertheless necessary to keep them until evening, when we went ashore to make camp and set up their cooking kettle and ours. While disembarking, yet another two of the most handsome ones died.[117]

[95] We spent the night in this place, and at daybreak we took to the river again. We had all the trouble in the world that day to make it to that night's stop because of the rapid flow of the river and also because of my crew, who were worn out. Meanwhile, I arrived at the meeting place, where the other boats were, one hour after midnight. Extremely worn out, I ran to get some sea bread to appease the hunger that was devouring me. This place was as flooded as the preceding one, but that did not keep me from sleeping there on some branches I cut to get myself above the water.

The biggest problem we had was lighting the fire for the Negroes' cooking kettle, which was to cook large Windsor beans.[118] We spent that night as badly as the preceding one, and likewise the following ones, until the fifth day, when we arrived at the first plantation, which belonged to three soldiers who were living together. We had a bite to eat at their house, and we pushed off to try to make it to the next plantation to sleep. With an eye toward this outcome, I pressed the Negroes to row, but night surprised us, and we stranded ourselves on a tree, from which we had the worst difficulties imaginable to extricate ourselves. Finally, by dint of pushing, after getting afloat again and getting underway, I noticed that my boat was taking on quite a bit of water and that

---

117. Caillot's calculation of the number of slaves distributed among several New Orleans–bound conveyances is incorrect. Though the *Vénus* left Africa with 450 slaves, only 320 disembarked at the Balize. Eighty-seven slaves died en route to Louisiana during the Middle Passage, and forty-three more were traded at Biloxi. From Caillot's report, it is clear that a number of slaves arrived in poor health; at least six bondsmen died between the Balize and the first stop on the trip upriver. *TASTDB*, s.v. "*Vénus*" (32909). On slave ships and sickness of captives and crew on disembarkation, see Hall, *Africans in Colonial Louisiana*, 79–80, 83–86; Emma Christopher, *Slave Ship Sailors and Their Captive Cargoes, 1730–1807* (New York: Cambridge University Press, 2006), 205–8; Marcus Rediker, *The Slave Ship: A Human History* (New York: Viking, 2007), 273–76; Usner, *Indians, Settlers, and Slaves*, 37–41.

118. The Windsor bean is the most common variety of broad, or fava, bean.

it was punctured. I had time only to have some of the Negroes get off onto the trees that had become stuck in that location, and to have the others get onto a boat that was luckily not far from mine. Never had I found myself in a situation like that. The boat, which had just taken some of my Negroes, kept on going and left us perched in our trees, where we remained not even a quarter of an hour when our boat sank to the bottom. While waiting for help from the boats that were coming behind us, I settled myself into the roots of one of those trees, which formed a sort of armchair, and told the coxswain to wake me when the boats were approaching.

[96] They arrived around three thirty in the morning. My friends were very surprised to see me in that state. Each of them took the rest of my Negroes, and, after I got on board with them, I told them how the accident had come about. They told me that they had also gotten stranded on the same tree, but that they had not sustained any damage. Since all of these things had slowed us down immensely, we were unable to go meet up with the boat that was carrying our provisions that day, and we were forced to put in to shore about nine in the evening at the first plantation a quarter of a league downstream. We went ashore, and the master of that place came to offer us his house.

We got the cooking kettle set up for the Negroes and afterward we went into the house, where we were graciously offered supper. Decide for yourself whether I acquitted myself of my duty, after not having eaten for two days. We did not lack for bread, but it was made of pure rice.[119] It was there that I first tried fish native to that country, which I found excellent. At another time I would not have wanted to try them for anything in the world, for fear that they would make me sick. We were welcomed quite warmly by the people there, but when it was time to go to bed, the only bed we had was a bearskin stretched out on the floor to cover ourselves with in order to protect ourselves from gnats and mosquitoes. In spite of how much I wanted to sleep, it was impossible for me to do so, because of those insects that were devouring us. There were so many of them that we were smashing them on our faces by the fistful.[120] Not being able to endure them anymore, I went to find the master of the plantation and borrowed one of his pirogues.

---

119. Rice was a staple in Louisiana, where it was used in everything from bread to desserts. On rice production and its culinary uses, see Antoine-Simon Le Page du Pratz, *Histoire de la Louisiane* (Paris: De Bure, l'aîné, 1758), 2:8, 346–47; Nancy Miller Surrey, *The Commerce of Louisiana during the French Régime, 1699–1763* (New York: Columbia University Press, 1916), 267–69; and Hall, *Africans in Colonial Louisiana*, 121–24. Also useful for information on the culinary habits of French colonial Louisianians is Shannon Lee Dawdy, "'A Wild Taste': Food and Colonialism in Eighteenth-Century Louisiana," *Ethnohistory* 57 (2010): 389–414.

120. The overwhelming presence of gnats (specifically biting midges, also known as no-see-ums) and mosquitoes is a reoccurring complaint in memoirs from early French colonial Louisiana. Hachard provided a similar account of her first encounters with "Monsieurs Mosquitoes" and "Frappes d'abord," the latter of which came "in such great numbers that one could cut them with a knife." Marie-Madeleine Hachard to Jacques Hachard, 27 October 1727, *Voices from an Early American Convent*, 56, 68.

I had my crew reembark with me, and I, with my legs almost ruined from scratching so much, forced my Negroes to row in order to rejoin the caravan, which I reached around seven thirty in the morning. They had waited for us until that time, not knowing how I would set myself up. I went to the house, where I found [97] our gentlemen, who, while waiting for us, were having some fun. When they saw me, they asked if I had eaten well at my stop. I told them how I had managed and what I had eaten. They told me that I had done better than they; that they had eaten only some sagamité, in other words, some rice in water, because they had not found anyone in the plantation.[121]

This news did not please me one bit, because I felt like I was at least as hungry as they were. While our Negroes were laying waste to the corn, seeing that there was no more bread or wine, I cooked some new rice with three snakebirds that I had killed, and a few swallows. I put them in all together with some large peppers instead of regular pepper, and no salt.[122] I succeeded in making a hash that had us licking our fingers. Seeing us, one would have said we were like a pack of hunting dogs scrambling after the spoils.

We reembarked and traveled until ten o'clock. My crew, which had always been last, found themselves first, since we had twelve oars on board and everyone was a good rower. We also had two small sails. I arrived at the place we were to sleep that night two hours before the others. It was at the house of a *gros habitant* from Paris named Tixerant, who had been an ironmonger at the end of the Pont Neuf.[123] He had been notified that we were supposed to be stopping at his house that night. I went ashore and had the Negroes stay in the boat so that they wouldn't take anything. I had no sooner given my orders when, turning my eyes toward the house, I saw in the distance what looked like a little enchanted palace. Lit by many torches, I saw a room in the middle of

---

121. "Sagamité" is a term used to describe a number of dishes with a corn (not rice) base, ranging from hasty puddings to broths. Dawdy, "'A Wild Taste,'" 393; Richard Campanella, *Bienville's Dilemma: A Historical Geography of New Orleans* (Lafayette: Center for Louisiana Studies, 2008), 240–43; and "Sacamité" in William A. Read's *Louisiana Place Names of Indian Origin: A Collection of Words* (Tuscaloosa: University of Alabama Press, 2008), 117–18.

122. "Large peppers" refers to bell peppers.

123. The terms "*gros habitant*" and "*petit habitant*" were used to describe French colonists at opposite ends of the socioeconomic spectrum. In the English colonial world, *gros habitants* are often referred to as planters: influential, powerful, and often wealthy property owners. Conversely, *petits habitants* were colonists of limited means: laborers, those without property, and some craftsmen, who were often dependent on the patronage of wealthier colonists for their own advancement. Louis Tixerant (also spelled Tisserand) arrived in Mobile, where he served first as a company warehouse guard, in the early 1720s. He later served as storekeeper of the warehouses at Biloxi until he was dismissed following an inventory scandal. His 1724 marriage into one of the largest planter families in Louisiana, the Carrières, meant that, by the time of Caillot's arrival, Tixerant had accumulated enough land and slaves, including forty-five Africans and two Indians, to be considered a *gros habitant*. Charles R. Maduell Jr., ed. and trans., "Census of the Inhabitants along the River Mississippi Dated 1731," *The Census Tables for the French Colony of Louisiana from 1699 through 1732* (Baltimore: Genealogical Publishing Co., 1972), 114; Jacques de La Chaise to the Directors of the Company of the Indies, 8 March 1724, *Mississippi Provincial Archives*, ed. and trans. Dunbar Rowland and A. G. Sanders (Jackson: Press of the Mississippi Department of Archives, 1932) 2:303, 336.

which there stood a large table all set for a meal. At that delightful sight, I felt a certain something in my heart, which then made me forget half the troubles I had endured, and after [98] a bit I soon forgot the rest. When a young and beautiful lady dressed in muslin, followed by four slaves who lighted her way, came before me at my boat, requesting me with a gracious and charming air to go rest, I paid her a small compliment and followed her. She led me to the place I had seen, and while walking with her I could not help but examine her charming form, her free and lighthearted air, and her great manner, such that I was like a spellbound man. But my stomach, which was quite empty, and my entrails were not reconciled to that and would not have approved of my way of acting one bit. But luckily, turning my head to the side, I saw by chance a place where I heard a great clatter of pots and pans, which reunited me completely, body and soul, with them. I can assure you that never was there a soldier more animated by the sound of the trumpets and drums than my insides were from this clatter. From that moment on, I was in such a happy mood that I felt as if I owned the entire universe.

I chatted with this woman, who I realized was the lady of the house. Concerning Monsieur Tixerant, he had gone to New Orleans, and she was expecting him at any moment. I took advantage of this fortunate absence to praise the charms of my incomparable hostess, but my pleasure did not last for long and was interrupted by the arrival of our fleet, which pained me, because I could no longer converse tête-à-tête, yet, on the other hand, I was delighted with it, because that meant supper would be sooner. I led her on board our boats, followed by her slaves, where she welcomed our gentlemen in her customary manner. We saw her husband arrive, and he did not contradict in the least the obliging manners of his wife. He is a man who is a friend of pleasures and good food. When we arrived at the house, since no one had a lack of appetite, we [99] sat down at the table, where we were immediately served with all the delicacy possible for the country and the season. At that moment I felt my heart beating almost like Sancho Panza's did, when, by chance, Don Quixote found himself at a country wedding, where his faithful squire filled his stomach for the time that he had been obliged to fast. What happened to me was more or less the same. The only thing lacking at this meal was wine, because half the year there is no wine, so we drank brandy.[124]

---

124. The importation of wine, in casks and bottles, to Louisiana proved a tricky endeavor. Though wine arrived on nearly all company ships, the quantity and quality varied significantly depending on available room and storage conditions in the hold. Wine at sea in the summer months often spoiled before reaching its destination. This was the case with the hogsheads of wine that arrived on the *Durance*. In a letter to company directors, Jacques de La Chaise reported his "fear that the wines" from the *Durance* "will be spoiled by the great heat . . . in the hold," which was worsened, according to Captain Aubin Du Plessis, by the placement of the cook's galleys between decks (translation my own). Etienne Périer and Jacques de La Chaise to company directors, 26 August 1729, ANOM, C13 11, fo. 351–65.

We spent the rest of the evening very pleasantly, and when the time came to reboard the boats and we had to leave, it was not without regret. We pushed off at about two o'clock and traveled the whole night, the next day and night, setting foot on land that night, or at daybreak, at the house of one of the gentlemen who had gone up the river with us. We had some food and drink there, and changed clothes to be able to appear in New Orleans, which was no more than two leagues from where we were. He loaned us one of his pirogues, and from then on we were done with the war, plague, and famine we had faced during this little trip. War, because it had been necessary for us to have stick in hand to keep the Negroes under control; plague, for the stench that the scurvy-ridden people had given us; and famine, because as a rule we had nothing to eat.

On July 13, at about 9:30 in the morning, we arrived in the city of New Orleans, where we found ourselves like veritable greenhorns, not knowing where we were going to stay. Monsieur De Bussy, our bookkeeper, who had come along with us, said he had a letter for a certain Monsieur Chastang, inspector of the books, that we should all go with him and make arrangements for ourselves according to what he said to us.[125] We found out where [100] this man resided. Finally, after making many turns, we arrived at his house. He asked us without much conviction to dine with him, but seeing that we were not at all reluctant, that we had freely accepted the invitation, and that each of us was also talking about having our baggage brought to his house, this frightened him and he was very apprehensive that we would stay in his house several days, and so for that reason he saw to finding us lodging elsewhere.[126] He notified a certain Jarry of our arrival, an innkeeper at whose place we slept starting that very night.[127]

The next day we got dressed to go see Monsieur de Périer, who is the commanding general of the Province of Louisiana, where we were very well received.[128] He promised that he would do everything in his power to help us out, and that he would do so willingly. We took our leave of him, and then we went to the company headquarters, where Director-General Monsieur de La Chaise and his daughters welcomed

---

125. François Chastang was chief inspector of the company's accounts in Louisiana and the newly arrived employees' superior.

126. In the five years before Caillot's arrival, several scandals involving dissolute clerks had unfolded. In 1724 a bookkeeping clerk was dismissed from his post and jailed for writing "verses against the honor of the ladies of New Orleans." In 1728 six clerks ran amok. Three were involved in a forgery scheme. Two more were dismissed for being lazy and drunken, and the sixth was involved in a brawl that resulted in the death of one clerk at the hands of another. Past experience with company clerks may help explain Chastang's reluctance to welcome the new recruits into his home. Greenwald, "Company Ships and Tropical Baptisms," 156–59.

127. Louis and Anne Jarry ran an inn on Royal Street. Their establishment was popular among visiting ships' officers and company employees.

128. Etienne Périer served as Louisiana's military commander and governor between 1726 and 1732. All newly arrived officers and company employees were required to register their arrival in the colony with him. "Ordonnance pour les Apointemens des Officiers et Employés de la Louisianne," 30 September 1726, ANOM, B 43b, fo. 652–53.

us very warmly.[129] I gave them some letters from their relatives, and then they offered us coffee. After conversing for two hours, we withdrew. The next day we took our places in the offices.

That is the account of my trip from Paris to Louisiana. I am now going to relate to you an account of that country, of the peoples who inhabit it, and in what manner they govern themselves. Following this I will recount everything that happened during my stay in this country.

---

129. The company's Louisiana headquarters were located in the square block bounded by the Place d'Armes, Chartres and Toulouse Streets, and the riverfront. Between 1723 and 1730 Jacques de La Chaise served as the company's chief financial officer in Louisiana. Beginning in 1725 he was also the colony's *commissaire-ordonnateur*, or king's commissioner, who shared supervisory duties with the governor. The *commissaire-ordonnateur* was responsible for civil justice, provisioning, trade, and finances.

An Account of the Mississippi Country and the Indians Who Inhabit This Land

I will begin with the principal town, called New Orleans, where the Superior Council and Governing Council are held, composed of the following gentlemen, namely:

Superior Council:

Messieurs:

de Périer, general of the whole province of Louisiana

de La Chaise,[130] previous director-general and commissioner appointed by the king

MacMahon, present director-general and first councilor

Bruslé,[131] extraordinary commissioner of the troops and second councilor

Dausseville,[132] chief administrator of the navy and third councilor

Prat,[133] physician-botanist paid by the king, and fourth councilor

Le Baron,[134] astrologer and fifth councilor

Fleuriau,[135] king's prosecutor and civil judge

---

130. In the margin to the left of La Chaise's name, Caillot noted that La Chaise was dead (see plate 5); indeed, he served as director-general and first councilor until his death, on February 6, 1730. Senior councilor Antoine Bruslé filled the role in the interim between La Chaise's death and the April 17, 1730, appointment of merchant Laurent Patrice MacMahon to the post. MacMahon served as director-general until October 1731, when he was replaced by the king's appointed *commissaire-ordinateur*, Edme Gatien Salmon.

131. One of the council's original members, Bruslé managed the colony's finances.

132. Raymond Amyault, sieur Dausseville, received his commission as a member of the Superior Council on August 24, 1726. "Commission de 2. Conseillier au Con. de Regie de la Louisianne pour le Sr. Amyault d'Ausseville," ANOM, B 43, fo. 619.

133. Doctor Louis Prat, king's physician and Louisiana's official botanist, received an honorary commission as a nonsalaried member of the Superior Council in 1725. His appointment was intended to ensure that the council had enough members on hand to validate judicial outcomes.

134. The king's mathematician Pierre Baron, along with Ignace-François Broutin, succeeded the royal engineer Adrien de Pauger following Pauger's death in 1726. Baron was commissioned as the Superior Council's fifth member in 1728. On Baron's family background and service in Louisiana, see Giraud, *History of French Louisiana*, 5:244–47, 251–55.

135. François Fleuriau was appointed to the council in 1722. He served as the king's prosecutor (attorney general), collected company debts, and enforced judicial ordinances; he also managed the colony's hospital.

[102] Sieurs:

Rossard,[136] clerk of court and assessor of unclaimed property

Dargaray,[137] bailiff

The Governing Council is composed of the aforementioned with the exception of the following Messieurs: Prat, Le Baron, Fleuriau, Rossard.

The city was planned out in September 1718 and was on its way to becoming well established by 1721.[138] First you see the parish church, built of wood and bricked inside, 144 feet long and 60 feet wide, of a terrible wood that is found in this aforementioned place. One can sing the praises of the engineers who drew up the plan for this town, for it is a very fine creation for the country. It will become better and better, as much for the beauty of its buildings, which are being constructed, as for the layout of its streets, and also for its long levee, a quarter of a league long and 22 feet wide, which protects the city from river flooding. Along this levee is the customary promenade, and on one side there are two storehouses, each 220 feet long and 40 feet wide.

The company headquarters are also very well built, both grand and spacious, consisting of an apartment for the director, a very proper main hall for hearings, and three offices joining it. They are as follows: one for the council, where the secretary and two assistants work; the second for the chief bookkeeper and his eight employees;[139] and the third for the private accounts of the former administration, which has seven employees. What makes this building even more beautiful are two pavilions that have fine wrought-iron balconies. The munitions storehouse is found to the left of this building, and to the right you can see an arsenal, all situated opposite the river.

The river, which we call the Mississippi and the natives call Balbancha, is (and this I can say without having traveled very far along it) one of the deepest, for there are places where it is up to one hundred fifty or two hundred [103] fathoms, which is one thousand feet. Many travelers have searched for its source without ever finding it, even

---

136. Michel Rossard, New Orleans's royal notary, also served as the Superior Council's registrar, beginning in 1724. Two years later he took on additional duties as police inspector and unclaimed property assessor.

137. Pierre Dargaray, a native of Rennes, France, came to Louisiana as an indentured servant around 1720. After completing his contract at the Sainte-Reyne concession in the Tchoupitoulas district (an east-bank settlement approximately four leagues upriver from New Orleans), Dargaray moved his family to New Orleans, where he accepted the post of bailiff.

138. Clearing of the site destined to become the French capital began in 1718, but New Orleans remained a muddy tract containing just a few scattered houses until 1721, when royal military engineers Pierre Leblond de La Tour and Adrien de Pauger implemented the layout of the sixty-six-block grid now known as the French Quarter. On the establishment of New Orleans and the careers of Leblond de La Tour and Pauger, see Gilles-Antoine Langlois, *Des Villes pour la Louisiane française: Théorie et pratique de l'urbanistique coloniale au 18e siècle* (Paris: l'Harmattan, 2003); and Dawdy, "*La Ville Sauvage*: Nature and Urban Planning" in *Building the Devil's Empire*, 63–98.

139. During his tenure in Louisiana, Caillot worked in one of the bookkeeping offices headed by François Chastang (see fig. 2).

after going upriver more than nine hundred leagues.[140] They have been constrained to renounce their intentions because of the quickness of the current and the horrible deserts,[141] where they were unable to find anything that could sustain them. This river passes before the town and flows into the sea thirty leagues downriver, which is very troublesome for the vessels that come to bring merchandise and supplies. These vessels are obliged to come upriver to New Orleans, which sometimes takes them one and two months to reach, and during this time they lose a part of their crew due to the great hardship they have. This river begins to rise in April and falls toward the end of July. It doesn't take long to rise, but in less than eight days it drops more than fifty feet.

There are fourteen streets in this town [see plate 19], not counting the quay, and they are all laid out perfectly straight. The houses are built of wood, due to the lack of stones, but for one year now people have been taken with the fashion of building in brick. Instead of plaster, they use lime, which is made with shells, and a good number of residents benefit considerably in making brick and lime, for which the company pays three livres per quarter pound.

You will also find two hospitals, which are each 135 feet long and 45 feet wide, each having 25 beds. At the end of the quay you can observe the large quarters (formerly belonging to the deceased Monsieur de La Tour,[142] brigadier of the engineers, knight of the military order of Saint Louis, and lieutenant general for this province), which are used today as a hospital for Negroes.

On Chartres Street there is a convent of Ursuline nuns, who are seven in number.[143] There should be twelve more coming from France, and the convent will be at the other end of town, on the quay. They teach the young people without profit or anything else

---

140. Explorers continued to search for the Mississippi's headwaters until 1832, when American ethnologist Henry Rowe Schoolcraft identified northern Minnesota's Lake Itasca as the river's source.

141. The French word "*desert*" ("desert") was often employed to describe plots of land or fields inhabited or used by Indians. In this instance, however, Caillot may be using "*deserts*" to describe plains.

142. Leblond de La Tour died in October 1723.

143. La Chaise initially attempted to secure gray sisters (*hospitalières*) from the Daughters of Charity to staff New Orleans's hospital, but none was available to take up a new mission in Louisiana. Instead, in 1727 a group of twelve Ursuline nuns from Rouen, France, traveled to New Orleans, where the company hoped they would run the capital's hospital. These early Ursulines are best known not for hospital ministrations, however, but for the establishment of the first school for girls in the Mississippi Valley. Beginning in the fall of 1727, the Ursulines opened the doors of their temporary residence to girls of African, French, and Indian descent. Seven years after their arrival, on July 17, 1734, the Ursulines moved their school and boarders to a new convent constructed at the edge of town, in the block bounded by Chartres and Arsenal (now Ursulines) Streets, the quay, and what Caillot called "rue des Religieuses" (now Governor Nicholls Street). Note that on his February 1731 map of New Orleans (see plate 19), Caillot confused the future location of the Ursuline convent with that of the arsenal, possibly because the engineers' original plans called for construction of the convent on the arsenal site once the arsenal was moved to the Place d'Armes. On the Ursulines in New Orleans, see Hachard, *Voices from an Early American Convent*; and Emily Clark, *Masterless Mistresses: The New Orleans Ursulines and the Development of a New World Society, 1727–1834* (Chapel Hill: University of North Carolina Press, 2007).

except for what people willingly want to give them. They have some boarders who pay [104] room and board. Outside town at a distance of a musket shot, you will find the Jesuits, who intend to have a church built there, 130 feet long by 45 feet wide.[144] There are only two of them at present, for the others have gone away—one to perform missionary work and serve as parish priest among the Illinois, another to the Arkansas, one to the Natchitoches, and another to the Choctaw.[145] They are very powerful and they have a magnificent brickyard.

If you count all the people in the town, from the youngest to the oldest, there are sixteen hundred inhabitants, of which four hundred are arms-bearing men, without counting the employees, who are thirty in number.[146]

There is also a garrison of two hundred men who make up four companies, namely, the First, Gauvry;[147] the Second, Dartaguiette;[148] the Third, Dutisné;[149] and the

---

144. A 1704 decree awarded the exclusive right to shepherd Louisiana's native and colonial souls to the Capuchins, a move contested by the Society of Jesus and its supporters. In 1723, company directors in France agreed to a compromise that allowed the Jesuits to establish a missionary presence north of Natchez. Despite the geographic proscriptions of the 1723 agreement, the Jesuits maintained an active presence in and around New Orleans throughout the years of company rule. Caillot's commentary on the Capuchins and Jesuits in New Orleans reveals a decidedly pro-Jesuit stance. On interorder infighting in early Louisiana, see Charles Edwards O'Neill, *Church and State in French Colonial Louisiana: Policy and Politics to 1732* (New Haven: Yale University Press, 1966).

145. By 1729 the number of Jesuits conducting missionary work among Louisiana's numerous Indian groups far outnumbered the Capuchins, whose superior, Father Raphaël, a Luxembourg native, failed to increase either the number of Capuchins active in the colony or the number of Capuchin-led evangelizing missions. A 1729 company expense report shows the Capuchins ministering almost exclusively to French colonists across seven sites stretching from the Balize to Natchez, while the Jesuits counted nine evangelizing missions among the Alabamas, Chickasaws, Choctaws, Illinois, Koroas, Quapaw (Arkansas), Yazoos, and others. "Etat general des Dépenses," 1729, ANOM, B 43b, fo. 826.

146. Caillot inflated the number of New Orleans's permanent inhabitants. A 1727 census of New Orleans and the route along Bayou Saint John captured a total of 1,030 residents, including 781 free whites, 48 indentured servants, 181 blacks, and 20 Indian slaves. As was typical of colonial census records, this number did not include transient populations of soldiers, sailors, or officers. Also excluded were free Indians and the population across the river at the company plantation (present-day Algiers Point), which in 1731 included 149 enslaved men, women, and children, and a handful of white administrators and plantation managers. Slave laborers clearing trees on the company plantation can be seen in the foreground of plate 11. Maduell, "Census of New Orleans as Reported by M. Perier, Commandant-Général of Louisiana," 1 July 1727, in *The Census Tables*, 82–95; and "Inventaire de l'habitation de la Comp. des Indes sur le fleuve St. Louis vis avis la Nouvelle Orléans et de tous les Batimens, marchandises, denrées, ustensils, Negres et Bestiaux à la charde de S. Le Page," 2 September 1731, ANOM, C 2 24, fo. 183–86.

147. Captain Joachim de Gauvry capped off a long military career in France with service in Louisiana, beginning in 1716. By 1727 he had established a small plantation along Bayou Saint John, worked by five slaves. Among Louisiana's military officers, Gauvry's wealth was fairly exceptional. Officers' meager pay rarely afforded them opportunities to purchase land or slaves. Even commanding officers made less than 1,200 livres annually.

148. Captain Pierre Dartaguiette d'Itouralde, the younger brother of company director Jean-Baptiste Dartaguiette Diron, owned and managed a plantation and more than fifty slaves in Cannes Brulées, Louisiana, with another of his brothers, Bernard Diron Dartaguiette, who served as king's lieutenant in the colony at an annual salary of 4,000 livres.

149. Claude-Charles Dutisné began his Louisiana career as commandant of the Illinois country in the early 1720s. In 1725 he was given command of the Natchez settlement, a post he held until 1728, when he was replaced by Commandant de Chépart (also D'Etcheparre, first name unknown) and reassigned to Plantin's company.

Fourth, Renauld d'Hauterive.[150] The garrison commander is named de Louboey, knight of Saint Louis.[151]

The prison is next to the guardhouse, and it is the most beautiful building in the town, after the one Monsieur Le Baron had constructed for himself while in the government. I forgot to say that there is also a monastery of Capuchins. There are three priests residing there, of which the warden is vicar general of the bishop of Quebec, and has received the pectoral cross.[152] There are those who carry out the parish functions, and there are two more who have gone to perform missionary work.[153] Their building is quite beautiful but too small for a monastery. Their garden is large and well cared for. These are the priests who teach the youth, especially the Reverend Father Raphaël, the father superior, who applies himself entirely to this task. He is a holy man, and, though disturbances are quite frequent in this colony and vice triumphs here with so much impunity, it is not for lack of being reprimanded by frequent sermons, which he preaches with zeal, for the promotion of Divine Glory. I can attest that he has his hand in as many things as possible, and it is partly because of him that justice is not completely abolished.

It is not the same with the other priests, who secretly lead very excessive lives, [105] of which it is not necessary to make an account. Here in New Orleans they each wear shirts with lacy cuffs, silk stockings, and slippers, and carry money, a snuffbox, a watch, and a parasol.

For a small place like this town, one cannot fail to say that there are nonetheless lots of warrants issued. The cause of all this disorder arises from the fact that they have sent to this land many young people who, in order to avoid a shameful death in France, where they would have undoubtedly dishonored their families, have come here as the lowest rung of their iniquities and to receive a just punishment.[154]

---

150. Renauld d'Hauterive arrived in Louisiana, where he served as a company commander at Natchitoches, in 1720. He later received a commission as captain and went on to win the Cross of Saint Louis for his service in the 1736 Chickasaw war.

151. Henri de Louboey arrived as a military officer in Louisiana in 1716. From 1721 to 1728 he held commissions as captain and commander at Biloxi and Mobile before being commissioned as major of New Orleans in 1729. Louboey also led the charge against the Natchez Indians following the Natchez attacks of late 1729.

152. High-ranking clergymen, including those holding the rank of bishop or above, wear an elaborate cross suspended from a long chain that extends just below the heart. Crosses worn in this fashion are known as pectoral crosses.

153. For most of 1729, Capuchin Fathers Raphaël and Theodore and Brother Cyrille ministered to New Orleans's colonial population, while Fathers Philippe, Gaspard, Mathias, Maximin, and Philibert served the settlements of Tchoupitoulas, the German Coast, Balize, Mobile, Natchitoches, and Natchez. Father Victorin of the Recollet order was the only priest under the Capuchin umbrella to establish an evangelizing mission. He did so among the Apalachees along Mobile Bay. Company Expense Reports, 1728 and 1729, ANOM, B 43b, fo. 775–77, 825–26.

154. Here Caillot refers to those sent to French colonies under *lettres de cachet*, official decrees issued by the

The executioner is a Negro who was supposed to have been hanged. They accorded him a pardon on the condition that he would exercise this employment. He earns the same wages as men from France, although he is very unskilled in his line of work. He lives outside the town.[155]

At a fourth of a league's distance from town, there is a very nice brickyard, belonging half to Monsieur de Périer and half to a man named Morand,[156] and a little farther away there is an earthenware factory that never produces any genuine pottery. There is someone named Foussy from Rouen who makes a lot of it, but not near as beautiful as what is made in France, because the earth is not good for this. At three-fourths of a league's distance on the left you will find a hamlet called Bayou Saint John, where there live five or six inhabitants very rich in livestock.[157] Before New Orleans was built, there was a nation of Indians called the Colapissas, who went to take refuge ten leagues above this spot.[158]

---

king that provided an alternative to incarceration for individuals (typically young men) from noble or well-connected families caught up in any number of scandals, ranging from theft and gambling to sexual peccadilloes. *Lettres de cachet* resulted in the wayward individual's being sent to the colonies, where it was hoped he would seize the opportunity for self-reform. A number of individuals sent to Louisiana in semi-exile arrived under circumstances never formalized by the issuance of an official *lettre de cachet*. See Dawdy, *Building the Devil's Empire*, 151; and Brian Strayer, Lettres de Cachet *and Social Control in the Ancien Régime, 1659–1789* (New York: Peter Lang, 1992). Historians continue to debate the appropriateness of characterizing Louisiana's colonial population as debauched. Emily Clark argues that critiques of middling and poor colonists made by members of the elite (administrators, clerics, military officers) should be viewed with skepticism. Clark points to the large number of nonelite women who actively participated in New Orleans's laywomen's confraternity, known as the Ladies Congregation of the Children of Mary, as a counterpoint to elite claims. See Clark, "'By All the Conduct of Their Lives': A Laywomen's Confraternity in New Orleans, 1730–1744," *William and Mary Quarterly*, 3rd ser., 54 (1997): 786–90. The perceived havoc wrought by the failure of both the Crown and charter companies to attract sizable numbers of stable colonists to Louisiana has been well documented in James D. Hardy Jr., "The Transportation of Convicts to Colonial Louisiana," *Louisiana History* 7 (1966): 207–20; Mathé Allain, "L'Immigration française en Louisiane," *Revue d'histoire de l'Amérique française* 28 (1975): 559–64; Allain, "*Manon Lescaut et Ses Consoeurs*: Women in the Early French Period, 1700–1731," in *Proceedings of the Fifth Meeting of the French Colonial Historical Society*, ed. James J. Cooke (Lanham, MD: French Colonial Historical Society, 1980), 18–26; and Marcel Giraud, *Histoire de la Louisiane française*, vol. 4, *La Louisiane après le système de Law, 1721–1723* (Paris: Presses Universitaires de France, 1974), 176–82.

155. Skilled labor was a prized commodity in the fledgling colony; slaves with highly specialized skill sets could sometimes parlay their abilities into freedom. Such was the case with African slave Louis Congo, who in 1725 bargained for his freedom and that of his wife, Suzon, plus a two-arpent tract of land in Chantilly (now Gentilly) and an annual allotment of rations from the company worth over 300 livres. In exchange, Congo agreed to serve as the settlement's executioner.

156. Chevalier Charles de Morand began his career in Louisiana as a public-works inspector. In 1726 he was charged with overseeing a company-owned brickworks outside the capital, near the present-day Gentilly neighborhood. After the retrocession of Louisiana to the Crown in 1731, Morand became the brickworks' sole owner. On the production and shortage of bricks in and around New Orleans, see Marcel Giraud, *Histoire de la Louisiane française*, vol. 3, *Epoque de John Law, 1717–1720* (Paris: Presses Universitaires de France, 1977), 239–41, 248–50.

157. In 1727 the population along Bayou Saint John totaled 121, including forty-one whites, three indentured servants, seventy-three blacks, and four Indian slaves. Maduell, "Census of New Orleans," 1 July 1727, in *The Census Tables*, 95.

158. As early as 1702 many Colapissa moved from their villages along the lower Pearl River (in present-day

At a quarter of a league downriver, there is a brewhouse that functions as a place of recreation for taking promenades, and at this place you can also drink this beer that is brewed with roasted maize, also known as Turkish wheat.[159] It is not one of the best, but when wine is lacking, it is good. This place has the feel of an open-air café in Paris where countless numbers of people go [106] to have fun. There are also several inns and taverns where one is not very well served but instead well swindled.

There are also several shops selling various types of merchandise that they buy from the ships, no matter that it is against company orders. These traders have wives who sell in the streets.[160]

In front of the parish church, there is a large parade ground, quite spacious and surrounded by palisades with two barriers—one at one end and the other at the other end. Next to this parade ground is the government building, surrounded by brick walls. At the end of the courtyard you will find the house of Monsieur Le Baron, of whom I have already spoken. This house is built of brick and roofed with tiles. It is the only house roofed in this way, since it is the first time that this has been tried. This Monsieur Le Baron is a man who was sent from the court to make his observations both of the stars as well as of medicinal herbs. He is a man of superior intelligence who lives like a good philosopher, not worrying himself about anything.[161]

There are always two brigantines in front of New Orleans, which are used in order to bring supplies and merchandise to Mobile. In addition, there is a boat, three flat-boats, and fifty pirogues, which are used to go upriver to the more distant outposts. There used to be a seven hundred ton flute that had been condemned to remain in the river six years ago and that has just been torn apart. There is also an eighteen-oar galley. There used to be two of them, but one was burned by the savages during the first Natchez war, about which I will speak here above, that is, I mean later.[162]

---

southwestern Mississippi) to multiple sites around New Orleans. The largest village could be found on the north shore of Lake Pontchartrain. Ives Goddard, "Colapissa," in *The Handbook of North American Indians*, ed. Raymond D. Fogelson, vol. 14, *Southeast* (Washington, DC: Smithsonian Institution, 2004), 177–78.

159. Caillot is referring to the brewery just outside New Orleans, run by the Dreux brothers, Mathurin and Pierre. The brewery is the first east-bank property downriver from New Orleans on the "Carte particulière du fleuve St. Louis dix lieüs au dessus de la Nouvelle Orléans," ca. 1723, Newberry Library, Ayer MS map 30, sheet 80 (see plate 12); see also Maduell, "Census of New Orleans," 1 July 1727, in *The Census Tables*, 98.

160. The company's monopoly on trade in Louisiana made trade of nonlocal goods between individuals illegal, though company officials on the ground did little to prevent such transactions. Caillot makes clear that private citizens openly conducted petty trade on the streets of New Orleans, whether in surplus ships' provisions or manufactured goods.

161. Two words, "*mais impie*" ("but impious"), appear to have been added to the end of this sentence at a later date. The words are in the same hand but in a lighter ink.

162. Caillot's reference to the Natchez war, which began in December 1729 and continued throughout 1730 into 1731, is one of several instances indicating that the manuscript was written out in full after his return to France.

In the hamlet about which I have just spoken here above, there is a small river that has the same name as the hamlet—Bayou Saint John—and it flows out of a cypress swamp. There are three boats and one longboat on this bayou, which are used to go to Mobile by way of Lake Pontchartrain. [107] This lake has around thirty to thirty-five leagues of turns, which lead to the sea. It is seven leagues across. On the other side of this lake there are three plantations rich in livestock and timber, which they have in their cypress groves.[163] Innumerable little rivers and bayous feed into the lake, and during the winter many inhabitants go up them as far as seven or eight leagues to go hunting. They kill bison, deer, turkey, and other game, which they bring to the city to sell. They earn more than 200 percent profit on this, even including their expenses. You should know that, in addition to these hunters, close to two hundred to three hundred Biloxi Indians come here every winter to go hunting. You barter something for a piece of game. For example, for a pinch of vermilion, some will give you four to five ducks. For myself, I got fifteen ducks and a deer for three musket balls.[164]

If, among the inhabitants who go hunting, there are some who find profit, there are also some who find many risks, including storms, which are frequent on this lake, where the waves are rough and very choppy. On the other hand, when there is no wind, the hot air makes the meat go bad, and they are obliged to go hunting again as if they had not killed a thing.

Concerning the Balize

The Balize is a place swamped by the sea, so swamped that, when the sea is heavy, you are forced to walk on planks. There are not even eight arpents that are not inundated every day. There is a *comptoir*[165] with a keeper, a church formerly pastored by a Capuchin, the late Reverend Father Gaspard, a troop of thirty men with a sergeant, a commander, a surgeon major, and forty laborers who work continually to fortify this place, since it is the key to the country.

---

163. Efforts to increase Louisiana's timber production on the north shore of Lake Pontchartrain were led by carpenter and former indentured servant Etienne Duchesne, who in 1724 received a company contract for the construction of two half-galleys. Louisiana timber was also used as ballast for company ships returning to France. On the timber industry in early colonial Louisiana, see Giraud, *History of French Louisiana*, 5:141–44.

164. In a 1726 memoir, Governor Jean-Baptiste Le Moyne de Bienville noted that the Biloxis and Pensacolas "established on the Pearl River . . . are very laborious and good hunters. They furnish an abundance of meat to all the French who are near enough to trade for it." *MPA*, 3:535. On the regular trade of foodstuffs in exchange for goods between Indian hunters and European settlers, see Usner, *Indians, Settlers, and Slaves*, 191–201, 204–13.

165. "*Comptoir*" was the word used to describe a company-administered trade outpost. In Louisiana the capital *comptoir* was New Orleans. All other, smaller outposts reported back to offices in the capital.

The company keeps convicts there, namely Maisonneuve, previously employed in New Orleans (in perpetuity) for having [108] forged a number of signatures and other knavish tricks,[166] and the Chevalier des Tourettes, for having robbed the company baker. This last one is only there for ten years. Hunting for fowl is very easy in this place in the months of November, December, January, February, March, and April, but the rest of the year you die of hunger. From here to New Orleans there are thirty-five fairly well-built plantations, but fifteen to twenty of them are quite substantial, both for the number of slaves as well as cattle found there [see plate 12].

From New Orleans, going upriver two hundred leagues, there are as many plantations as concessions—one hundred fifty—among which twenty to twenty-five are very rich, including the Tchoupitoulas plantations, four in number, belonging to Monsieur de Kolly, Monsieur de La Fresnière, Monsieur de Lery, and Monsieur Dubreuil, who together hold more than 560 Negroes, 1,000 cattle, and many Indian slaves.[167] They are very well fortified. These four gentlemen and one named Monsieur Carrière *le gros*, who is six leagues downriver below the town, are the lords among the inhabitants.[168]

It is quite certain that if the Company of the Indies would send only two thousand Negroes with the same number of whites, you would see a second Saint Domingue reborn in this country, and better in terms of health, the air being more temperate. You would load ships with rice as beautiful as that which comes from the Levant;[169] maize, or Turkish wheat, grows marvelously well here, the indigo found here is admirably beautiful, and the millet too. French wheat grows here, too, in the Illinois country, which is five hundred leagues from this city. The bread made from it is brown but has an excellent flavor. Flour cannot be kept for more than six months, but it is harvested twice each year.[170]

---

166. In 1728, company clerk Maisonneuve was implicated as ringleader of a scheme to circulate among the colonial population banknotes forged with Director-General Jacques de La Chaise's signature. He confessed under torture and was sentenced to life in prison. On the Maisonneuve affair, see Greenwald, "Company Towns and Tropical Baptisms," 101–2.

167. In 1727 the three Canadian-born Chauvin brothers, Nicolas Chauvin de La Fresnière, Joseph Chauvin de Léry, and Chauvin de Beaulieu, owned a combined total of 198 African slaves and 12 Indian slaves, while neighboring planters Claude-Joseph Villars Dubreuil and Jean-Daniel de Kolly owned an additional 1 Indian and 118 African laborers (see plate 12). De Kolly was also a stakeholder in the Natchez area's Sainte Catherine concession. Given that more than 1,600 slaves arrived in the colony from Africa from 1727 to 1729, it is possible that these five *gros habitants* had increased their slave holdings to Caillot's estimate of 560 by 1729. Dawdy, *Building the Devil's Empire*, 183; Maduell, "Census of New Orleans," 1 July 1727, in *The Census Tables*, 98–99; *TASTDB*.

168. Like the Chauvin brothers upriver, the three Carrières (also Canadian), André, Joseph, and François, developed large neighboring plantations downriver from New Orleans (see plate 12). By 1729 André had died, and his widow, Marie Arlut, had married Louis Tixerant, who continued to run the deceased's plantation. The other two Carrières maintained extensive land and slave holdings, with François owning more than double the number of laborers his brother owned. It is likely François whom Caillot referred to as *le gros*.

169. The term "Levant" referred to the Near East, or the lands along the east coast of the Mediterranean Sea.

170. Flour shortages provoked continual complaints from Louisiana's inhabitants. Wheat did grow in the

[109] Butcher's meat in New Orleans is quite good, but they do not eat mutton at all because of its rarity.

The Diverse Nations That Live Along the River [171] [see fig. 15]

Five leagues below the city, there is an Indian village called Chawasha, which has sixty men and women, and one league below this place is the village of the Washa, thirty-five in number.[172]

Ten leagues above the city is the village Des Allemands, where there are, in fact, 100 German families,[173] and next to them there are the Colapissa Indians, numbering 110.

Illinois country, but supply could not keep up with demand, especially in times of political unrest between the French and their Indian neighbors, which disrupted trade lines between upper and lower Louisiana. Wheat stores from France often arrived damaged or rotten after months in ships' holds, and colonists in lower Louisiana had great difficulty coaxing newly sown wheat to maturity. To lessen the impact of wheat-flour shortages, bread was often made with cornmeal or a combination of wheat and rice. On provisioning ties between upper and lower Louisiana, see Cécile Vidal, "Antoine Bienvenu, Illinois Planter and Mississippi Trader: The Structure of Exchange between Lower and Upper Louisiana," in *French Colonial Louisiana and the Atlantic World*, ed. Bradley G. Bond (Baton Rouge: Louisiana State University Press, 2005), 111–33.

171. The first quarter of the eighteenth century was one in which the Indian groups of the colonial Southeast struggled to recover from severe population losses due to disease, slaving, and warfare experienced in the previous century. Despite these losses, however, historian Kathleen Duval estimates that in the mid-1720s Louisiana's native population outnumbered the French by a ratio of fourteen to one. Duval, "Interconnectedness and Diversity in 'French Louisiana,'" in *Powhatan's Mantle: Indians in the Colonial Southeast*, ed. Gregory A. Waselkov, Peter H. Wood, and Tom Hatley (Lincoln: University of Nebraska Press, 2006), 138. Caillot likely derived much of the detail he provided on Louisiana's Indian groups from official trade and military reports, maps, and censuses that circulated through the company offices in which he worked, as well as word-of-mouth and unofficial accounts penned by his contemporaries. Caillot lacked firsthand knowledge of most Indian groups and customs discussed here and so acted more as collector and chronicler of others' stories than as a witness, which is to say that not all of Caillot's observations may be true. Descriptions provided in this chapter's notes are intended to guide the reader by providing basic information on each group. For more-thorough treatments of southeastern Indians, see Charles Hudson, *The Southeastern Indians* (Knoxville: University of Tennessee Press, 1976); Fred B. Kniffen, Hiram F. Gregory, and George A. Stokes, *The Historic Tribes of Louisiana, from 1542 to the Present* (Baton Rouge: Louisiana State University Press, 1987); Usner, *Indians, Settlers, and Slaves*; Usner, *American Indians in the Lower Mississippi Valley: Social and Economic Histories* (Lincoln: University of Nebraska Press, 1998); Robbie Franklyn Ethridge and Charles Hudson, eds., *The Transformation of the Southeastern Indians, 1540–1760* (Jackson: University Press of Mississippi, 2002); Alan Gallay, *The Indian Slave Trade: The Rise of the English Empire in the American South, 1670–1717* (New Haven: Yale University Press, 2002); Paul Kelton, *Epidemics and Enslavement: Biological Catastrophe in the Native Southeast, 1492–1715* (Lincoln: University of Nebraska Press, 2007); and Waselkov, Wood, and Hatley, eds., *Powhatan's Mantle*.

172. Closely affiliated with each other and both having ties to the Chitimacha, the Chawasha and Washa lived historically in the area between the Mississippi River and Atchafalaya Bay. By 1722, however, both groups had relocated to villages downriver from New Orleans on the Mississippi's west bank. Ives Goddard, "Washa, Chawasha, and Yakni-Chito," in Fogelson, *Handbook of North American Indians*, 14:188–90.

173. Efforts to attract German settlers to Louisiana began with a propaganda campaign sponsored by the Company of the West in 1719. By the end of 1722, approximately sixteen hundred immigrants had arrived in Louisiana to work the concessions owned by John Law. After the collapse of Law's system, however, Governor Bienville granted the Germans concessions along the west bank of the Mississippi in an area that quickly became

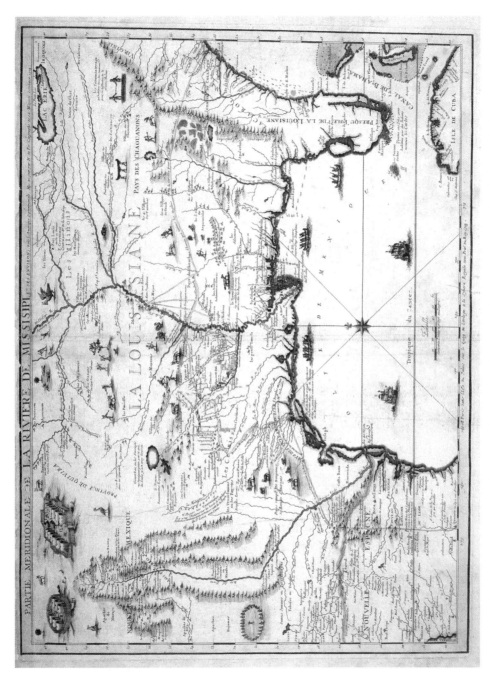

Figure 15. This 1718 map provides a visual complement to Caillot's descriptions of Louisiana's Indian populations. *Partie meridionale de la rivière de Mississippi, et ses environs, dans l'Amérique Septentrionale,* by Nicolas de Fer, 1718. (The Historic New Orleans Collection, 1971.20.2)

Five leagues from this village you find the Taensa, among whom there are seventy men.[174]

Seven leagues farther there is a nation called the Houma, which is about 130 in number.[175]

Eight leagues beyond them are the Bayogoulas, who are two hundred in number, including women.[176]

Forty-two leagues farther there is the village of the Little Tunicas, who are 210 in number.[177]

Two leagues higher you find a river that is called the Red River. According to travelers, its source is in New Mexico, where there are silver mines. Going up this river you will find an Indian village named Natchitoches, numbering one hundred fifty inhabitants, and facing them there is another fortified French village with a good fort, a commander, two officers, and a troop of thirty-five men.[178] There is also a church with

known as the Côte des Allemands (the German Coast), or simply Des Allemands. On German immigration to French Louisiana, see René Le Conte, "The Germans in Louisiana in the Eighteenth Century," in *A Refuge for All Ages: Immigration in Louisiana History* trans. and ed. Glenn R. Conrad (Lafayette: Center for Louisiana Studies, 1996), 31–43; and J. Hanno Deiler, *The Settlement of the German Coast of Louisiana and the Creoles of German Descent* (Philadelphia: Americana Germanica Press, 1909).

174. The Taensa were a Natchezan group historically located north of present-day Natchez, Mississippi. In 1706 the Taensa moved south to live among the Bayogoula (whom they promptly attacked and forced out) in order to escape increasingly frequent slave raids conducted by the Chickasaw and Yazoo. By 1715 the Taensa lived in scattered villages between Bayou Manchac and Mobile Bay. Kniffen, Gregory, and Stokes, *Historic Tribes of Louisiana,* 76–77; Patricia Galloway and Jason Baird Jackson, "Natchez and Neighboring Groups," in Fogelson, *Handbook of North American Indians,* 14:599–600. On Indian slave raids and slavery, see Gallay, *Indian Slave Trade*; and Robbie Franklyn Ethridge and Sheri M. Schuck-Hall, eds., *Mapping the Mississippian Shatter Zone: The Colonial Indian Slave Trade and Regional Instability in the American South* (Lincoln: University of Nebraska Press, 2009).

175. Concentrated mainly in the area south of Bayou Manchac, between the Mississippi River and Lake Pontchartrain, the Houma were allied with the French throughout the period of French governance in Louisiana. In the early 1800s the Houma relocated to lands south of the confluence of Bayous Lafourche and Terrebonne. Jack Campisi, "Houma," in Fogelson, *Handbook of North American Indians,* 14:632–34.

176. Until being forced out of their villages by the Taensa in 1706, the Bayogoula lived near the confluence of Bayou Lafourche and the Mississippi, on the river's west bank. Taensa attacks forced them downriver, near the Houma settlements. Ives Goddard, "Bayogoula," in Fogelson, *Handbook of North American Indians,* 14:175–76.

177. Historically the Tunica lived along the Yazoo River in parts of present-day Arkansas and northwest Mississippi. In 1706 the Tunica relocated south, to a village formerly occupied by the Houma. By 1721 Charlevoix noted that the Tunica were living in three villages, one of which Caillot described here. Jeffrey P. Brain, George Roth, and William J. De Reuse, "Tunica, Biloxi, and Ofo," in Fogelson, *Handbook of North American Indians,* 14:586–88.

178. Trade relations between the Natchitoches and the French date to 1714, when the French established an eponymous trading post among them. In 1726 the French population at Natchitoches numbered one hundred settlers, including six indentured servants. J. Daniel Rogers and George Sabo III, "Caddo," in Fogelson, *Handbook of North American Indians,* 14:616–18; Maduell, "General Census of All Inhabitants of the Colony of Louisiana," 1726, in *The Census Tables,* 60–61. For a recent overview of French-Indian relations in colonial Natchitoches, see H. Sophie Burton and F. Todd Smith, *Colonial Natchitoches: A Creole Community on the Louisiana-Texas Frontier* (College Station: Texas A&M University Press, 2008).

a Jesuit who says Mass and who is a missionary to the Indians.[179] There is also a large storehouse and about forty to fifty inhabitants.

[110] Seven leagues from the Natchitoches, there is a Spanish post where there is a troop of one hundred men, a commander, and two officers. There is also a church with a padre who is the parish priest there. There are many French people who go there to trade in order to get *piastres*, however, with the permission of their commander.[180]

Eighty leagues from the town, taking the river again from that point, you find the large village of the Tunica, where these Indians are 260 in number. The great chief is a Christian, but I think it is more in appearance than anything.[181] Nevertheless, it seems that he likes the French. This nation had as a missionary Monsieur Davion, who lived there for six years in order to instruct them in our religion, without having been able to convert them, except for the chief.[182]

Two hundred leagues from there, or one hundred from New Orleans, you find the Natchez nation, where there is a small town. The parish priest is a Capuchin.[183] There is a commander, two officers, a garrison of fifty men, with a *comptoir général*. That is to say, the neighboring posts deliver their accounts to this one, and this one delivers these to the New Orleans *comptoir*, which is the main one. This is the place where they grow good native tobacco, and each harvest weighs up to one hundred fifty thousand pounds.[184] The company accepts it from the inhabitants at the rate of six *sous* per pound, for which they are paid either in merchandise or in letters of exchange by the company in Paris. There is also, just like in New Orleans, a notary and a court recorder.

---

179. According to company records, the priest ministering to settlers at Natchitoches was Father Maximin, a Capuchin, not a Jesuit. "Etat general des Dépenses," 1729, ANOM, B 43b, fo. 826.

180. Los Adaes, located approximately twelve miles from the French post at Natchitoches, was Spain's easternmost Texas settlement. Because of its geographic isolation from other Spanish settlements, Los Adaes was heavily dependent on French Louisiana—and on traders at Natchitoches, in particular—for provisions and trade goods. On Presidio Los Adaes, see Francis X. Galán, "Last Soldiers, First Pioneers: The Los Adaes Border Community on the Louisiana-Texas Frontier" (PhD diss., Southern Methodist University, 2006); and David J. Weber, *The Spanish Frontier in North America* (New Haven: Yale University Press, 2009), 130–33.

181. Tunica Chief Cahura-Joligo was known for dressing in the French style and for his adherence to Christianity.

182. Jesuit Father Antoine Davion established the first permanent mission in the lower Mississippi Valley among the Tunica in 1699. With the exception of a two-year hiatus from 1702 to 1704, Davion presided over the mission until 1720. He later served briefly as priest at the Balize post, before being recalled to France in 1724. O'Neill, *Church and State*, 15–17, 49–51, 150–51.

183. Capuchin Father Philibert Vianden from Luxembourg began serving Natchez's settler community in 1726.

184. Situated about ninety leagues upriver from New Orleans, the area surrounding Fort Rosalie (established 1716; now Natchez, Mississippi) benefited from the Mississippi Valley's rich alluvial soils and its location atop a flood-resistant bluff. Efforts to encourage tobacco production there began under John Law in 1717, but at peak output in 1728, Natchez tobacco planters managed to produce only one hundred fifty thousand pounds of tobacco, and most of this was of very poor quality. Tobacco production in Louisiana never approached the company's projections of three hundred thousand pounds annually.

There are 160 inhabitants.[185] In this place, one finds many medicinal plants that are good for many things, according to the natives who use them. Some of them are familiar to surgeons.

Near the town of Natchez, there is a nation that has the same name.[186] They are seven to eight hundred in number, including women. They comprise four villages under the domination of a great chief, whom they call great sun. I will speak later about the ceremonies they observed at his death six years ago,[187] when we had a war with them that lasted two months.[188] We killed about twenty of them, took five women and two children as slaves for us, whom they bought back with corn and chickens. Since then they are eager [111] to like the French. Later I will speak more fully of their character and their treachery.

At the death of the great sun, there were four war chiefs, or, you could say, four lieutenants general.[189] These chiefs are regarded with great veneration among their people. After these nobles, there are twenty to thirty worthies;[190] these are the friends of the

---

185. In 1726 the non-Natchez Indian population numbered 148 whites, 65 African slaves, and 6 Indian slaves. The largest plantations in Natchez were the Sainte Catherine and White Earth concessions, which were worked by 38 French indentured servants, 50 African slaves, and 4 Indian slaves. Located between these two concessions was the Grand Village of the Natchez, the Natchez Indian ceremonial center. Another 44 French households were scattered in and around the Natchez settlement. Maduell, "General Census of All Inhabitants of the Colony of Louisiana," 1726, in *The Census Tables*, 56–57.

186. The Natchez Indians inhabited some of the lower Mississippi Valley's choicest agricultural land, making the area a desirable settlement locale for French would-be planters. Their lands also stood at the crossroads of trade for neighboring Indian groups and French and English traders.

187. This temporal reference suggests that Caillot wrote his account of Louisiana in 1731, the year he returned to France, six years after the funerary rituals he described here.

188. From 1716 to 1730 the Natchez and French engaged in a series of skirmishes, sometimes referred to as the Natchez wars, over land and trade goods. The first took place in 1716 and resulted in a settlement that allowed the French to construct Fort Rosalie. The second and third Natchez wars began in 1722 and ended late the following year. It is to one or both of these conflicts that Caillot referred, given that some historians see the third war as an extension of the second. On the Natchez wars, see Arnaud Balvay, *La Révolte des Natchez* (Paris: Éditions du Félin, 2008), 68–74, 95–115; and James F. Barnett Jr., *The Natchez Indians: A History to 1735* (Jackson: University Press of Mississippi, 2007), 65–72, 84–94.

189. In his account, Caillot confused the great sun, hereditary chief of the Natchez, with his younger brother Tattooed Serpent (Serpent Piqué), also a sun, who died June 1, 1725. Caillot may have confused the two men due to Tattooed Serpent's high-profile relationship with the French as the Natchez's diplomatic envoy. Tattooed Serpent is sometimes referred to in contemporary accounts as the Natchez "war chief," although historian James F. Barnett Jr. sees him more as "peacemaker" and "the tribe's ranking negotiator" than military leader. Barnett, *Natchez Indians*, 86. For additional contemporary French sources, see Le Page du Pratz's eyewitness account in *Histoire de la Louisiane*, 3:28–60; and Jean-François Benjamin Dumont de Montigny's secondhand account in *Mémoires historiques sur la Louisiane* (Paris: C. J. G. Bauche, 1753), 208–38. Also useful are John R. Swanton's *Indian Tribes of the Lower Mississippi Valley and Adjacent Coast of the Gulf of Mexico* (Washington, DC: Government Printing Office, 1911), 138–57; Gordon M. Sayre's *The Indian Chief as Tragic Hero: Native Resistance and the Literatures of America, from Moctezuma to Tecumseh* (Chapel Hill: University of North Carolina Press, 2005), 216–40; and George Edward Milne's "Rising Suns, Fallen Forts, and Impudent Immigrants: Race, Power, and War in the Lower Mississippi Valley" (PhD diss., University of Oklahoma, 2006), 153–55.

190. "*Les considerés*" has been translated as "worthies" throughout.

deceased and warriors, or, you could say, captains. He has many stinkards, otherwise known as servants.[191]

It is worth noting that when the sun is about to die, his wives, who are seven to eight in number, and his servants, who are about twenty, all offer themselves up to death, as well as his relatives and his friends, in a sad and cruel manner, nevertheless with unequaled constancy. Among them it is an honor to lose their lives with their chief in the following way.

As soon as the great sun has breathed his last breath, they dress him in his most beautiful clothes, which consist of a pair of Indian shoes, which are two pieces of deer-skin in which they wrap their feet. Nonetheless, they are very well made. After, they have a pair of leggings, which serves as hose, a piece of animal skin that hides their nakedness, which they call a breech cloth. This serves as breeches. Then a bison hide with calumets[192] painted on it serves him as a suit of clothes. He has pierced ears, as do all the warriors, having two bits of iron going through them, which show that he was a great warrior. They weigh at least a pound and a half. He also has a pierced nose, with a bird feather passing from one side to the other. His face is painted black, red, blue, etc., the same as if he was going to war. As a hat, he has feathers artistically arranged on top of his head; his quiver is filled with arrows at his side; and he has his bow in hand, ready for combat.

It is a custom among the natives that, before undertaking anything, they must paint or besmear themselves, and they dance the appropriate dance for their plans, because each undertaking has its own dance. Returning to the deceased, they put him on a ceremonial bed, which, since we began trading with them, has been covered with red or blue cloth. This bed is ornamented with bird feathers of all [112] colors, and even with animal skins, which they glue on top. It is raised on four staffs, and there are mats of woven rush serving as covers and sheets. As a cover, there is a very finely painted bison skin.

He lies on that bed for seven days, during which time the people of his nation make a great fire, and then two at the head and two at the feet stand guard. They are relieved every thirty minutes. During this period, others serve him food more conscientiously

---

191. Caillot and his contemporaries often used the term "*loué*" to describe a servant or domestic within the Natchez polity, though "*puant*" was also used; "stinkard" is the closest English-language approximation of this term. On social stratification and hierarchy among the Natchez, see Douglas R. White, George P. Murdock, and Richard Scaglion, "Natchez Class and Rank Reconsidered," *Ethnology* 10 (1971): 369–88; and Dumont de Montigny, *Regards sur le monde atlantique*, 360.

192. A calumet is a pipe used by many Southeastern and Mississippi Valley Indians in greeting, or welcoming, ceremonies. On the calumet and its role in establishing and maintaining relationships, see Gallay, *Indian Slave Trade*, 102–10.

than when he was living, by continuously making a harangue to him with a long verbiage that always means the same thing, touching on the great journey he will take, for they believe that you never die, and that they are going on a journey when they die. That is why they leave him his bow, his arrows, his musket, and lots of ammunition for war, so that, as they say, during his journey he can kill his enemies if he should happen to meet them, and also so he can hunt bison and other beasts necessary for life.

At the end of seven days, his wives, relatives, friends, and servants, who are destined to die and are all painted as properly as they are able, go into the temple, where they begin to dance in their style, contorting themselves in a way that inspires more fear than admiration. The death cries, which they make to the sound of an old earthen pot covered with a piece of goat skin, which they beat with a stick, produce a sound as lugubrious and extraordinary as their appearance. This dance lasts about eight hours, along with dreadful wails. Following this, they are served a feast consisting of smoked beef that is drier than leather, which they call beef *boucané*,[193] and some roe deer boiled with corn,[194] dressed with herbs that are very glutinous and so strong that, when they eat this, the fibers stick to the dish in strands. Most of them eat with their fingers, but the more civilized ones have a type of spoon they call a *mikwan*.[195] Their stews are as bizarre as the smell they emit.

Immediately after this feast, about sixty Indians arrive, all painted, of which thirty are holding a piece of cord in their hand. When they enter, the others stop eating and begin to dance again, for [113] an hour. Then the other thirty, who have come with those who hold the ends of the cords, advance and blindfold the victims with pieces of cloth, or something else, and they also cover them with a buffalo skin. When this ritual is finished, they make a long oration to them about their journey, about the glory that they will derive from it in exchange, and a thousand other discourses, which always go back to their first sentiments. When this is finished, two of them go to each victim, and they pass the ends of the cord around their necks and strangle them. During all of this, these unfortunate people, resigned to their fate, chant the death songs until they cannot speak anymore, and by then they pass from this world into the other [see fig. 16].

After such a dreadful spectacle and such a barbarous dispatch, the war chiefs and the worthies lift the great sun from his bed of honor and transport him ceremoniously to a place not too far from the village, suspending him in a kind of chest on four wooden

---

193. "*Boucané*," a word of Amerindian origin, means smoke-dried, or, simply, smoked.

194. Roe deer are indigenous to Europe and Asia, not North America. Caillot may have referred to the white-tailed deer.

195. A *mikwan* is typically large and made of wood.

Figure 16. This engraving by Antoine-Simon Le Page du Pratz depicts Natchez burial rituals conducted following the death of Tattooed Serpent. Note the family members and servants of the deceased lining each side of the death litter. From *Histoire de la Louisiane*, 1758. (The Historic New Orleans Collection, 73-17-L)

pilings. This chest is made of tree bark. When they have arrived at the designated place, they dance the departure dance, which they accompany with their death cries. What is most dreadful, in my opinion, is the following: when they have stopped dancing, there is a baby of seven or eight months that they have brought with them, all naked. When they start to make their harangue, they then slit the throat of this little innocent one, whom they hold by his two feet with his head hanging down, and they sprinkle the coffin with his blood by passing and repassing this little dying infant above and below this coffin. Then they enclose him with the great sun at the end of this ceremony, and, after, they go get all the other cadavers, which they bury all around the tomb.

The above-mentioned types of cruelties have not been practiced for five or six years, through showing them the fallacy of their thinking, but, nevertheless, in spite of this, they still continue in their errors in many things, and there are still those who sacrifice their lives.

This nation does not want to be instructed in our religion. They worship the rattlesnake, which is the most dangerous snake of all.[196] They understand, though in a confused way, that there is a spirit in the clouds that governs [114] everything and is the prime cause of all things on earth.[197] They also know that there is an evil spirit that seeks only to do them harm. This is why they pray to him, and most among them conjure, that is, speak to the devil. It is a terrifying thing to see them conjure. They fling blood in their noses, their mouths, and their ears (while in their postures howling), and this is what they do in order to know what the future holds. I have seen proof of it by asking them in which month ships will arrive from France. They told me, not only the month, but the day and the hour too. The priests and missionaries forbid us as strongly as they can to keep us from having them conjure. All the Indian nations have the same knowledge and are adept at conjuring.

I will speak about their ways, their customs, their clothing, and their food later. They are almost all alike as far as these sorts of things go.

One hundred forty leagues from New Orleans, going upriver, there is an Indian village of the Yazoo, who are 260 in number.[198] To express its joy, this nation cries tears

---

196. Charlevoix and Pénicaut also made reference to rattlesnake worship among the Natchez. Pertinent excerpts from their accounts can be found in Swanton, *Indian Tribes of the Lower Mississippi Valley*, 159–61.

197. The supreme deity of the Natchez Indians was a sky deity, which, according to Le Page du Pratz, the Natchez called Coyococop-Chill, or Great Spirit. Le Page du Pratz, *Histoire de la Louisiane*, 2:327. On Natchezan religion and sociopolitical organization, see Swanton, *Indian Tribes of the Lower Mississippi Valley*, 158–81; Galloway and Jackson, "Natchez and Neighboring Groups," in Fogelson, *Handbook of North American Indians*, 14:603–7.

198. Located just upstream from the Tunica on the Yazoo River, the once numerous Yazoo population had by 1725 been considerably reduced to two villages. The village described by Caillot was an amalgamated population of Koroas, Ofogoulas, and Yazoo, with an estimated 120 warriors. Usner, *American Indians in the Lower Mississippi Valley*, 49–50.

most copiously. Near this village, there is a French post, with a commander, an officer, a troop of thirty men, and twenty to twenty-five inhabitants.[199]

At 250 leagues there is the village of the Arkansas, where there are 270 Indians, including both men and women.[200] Previously there was a commander with some troops, and there may still be 10 to 12 inhabitants.[201] This place is very good for hunting bison.

At four hundred fifty leagues there is a place named the Wabash, where they want to send some people to establish a settlement. It is a very beautiful land where fruits grow, among which are apples and pears of an excellent flavor.

At 500 leagues from the city there is the Illinois post,[202] where French wheat is grown. This is a city whose houses are, for the most part, made of very hard stones that are extraordinarily difficult to cut but very [115] beautiful. There are perhaps 300 to 400 inhabitants, who are for the most part Canadian. There is a commander with a garrison of 130 men,[203] a *comptoir* with a keeper,[204] and a director,[205] which forms a less important council than the one in New Orleans. There is also a church with two or three Jesuits who perform parish duties there.[206] There is a windmill for wheat similar to those in France. They must build three more in order to be able to grind enough to provide New Orleans with as much as it needs when the ships do not arrive.

Nearby there is a nation of the Illinois, from which the town gets its name. They number one thousand and they love the French dearly.[207] They have men from six feet to six and a half feet tall. They are so nimble that they catch deer while running without much fatigue. Every day they go to war alongside us against the Foxes, who have destroyed many of their warriors, and some of the French, too, in a very barbarous manner, which means that, when we trap some of them, we pay them back.[208] When

---

199. The French established Fort Saint Pierre among the Yazoo in 1719, following the first Natchez war, in 1718.

200. In 1727 the Arkansas, now known as the Quapaw, inhabited three villages near the confluence of the Arkansas and Mississippi Rivers. Duval, "Interconnectedness and Diversity in 'French Louisiana,'" 135–38, 145–46; and W. David Baird, *The Quapaw Indians: A History of the Downstream People* (Norman: University of Oklahoma Press, 1980).

201. The Arkansas post was established in 1698 by Henri de Tonti.

202. Caillot refers to the Kaskaskia post.

203. Charles Desliettes took command of the Illinois country's Fort de Chartres in 1724.

204. Fort de Chartres's warehouse keeper was Nicholas Chassin.

205. Marc-Antoine de La Loire des Ursins served as chief clerk and director of the Illinois country until 1728, when he relocated to Natchez. It is unclear who replaced him during the last three years of company rule.

206. Jesuit Fathers Tartarin and Le Boulanger served settlers in Fort de Chartres and Kaskaskia.

207. On French-Indian relations in the Illinois country, see Richard White, *The Middle Ground: Indians, Empires, and Republics in the Great Lakes Region, 1650–1815* (Cambridge: Cambridge University Press, 1991); W. J. Eccles, *The French in North America, 1500–1783* (East Lansing: Michigan State University Press, 1998); and M. J. Morgan, *Land of Big Rivers: French and Indian Illinois, 1699–1778* (Carbondale: Southern Illinois University Press, 2010).

208. In the first three decades of the eighteenth century, tensions rooted in the expansion of French fur

these curs have taken a Frenchman, they attach him to a tree and four or five of them start to gnaw off the tips of his fingers, his hands, and his feet until no more blood, which they love dearly, comes out, after which they smoke the same fingers in pipes as if it were tobacco. There are no cruelties in existence more painful than those. Next they cut off an arm or a thigh, which they cook or, for the most part, they eat raw; the same with the other limbs. They have yet a number of other atrocities, about which I will speak next, in the appropriate place.

This is what happened not too long ago to a man, a woman, two little children, and an officer who left New Orleans to go to Missouri to establish themselves, and the officer going to command a detachment there. They were seen while they were going up there and attacked right away by those barbarous savages, who did not hesitate at all, because of their number, to make themselves masters of these people and their trans-port. They began by exercising their cruelties on the little children, whom they cut into pieces, which [116] served as a light meal for the twenty-two of them. To quench their thirst, they slashed the arms of these poor wretches many times with knives in order to suck their blood out. After this, they took the woman, who was seven months pregnant, opened her belly, took her baby, and roasted it in front of her. Next they went to the officer, to whom they had not yet done a thing and who was half dead from seeing such atrocities. He was not alive much longer than the others, because after they attached him by his feet with his head hanging down, they scalped him, meaning they flayed the top of his head, cut him into pieces, put these in their mouths, and ate them up.

This is the manner in which these savage beasts treat us when they catch us. This nation does not have a village and is nomadic. This is why they are called the Foxes, and also because of their cunning.

Eighty leagues above the Illinois, there is a French post with a garrison of twenty men and a commander, and, near this post, which is called Missouri, there is an Indian village from which this post gets its name.[209] The Indians number three hundred fifty. They fancy the French a great deal and are often at war against the Foxes, who, accord-ing to the slaves we took, are said to number between eight and nine hundred.

Near the Missouri, you can find mines that were believed to have silver, but Monsieur Renaud, who had been commissioned to undertake this great project and exploit it

---

trading operations in the Great Lakes region west of Detroit resulted in a series of wars with the Fox nation. Banks, *Chasing Empire*, 36–37; R. David Edmunds and Joseph L. Peyser, *The Fox Wars: The Mesquakie Challenge to New France* (Norman: University of Oklahoma Press, 1993); and William T. Hagan, *The Sac and Fox Indians* (Norman: University of Oklahoma Press, 1958).

209. Fort d'Orléans was established at the Missouri post in 1724 on the north bank of the Missouri River near the mouth of the Grand River.

with a company of miners and fifty Negroes that had been given to him, has found only lead, which sells for twenty-four *sols* per pound, net. Nevertheless, he is at this time still hoping to find the real silver mine, but, because of the small number of people Monsieur Renaud has to help him, it thwarts him from making this discovery.[210]

These are, more or less, the villages that border the Mississippi River. It may be that I have forgotten some little ones or, rather, that I did not want to describe them here for fear of boring the reader to no end. There are also some of which we have no [117] knowledge.

Indians are all tall and well formed, except for a nation that is called the Dwarfs, who are very short. Their skin is of a very deep reddish color. They are very adept at fishing and great lovers of hunting. Before they had any commerce with the French, they used only bows and arrows, but today they have muskets, which they use very skillfully.

With regards to the women, they are the same color. They occupy themselves only with their type of cooking, and they also grow corn, potatoes, squash (which are a type of pumpkin), and watermelons in their deserts, otherwise known as fields. The Indians have the advantage of enlarging their lands, as it seems suitable to them, without asking permission from anyone, quite different from France, where often one foot of land usurping one's neighbor's causes the ruination of families.

Only the people of the Illinois nation, of which I have just spoken here above, have whiter skin than the others, and their women are very beautiful, but very debauched, since they love the French excessively. As for the English, they are not loved by any nation, even though they give them presents. The cause of this hatred comes from the fact that the English wanted to have this colony before us. They used for this purpose poisoned brandy, which they had distributed to each village, but the Indians, seeing the effect this drink caused, refused to drink it anymore and began from that point to regard the English as their greatest enemies. Nevertheless they drink it nowadays, but only after they test it on animals.

There are also among the Natchez women those who go so far in their debauchery that they go to find the French, even in their beds, to assuage their ardent passion. They

---

210. Rumors of copper and silver deposits in the upper Mississippi Valley had been circulating in France since around 1695, when Pierre-Charles Le Sueur first recorded the presence of copper and lead traces along the Green (now Blue Earth) River. The rumors persisted through the first decades of the eighteenth century, but exploratory mining turned up only lead in significant quantities. The company helped support lead extraction efforts led by Philippe Renaud, but Renaud's efforts were stymied by a shortage of laborers to work the mine and goods to pay his existing workers. As late as 1753, Dumont de Montigny posited that the French failure to extract precious metals was due to a lack of interest in exploring. On French mining efforts in the upper Mississippi Valley, see Giraud, *History of French Louisiana*, 5:440–45; and Dumont de Montigny, *Mémoires historiques sur la Louisiane*, 71–74.

do not let you rest unless you have satisfied them. Most of the inhabitants buy only female slaves, Indian as well as Negro, in order to more conveniently lie with them.

[118] The French women of this country follow the native women around quite a bit, because even the girls, who should maintain some kind of chastity, act completely to the contrary and do not make a secret of losing it. You see them brag in public about their wicked conduct. Thus you can quite easily understand, for the reasons I state, that this colony's upsets and frequent wars derive only from the wicked life that the people there lead, and that the punishments God has sent to us are only too just, as you will see later.[211]

From the Natchez to above the Missouri, you find woods and also very beautiful plains of an excellent soil for planting crops. The land is elevated and has much more fresh air than in New Orleans, which is surrounded by woods and only has fresh air by clearing them out, which is what they have done and what they do every day, and also for the wideness of the river, which contributes a lot to it. I forgot to speak about New Orleans's windmill, which is a masterpiece for the country. If needed, it could serve two goals, the first to grind grain and the second to serve as a citadel. It is a very fine structure in the opinion of the laborers and builders, and it is of an ingenious style. Monsieur Le Baron was the one who designed it. Within it dwells a clerk who records what comes in and what leaves, whether wheat or rice. In this mill, at the bottom, there is a small mill that is turned by four horses in the event that there is no wind. This building is surrounded by an octagonal balcony, about eighteen to twenty feet above the ground, and it is plumb. At the four corners there is a gutter that throws rainwater off the mill. It cost the company eighty thousand livres.

There is another one [see fig. 17], on the other side of the river at the company plantation, which is used to saw planks by means of certain springs. It saws ten planks at a time. The same mill has at the other end eight pestles, which fall into sort of wooden

---

211. Repeated references to the dissolute nature of women in French Louisiana appear in contemporary accounts. Jacques de La Chaise objected to providing company rations to "a number of women . . . who are useless and do nothing but cause disorder." According to La Chaise, these same women were responsible for the spread of venereal disease among visiting sailors. Jacques de La Chaise to the Directors of the Company of the Indies, 6 September 1723, *MPA*, 2:315. Ship's captain M. Valette de Laudun wrote, "I think that most of the women sent here are so unhealthy and so used up by past relations that they are sterile before they even leave [France]," in *Journal d'un Voyage à la Louisiane, fait en 1720 par M.***, capitaine de vaisseau du Roi* (The Hague: Musier, Fils et Fournier, 1768), 255–56. In 1728 Marie-Madeleine Hachard informed her father that "As for the girls of bad conduct, they are closely observed here and severely punished by putting them on a wooden horse and whipped by all the soldiers of the regiment that guards our city. This does not prevent there from being more than would fill a reformatory." Marie-Madeleine Hachard to Jacques Hachard, 24 April 1728, *Voices from an Early American Convent*, 82. Antoine-François Prévost's fictional account, *Histoire du chevalier Des Grieux et de Manon Lescaut* (written in the 1730s, first published in its entirety in 1753), is perhaps the best-known depiction of Louisiana's female populace as thoroughly debauched.

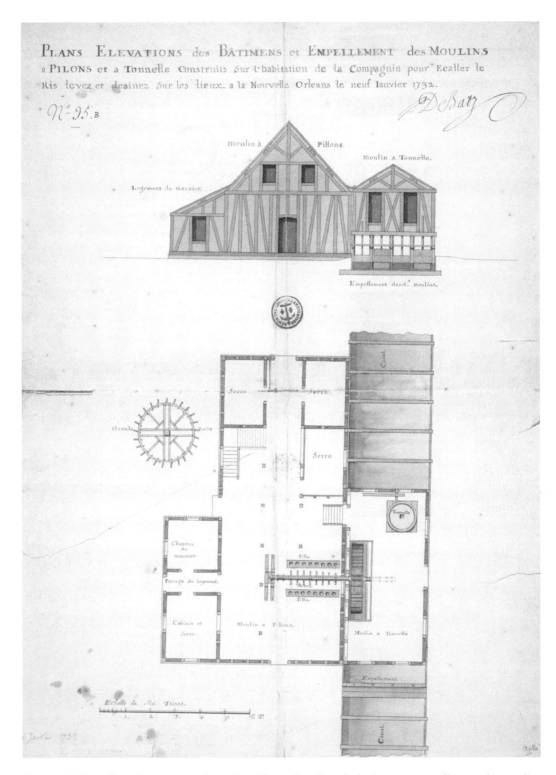

Figure 17. Rice mill at the company plantation; *Plans, elevations des batiments et empellement des moulins à pilons et à tonelle construits sur l'habitation de la Compagnie pour écaler le ris*, by Alexandre de Batz, 9 January 1732 (FR.ANOM. Aix-en-Provence. 04DFC 95B)

mortars [119] that are used to crush rice. On the same side, you see the company plantation, where the Negroes who arrive from Guinea are kept while waiting to be sold.[212]

A quarter of a league above, there is a country house belonging to Monsieur de Périer. It is very pleasant, built in brick and covered in brick, I mean in tile. The shutters and doors are painted green. They already hold social gatherings there.

I will now come back to a place called Dauphin Island [see fig. 18]. It is where the first ships that were sent to the colony came to anchor. Later they went to Biloxi, which is on the mainland, fifteen leagues distant from this island.[213] They had already built a town there, where the council and all the inhabitants were. This place is quite pretty, well elevated, but very difficult for anchoring vessels, which were obliged to anchor five leagues away, without being protected from any storm. The land there is very unpleasant, being but sand. The inhabitants, having seen that after blood, sweat, and tears they had not made any progress at all, made their case before the gentlemen of the council that they needed to abandon this country and that the settlement would be better along the riverbank. Their request was answered, and they were ordered to go establish themselves where they built New Orleans, which has been there since 1718. At present, Biloxi is deserted. It was high time to abandon it, since two years afterward it was submerged halfway and still is.

Two leagues from there are the Biloxis, who are on the seacoast, numbering 260. Eight leagues inland from there, in the lands of the same coast, are the Pascagoula, who are 170 in number.[214] Near them there are three or four quite-well-made plantations. There is no point in my describing here the passages, bayous, and little islands that are found there. This would only serve to bore the reader by the repetition of the same things.

Since they started taking people from Paris to send them to the Mississippi country, they have been putting them ashore, without giving them food, at Dauphin Island, otherwise known as Massacre Island. (They named it this because of the great quantity of people who were found dead there, as I will explain to you.) The only food they had

---

212. Across from New Orleans, on the west bank of the Mississippi River, the company operated a nearly four-thousand-acre plantation replete with rice-processing mill, brickworks, forge, slave quarters and hospital, and overseer's residence. The plantation was worked by approximately 125 adult slave laborers and housed an additional 25 enslaved children. Newly arrived slaves from Africa were held on site until they were deemed ready for sale. On company-owned slaves and their labor, see Greenwald, "Company Towns and Tropical Baptisms," 171–82.

213. Biloxi was Louisiana's official capital from 1719 until late December 1721.

214. The Biloxi and Pascagoula were two among several small coastal Indian groups present along the Gulf Coast. Because of their proximity to and close trade relationships with French settlements in Biloxi and Mobile Bay, these coastal Indians suffered extreme population losses—primarily caused by disease—in the first decades of the eighteenth century, though an influx of Indians driven out of other parts of the Southeast by warfare helped renew their numbers.

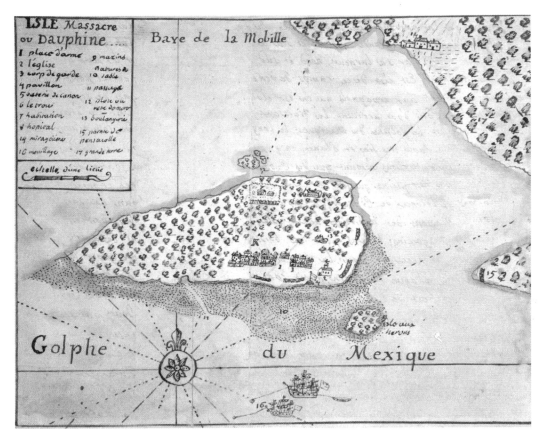

Figure 18. Dauphin (Massacre) Island; *Isle Massacre ou Dauphine*, by Jean-François Benjamin Dumont de Montigny, ca. 1747 (Courtesy of the Newberry Library, Chicago, Ayer MS 257, carte no. 2)

was what they could find, and, in the end, after looking for something [120] to live off of and not finding anything, some of them came to die along the coast while deploring their unfortunate fate, while others fell down dead. Still others stabbed themselves or threw themselves into the sea from despair. They counted five thousand dead on the sand. In the end, out of fourteen ships that had brought fifty-five hundred men and women, only five hundred were able to survive by eating grass, and many other things they found that were capable of killing them a thousand times.[215]

---

215. Caillot is telling tall tales about horrors on Massacre, or Dauphin, Island. Iberville named the island Massacre Island in February 1699, when he and his expeditionary crew found the decomposing remains of more than sixty individuals on the southwest end of the island. Though hunger and deprivation were realities for Louisiana's early colonists, there is no evidence that five thousand of fifty-five hundred colonists perished on the shores of Dauphin Island. See Pierre Le Moyne d'Iberville, 3 February 1699, in *Iberville's Gulf Journals*, ed. and trans. Richebourg Gaillard McWilliams (Tuscaloosa: University of Alabama Press, 1981), 38; and André Joseph Pénicaut, "Relation, ou annale véritable de ce qui s'est passé dans le païs de la Louisiane pendant vingt-deux années consecutifes . . .," Bibliothèque nationale de France (BnF), Français 14613, fo. 13–14.

After remaining a long time on this island, and even after constructing some huts and several houses for the officers and the council, they noticed that, day by day, the sea went beyond the limits and was claiming a considerable amount of land, which was cause for those who were still alive to quickly decamp. They risked everything, for it was risking a great deal, even their lives, to go back to the mainland at the mercy of so many savages who were unknown to us, and with so few of them remaining. Nevertheless, in order to prolong their lives, it was a risk they had to take. They thus went to the mainland, where they encamped at the village of the Biloxi, which was quite welcoming, and where they were better off than they had imagined.

The council did not want to abandon the island they had left, out of fear that, when ships finally arrived, and finding no one there anymore, they would return to France. For this reason they had a sergeant and three soldiers stay there. At the end of two months, upon returning there to bring them some provisions and to see if there had been any ships, they found only one soldier, who was eating the arm of one of his comrades since he had nothing else but that to eat. They asked him where the sergeant and the others were. He said that, after they were not able to find anything to live off of anymore, they had drawn lots to see who would be eaten first, and luckily for him he had remained the last. But, having only an arm left to eat, he would have brought an end to his days, too, by throwing himself into the sea, if he had not seen someone coming. They left him the provisions they had brought for him and his comrades. And those who had come returned to make their reports about what had happened among these soldiers.

[121] When the council heard this, they decided they should go find him again, and to this effect they sent a canoe charged with pecans and potatoes, which were the provisions they had found in Biloxi, and were a great help in making this little voyage. When they arrived on the island where this soldier was, they told him in the name of the council to get in the boat with them to go to the mainland. But when he saw that they had brought in the canoe something to live off of for seven or eight days, he took part of it to be able to subsist just until two ships that he had just seen (which were the ones they were waiting for, loaded with provisions) came to anchor at his island. In short, he continued to stay there from that time and never wanted to leave, such that at present he has a superb plantation where he lacks for nothing. They furnished him afterward with everything he wanted, both in slaves and livestock. Of Negroes he has twenty males, six females, and a few little children, and more than forty cattle, for which he does not owe a penny.[216]

---

216. Caillot's tale of soldier-on-soldier cannibalism on Dauphin Island is not substantiated in other accounts, leaving readers to wonder if he was unwittingly duped into believing the account by one of his contemporaries.

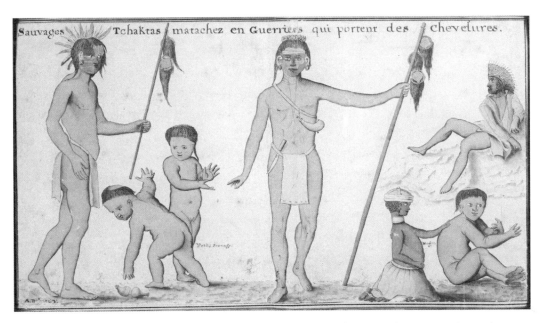

Figure 19. Choctaw warriors carrying trophy scalps; *Sauvages Tchaktas matachez en Guerriers qui portent des chevelures*, by Alexandre de Batz, 1735 (Courtesy of the Peabody Museum of Archaeology and Ethnology, Harvard University, 41-72-10/18))

It is to this man, who is called goodman Renaud,[217] that the ships arriving from France have recourse. He has in his little realm sixteen leagues all around. He has built a little fort, made only of earth and wood, and he has put four pieces of cannon along its ramparts. He has planted muscat grapes, which he got from the ships, that are of an exquisite flavor. He has enough of them to make one and a half barrels per year, which is all that he can drink.

Seven leagues above Biloxi, there is an Indian village called the Chacato [see fig. 19], who are 140 in number.[218] This nation is well loved by the French. They have equal parts of faithfulness and politeness. When a Frenchman goes to their home, they welcome him in their best-possible manner. They begin by making orations to him

217. The only Renauds present on Dauphin Island during the early French colonial period were members of the Canadian family headed by André Renaud, who maintained provisioning crops and a small herd of cattle.

218. Around 1704 the Chacato, often confused with the Choctaw, moved from lands in Spanish Florida to the Mobile Bay area. The Choctaw confederacy, centered in present-day Mississippi and western Alabama, was the largest in the lower Mississippi Valley, with an approximate population of fifteen thousand in the first quarter of the eighteenth century. The literature on the Choctaw is extensive. Useful overviews include Patricia Galloway and Clara Sue Kidwell, "Choctaw in the East," in Fogelson, *Handbook of North American Indians*, 14:499–519; Patricia Galloway, *Choctaw Genesis, 1500–1700* (Lincoln: University of Nebraska Press, 1998); Galloway, "'The Chief Who Is Your Father': Choctaw and French Views of the Diplomatic Relation," in Waselkov, Wood, and Hatley, *Powhatan's Mantle*, 345–70; Patricia Dillon Woods, *French-Indian Relations on the Southern Frontier, 1699–1762* (Ann Arbor: UMI Research Press, 1980); and Greg O'Brien's historiographic essay "The Coming of Age of Choctaw History," in *Pre-removal Choctaw History: Exploring New Paths*, ed. Greg O'Brien (Norman: University of Oklahoma Press, 2008), 3–25.

while making many curtsies to him, the way women do, then the chief sends some of them to go hunting and others to go fishing, and in less than an hour they regale you very well, though in their manner.

Three leagues above, you find the city of Mobile, which is very nicely situated.[219] It is on the shore of a big, wide river that has the same name as the city. It is very full of fish. Mobile is seven leagues from the sea. [122] It has a very pretty appearance. There are two forts at the two ends, and the houses there are very well built.[220] In winter the fogs are very thick, which causes illnesses. Life there is quite easy as far as game, which is very plentiful. There are 200 inhabitants, with a troop of 160 men. The two forts of which I just spoke are built of brick with four bastions, each having four pieces of cannon and many covered roads, with beautiful buildings that are enclosed within the forts. This is in case there is a war against the Spanish, English, and Indians; the whole city can take refuge inside while waiting for help. Monsieur Devin,[221] the engineer of the aforementioned place, drew up the plan for it, and Monsieur Diron, who is the brother of Monsieur Dartaguiette, director of the company, is commander and governor there. There is a little church, in which the Reverend Father Mathias, a Capuchin and a man quite zealous for the spiritual advancement of his parishioners, shows quite well by his conduct that he practices all that he preaches.

At five leagues' distance, you find an Indian nation that is called the Mobilians.[222] That is where the city gets its name from, and they number three hundred fifty men.

At fourteen leagues' distance inland, you will find the village of the Apalachees.[223] This nation would deserve rather to have the name Good Frenchmen and Good Christians, and not the name of savages, because they observe, with more exactitude than us, what they have been taught about our religion. One can speak more about the

---

219. Mobile was first established in 1702 several miles up the Mobile River from its current site, where it was moved in 1711. The best resource on old Mobile and Dauphin Island remains Jay Higginbotham's *Old Mobile: Fort Louis de la Louisiane, 1702–1711* (Tuscaloosa: University of Alabama Press, 1991).

220. Fort Louis de la Louisiane was built in 1702 to protect the old Mobile settlement. When the settlement was moved downriver, in 1711, a new, temporary fort, also called Fort Louis, was constructed south of the new site. New Fort Louis was replaced by Fort Condé in 1723.

221. Valentin Devin oversaw construction of Mobile's Fort Condé after the engineer Boispinel died, in 1723.

222. Settled along Mobile Bay, the Mobilians were in close contact with the French throughout the colonial period. Their proximity to Europeans led to a drastic population decline following a "plague" brought ashore by sick sailors, soldiers, and settlers in 1704. Other groups decimated by the 1704 epidemic included the Tahomé, Pascagoulas, Choctaw, and Apalachee. George E. Lankford, "Chacato, Pensacola, Tahomé, Naniaba, and Mobilia," in Fogelson, *Handbook of North American Indians*, 14:668; and Kelton, *Epidemics and Enslavement*, 190–92.

223. Approximately four hundred Apalachee Indians, Christianized by Spanish Franciscans in the seventeenth century, settled along Mobile Bay in 1704, after fleeing English-sponsored slave raids in Florida. Gallay, *Indian Slave Trade*, 144–49; Usner, *Indians, Settlers, and Slaves*, 60–61; Usner, *American Indians in the Lower Mississippi Valley*, 38–39; and Gregory A. Waselkov, *Old Mobile Archaeology* (Tuscaloosa: University of Alabama Press, 2005), 44–46. On the successful Christianization of the Apalachee in Florida, see John H. Hann, *Apalachee: The Land between the Rivers* (Gainesville: University Presses of Florida, 1988).

missionaries who have made them good Christians and very assiduous about Mass. I think that the tale that I am going to tell, in shortened form, will of itself be capable of awakening the spirit of those who, for a long time, have remained lukewarm and apathetic toward the divine service.

Monsieur Huet was a missionary who had been sent to this colony in 1698, to do mission work among the natives and to be a parish priest of a little place named Mobile, today well fortified.[224] That pious nation was, in those days, no farther than a league from there, in a place called Sacutlaire.[225] The aforementioned Sieur Huet would go there often after he learned their language, having found in them a [123] great disposition and a great desire to be instructed in our religion, and continued to go there two times per week. Then he encouraged them to come attend Mass, which they did with an admirable example of piety, though they were still blind. But the desire that they had to be admitted as children of the church made them come receive instruction and catechism sometimes more often than Sieur Huet wanted, due to his duties as parish priest. Nevertheless, the eagerness with which they were washed in the waters of baptism meant that, in less than one and a half years, they all received baptism, and, as a sign of their joy and the thankfulness they had in receiving God's grace, they all asked unanimously to have a parish priest in their village.

This was accorded to them eight years later, but, seeing that they were being sent another priest rather than their accustomed curé, they asked again for Monsieur Huet. He was constrained to go there, where he lives very happily with them today. They love him and make sure that he does not lack for anything he needs.[226] I can tell you that they perform their duty more devoutly than we do. It is a true pleasure to see the manner in which these new converts pray to the Lord. Their zeal alone is capable of inspiring devotion in the most villainous of people. They have a mass every day, and, if they cannot attend it all together, there is at least one from each house who goes to attend while the others work at cultivating the land. They especially pay great

---

224. Alexandre Huvé served as a priest in Mobile beginning in 1704. In October of that year he baptized the first child of European descent born in Louisiana. A member of the Foreign Missions order, Huvé was also an active missionary among the area's Indian groups, including the Apalachees, though his contemporaries questioned his effectiveness; he had a pronounced speech impediment that rendered his preaching difficult to decipher, and he was unwilling to learn Indian languages. That Caillot calls Huvé "Huet" suggests that he may have read André Pénicaut's manuscript account of his travels in Louisiana, in which Huvé is erroneously referred to as Huet. See André Pénicaut, *Fleur de Lys and Calumet: Being the Pénicaut Narrative of French Adventure in Louisiana*, ed. and trans. Richebourg Gaillard McWilliams (Tuscaloosa: University of Alabama Press, 1988). McWilliams suggests that Pénicaut may have left finished manuscript chapters in Natchez when he left for France in 1721. On Huvé's role as missionary and priest, see Higginbotham, *Old Mobile*, 187–89, 204–6, 277–79, 412–13.

225. Sacutlaire, or Sacullaire, may refer to one of the two Apalachee towns located on the Mobile River.

226. Huvé returned to France in 1727. Recollet Father Victorin, who joined the Apalachee mission in 1725, was the sole priest ministering to them at the time of Caillot's travels.

attention to the sermons. You would kill them more easily than you would make them miss a single word of these. The first Sunday of every month and New Year's Day, they approach the altar, and you do not see any of them hesitate to approach the sacraments by a misplaced shame of having committed sin. In the end, I can say, to the shame of countless Frenchmen, that they serve as an example.

If Frenchmen go to their houses, they are made very welcome, especially when they talk to them about God. They have a custom, which they got from the Spanish, of wearing the rosary around their necks. They number from four to five hundred.

From the Apalachees, you leave the Mobile River and enter into a bayou three leagues away to reach a village that is named for the Taensa. They are [124] sixty in number. They have a law among them, which is that in their village they have a large hut where an Indian lives day and night. He gets up at intervals to keep a fire going, which is continually ablaze. If by chance it happened to be extinguished, as has happened, there would be a worthy and four other Indians who would leave by land to go to the Natchez, who are one hundred fifty leagues away, in order to get more fire. During the voyage, which is only nine to ten days at the most, the ones who stay in the village continually whip the Indian who let the fire go out. When they decide that the travelers will soon be arriving, they pull out his tongue and attach him to a post, and when they arrive, if this wretch still has a bit of life in him, they make him light the fire. When it is burning well, they make him eat it while they chant death cries, and then they throw him in the fire. We do not know the reason for this superstition.[227]

Eighteen leagues from Mobile, on the same river, you will find the Indian nation that is called the Tohomé, who number 130.[228]

Two leagues above is the village of the Aniaba, who number eighty.

Seventy-five leagues away is the village of the Jutits Alis Indians, who number 160.[229]

At one hundred fifty leagues you find the Great Alabamas, an Indian nation that numbers four hundred fifty.[230] Near there is a French post with a garrison of eighty men, a commander, one major, two officers, and fifty inhabitants.[231]

---

227. The removal of the tongue is an act of extreme disdain toward the person being tortured because it prohibits the victim from chanting his or her mourning song on facing death. Placing the disembodied tongue back in the victim's mouth is a further act of contempt.

228. The Tahomé (Tomé) Indians were one of three culturally similar but distinct coastal tribes living around Mobile Bay; the other two were the Mobilians and Naniabas (Aniabas). All three groups were part of the Choctaw confederacy. Lankford, "Chacato, Pensacola, Tahomé, Naniaba, and Mobilia," in Fogelson, *Handbook of North American Indians*, 14:664–68.

229. It is possible that this was the "Little Alabamas," a group who remained friendly with the French while the other Alabamas were not. The manuscript clearly reads "Jutit Alis," a possible mistranscription of "Petits [Little] Alis."

230. The southernmost group of Upper Creeks, the Alabamas are often seen as a barrier tribe separating French Louisiana from English Carolina. They were not allied with either European power but traded with both.

231. Fort Toulouse, also called Fort des Alibamons, was established in Alabama territory in 1717 at French

Fifty leagues above the Great Alabamas, or Alis, you find the Indian nation of the Tallapoosa, numbering two hundred fifty.[232] They are very evil, barbaric, and cruel.

Twenty leagues above the Tallapoosa are the Cowetas, where the French and the English, up until present time, have together traded cows, of which they make great commerce. There is among them a great chief called emperor, who has not only that nation obedient to him, but all the other Indian villages of North America as well. There are close to ten thousand of them in their village, but they are in truth about one league from one another. When this emperor leaves his house, he is always accompanied by eight hundred Indians. [125] He is very advanced in age. We are the nation they like best. His son is quite different from him, because he is entirely taken with the English.[233]

When you go to this emperor's house, you are served with silver vessels and treated magnificently, not at all in the manner of the Indians. He also dresses in a French manner when he is with Frenchmen, and in the English manner when he is with Englishmen. He receives presents that are sent to him every year, and sometimes he comes walking along himself to get them.

When he came to New Orleans he was very well received by the commander, with whom he dined. During the meal, he examined everything in order to have himself served the same way. When he returned from there, they made him a present of several suits embroidered in gold and silver, and others in silk, which the company had sent for him in order to maintain his friendship with us, which is of no little importance for the colony.

At the extremity of the southwest coast, at a distance of one hundred leagues from Mobile, we have another nation, which is called Choctaw. They are eighteen thousand in number. They like the French for all appearances, but it is only to get presents from them, because, if they were as brave as they are numerous, they would do well to show the contrary, but they are extremely cowardly. (They are nicknamed Parisians.) Of all

---

Louisiana's eastern border with the Carolinas in hopes of preventing English encroachment into Louisiana. The fort, located at the present-day site of Wetumpka, Alabama, was at the crossroads for Indian trade among the Alabamas, Creek, Chickasaw, Choctaw, and Mobilians. For more on Fort Toulouse, see Daniel H. Thomas, *Fort Toulouse: The French Outpost at the Alabamas on the Coosa* (Tuscaloosa: University of Alabama Press, 1989).

232. Part of the Creek confederacy, the Tallapoosa and neighboring groups living along the Coosa, Tallapoosa, and Alabama Rivers are often referred to as Upper Creeks.

233. The Coweta, a Lower Creek group located south of the Chattahoochee River, in present-day eastern Alabama and western Georgia, joined forces with the Yamassee in 1715 against the British in Carolina. The Coweta chief, Emperor Brim (or Brims), was an astute politician whose favor shifted between the English, French, and Spanish depending on political and economic expedience. Some historians believe Brim played a key role in initiating the Yamassee war. The son Caillot referred to was probably Malatchi, who succeeded Brim as emperor of the Cowetas. On the Coweta and larger Creek Confederacy, see Steven C. Hahn, *The Invention of the Creek Nation, 1670–1763* (Lincoln: University of Nebraska Press, 2004).

the Indians, in general most of them are people whom you should never trust.²³⁴ The Choctaws have, like the other nations, their great chief, their sun, their war chief, their worthies, etc. They make up about twenty villages, one after the other, which form a circuit of fifty leagues. They have skin that is more blackish than the others because of the longleaf pine that they burn to warm themselves and heat their food. They also extract pitch and tar from this wood. These are the Indians who fear water the most, to such an extreme that in order to travel a distance of ten leagues by water, they prefer to make a detour of a hundred leagues.

The Chis, or Chickasaws (neighbors of the Choctaws), number three hundred.²³⁵ These Indians are very adept at hiding themselves. This is how they kill their enemies: when Frenchmen go to trade some fowl or [126] other things in their village and they do not keep up their guard, they are as good as dead, because, when they see you coming from afar, they hide behind a tree, where it is impossible to see them. When we get close to them, they seize us or shoot arrows at us. If they miss, they flee into the woods, making horrible howls; but also, if you are surprised by them, they begin to make death cries at you and scalp you from your forehead to your neck. They do this procedure very quickly with a little knife, a gun flint, or with their tomahawk, which is a type of small ax. When they have done this operation, they sometimes leave you to die like that. But ordinarily they drive four to five blows of that ax into your back. The Choctaws, their enemies, treat them the same way when they catch them.

There is a man in this colony who found himself in a great deal of trouble, having been surprised by the Foxes and close to being scalped. This is how he was able to get himself out of that situation and at the same time make himself feared by those wretches: Monsieur Dutisné, captain in Plantin's company, being at the head of a detachment he was leading to the Illinois and taken with the desire to go into the woods accompanied only by his manservant, had gone a distance of only three musket shots when he was attacked by about twenty Foxes. (This is a nation as cruel as it is carnivorous, especially for the flesh of the French, which they prefer over all others, and

---

234. The notion of Choctaws as cowards comes up repeatedly in both French and English accounts. Historian Alan Gallay argues that the Choctaw reputation for cowardice was ill-deserved, and that in fact they were feared by all their neighbors but earned this reputation from their manner of warfare, which sometimes included nighttime raids that allowed the Choctaw to catch their enemies unaware. Gallay, *Indian Slave Trade*, 180–83. The Choctaw were the largest Indian group in French Louisiana and were French allies throughout the colonial period. Caillot's own opinion of the Choctaw may have been colored by the perception that they had acted duplicitously during the Natchez war of 1729–30.

235. Located north of the Choctaw in present-day northern Alabama, northern Mississippi, and western Tennessee, the Chickasaw were generally allied with the English, especially with Carolina traders, and in Louisiana were often perceived as predatory because of their repeated raids against French-allied tribes. On the Chickasaw, see Robbie Franklyn Ethridge, *From Chicaza to Chickasaw: The European Invasion and the Transformation of the Mississippian World, 1540–1715* (Chapel Hill: University of North Carolina Press, 2010).

they eat their own people.) These savages began by stripping off his clothes until he was completely naked, and divided the spoils among themselves. One got a sleeve, another the breeches, another the other sleeve, etc. After this, they set themselves to the task of scalping him. You decide whether he was in a difficult situation, finding himself so close to death.

In the meantime, he resolved himself to risk death, since he was going to die anyway, and intended to try to execute a plan that came to him. To that effect, as they were going to put their hands on his head, he said to them, in their native tongue, "Envna," which means "wait," and then he made them an oration in which he made them see that there was no value in taking his scalp. To give them proof of this, [127] he told them he would do it himself. At that moment, he threw his hat on the ground, and, since he was wearing a wig, he took it by the knots and, pretending to be making an effort doing this, threw it at their feet. As soon as these barbarians saw that, they remained completely speechless, but what surprised them the most about this was not seeing any blood running down his head, which had just been freshly shaved. They could not keep from crying out, all of them trembling, that this was a man of great valor, and, for its very great rarity, they took that wig, which they have preserved in their village as a prodigious thing.

After this action, Monsieur Dutisné, seeing that his affair was going well, showed them a magnifying glass, which he brought close to his clothing, to astonish them even more. He burned a small patch, and, to make it more perceptible to them, he held the glass directly over their skin. When they felt that this thing was burning them keenly, they started crying out and taking flight, but Monsieur Dutisné, reassuring them, said to not be afraid, that he did not want to do them any harm. They came back, to the great regret and against the wishes of his servant, who was three-quarters dead. When they returned, he used the same magnifying glass to burn some gunpowder. Then they threw themselves face down on the ground, all believing themselves to be exterminated.

At Monsieur Dutisné's words, they got up again, knowing no longer what posture to maintain in front of him. They would have liked to have never seen that man. He made them look through a microscope, which increased their surprise even more. But what frightened them most was that, upon finding a little pool of water, Monsieur Dutisné told them that in a moment he was going to dry up this pool as easily as he would dry up the Mississippi River. They begged him not to do anything, for they would die if he did it. He brought them with him along the shore of the river, where, without their seeing, he poured some brandy in a mess kit and told his servant to give him a mess kit full of water. The servant, who had been present at all of his master's tricks, pretended to get some water from the river and brought it to Monsieur Dutisné, who told them,

"If you or anyone of your nation harm the French anymore, I will burn you all up and I will dry up the Balbancha" (which is what they call the river). [128] At the same time, he put fire in the brandy to show them the truth of what he was saying, but they could no longer endure so many wonders, which made them all prostrate themselves at the feet of the aforementioned gentleman, and they begged him not to do anything else, which he did, and he let them go. This is how he escaped from such a bad predicament, and his servant too. From that moment they have always feared him, believing that he was the Great Spirit, which is what they say when speaking about God.

Indians declare war between themselves in the following manner. They go to the village they want to strike, and they plant a staff there painted in black on top, and the other half in red, into which a tomahawk is driven. That is the way they declare war and that is the signal.

Indian Clothing and Customs[236]

The chiefs, worthies, and other warriors at the present time dress with clothes the company has had made for them, colored red and blue, trimmed with fake gold and silver braid according to their rank.[237] The other Indians are made a gift of loincloths, as I explained previously. They go about with bare feet and bare heads, with the exception of the chiefs, who have hats trimmed in fake braid. Each nation is known by its hairstyle, which is different from nation to nation. Some cut off all their hair, others only half, etc.

Concerning the women, they wear half an ell of limbourg, or otherwise a blue cloth, around themselves, and the rest of their body is completely naked. Almost all of them have long hair that they wear sometimes parted and sometimes braided, with a type of long fiber that hangs from the trees, which they call Spanish beard.[238] They rarely paint themselves except for special ceremonies. They are tattooed with a single little dotted

---

236. Much of Caillot's commentary on Indian clothing and customs resembles passages found in Le Page du Pratz's and Dumont de Montigny's memoirs. See Le Page du Pratz, *Histoire de la Louisiane*, 2:190–202; and Dumont de Montigny, *Regards sur le monde atlantique*, 360–91.

237. The number and variety of trade goods distributed among Louisiana's Indians in exchange for furs, pelts, provisions, and sometimes military alliance were extensive. A 1731 inventory of goods destined for the Indian trade in Louisiana includes defense- and hunting-related items such as bullets, flints, hatchets, muskets, and powder; but also more quotidian objects like sewing (or tattooing) needles, cooking implements, limbourg cloth, bells, baby blankets, handheld mirrors "laquered in the Chinese style," combs, nails, vermilion, red and blue socks, "trading shirts for men and women," feathers in a variety of colors, and hats trimmed in fake gold or silver braid. "Etat de marchandises propres pour la traite à presens des sauvages de la province de la Louisianne à envoyer de France," 1731, ANOM, F 1A 30.

238. Spanish moss

black line, which goes from the ears to the corners of the mouth, and another one from the top of the forehead to the bottom of the chin.[239] Other than that, they wear little pieces of cloth at the tips of their little feet, thinking themselves to be well ornamented. They also wear things like rings of iron on their arms, which signal the number of husbands they have had, and in their ears they wear shells passed through sideways.[240] Warriors paint themselves, as do the men.

[129] Girls and women who have given themselves to many Indians and whose debauchery is known by the whole nation or only by the village have their hair cut off and receive the lash, which is a great punishment for them.

An Indian becomes a warrior when he has killed someone and scalped him. They are known by the more than one and a half pounds of iron they wear in each ear and by their tomahawks, which they always carry in their hand.[241]

Concerning their marriages, the ceremony is performed early and the banns are published quickly, for when an Indian man and woman like each other, they take each other and get together without any other information. Likewise, when one of the two is not happy, they leave each other and go elsewhere to marry. Nevertheless, it is very rare for them to leave each other, because when they take one another, they truly love each other with a love that lasts a long time, without any vow or pretension of getting goods like three-fourths of the marriages in France.[242]

When they have children, they love them a great deal, and this is how they raise them: when they first come out of the mother's womb, they attach these newborns very securely to a board, and then they are not taken off it until they are weaned. When they begin to eat, they are untied and put on the ground until they know how to walk or until the time they crawl. When they have begun to walk, they make them little arrows, along with a bow proportioned to their strength, and you see these little cupids in the woods, at only four to five years of age. They are so adept at seven or eight that they kill their game with perfect ease. In brief, this is how they are raised. They are all tall men, well formed and straight of posture, because of the board that they were placed upon at birth.[243]

---

239. On tattooing among southeastern Indians, see also Dumont de Montigny, *Regards sur le monde atlantique*, 367; Le Page du Pratz, *Histoire de la Louisiane*, 2:196–97, 198–200; and Jean-Bernard Bossu, *Nouveaux voyages aux Indes occidentales* (Paris: Le Jay, 1768), 190–91.

240. According to Le Page du Pratz, these earrings were made from the center spiral of a large snail-shaped shell called a burgo. *Histoire de la Louisiane*, 2:196.

241. Le Page du Pratz adds that, in addition to iron earrings, warriors commonly wore belts adorned with bells or gourds. Ibid., 200–201.

242. On Indian marriages, see ibid., 385–93.

243. Le Page du Pratz also discusses native child-rearing practices in ibid., 309–19.

I shan't forget to describe to you how they perform the calumet ceremony when they come to the commander's house in New Orleans.[244] Sometimes they number one hundred fifty or two hundred and other times five hundred, counting the chiefs, worthies, and war chiefs. They also bring some women to cook for them during their travels. When they are about to arrive in the [130] city, they make their cries, and, before entering, they perform their dances, then they arrange themselves in a line, one after the other, and cry out at intervals, always the same cry. When they arrive at the governor's gate, they all sit on their bottoms, like monkeys, until they are let in. Although sometimes he is busy or with company, it does not matter; he leaves everything, and he and his company sit in a semicircle.

When the chiefs have entered, the noble advances with the others in his retinue and two or three Indians who are encumbered with presents for the governor. The principal chief comes forward, making a great show of reverence, and presents the calumet to the governor (by placing his hand in the governor's, and likewise with all the company) in order for him to smoke it a bit. It is a great sign of friendship among them. When Monsieur de Périer has smoked two or three puffs, he presents it to his wife, who, despite her wishes, takes one or two gulps, then she presents it to whomever seems good to her, so that all the company smokes at least one puff. This calumet is a pipe made of red clay, with a long tube of two and a half feet in length, very properly polished and decorated with numerous feathers from different birds. After this ceremony is done, he makes an oration in his language. The governor has a Frenchman who serves as an interpreter. Here are the words of his speech, more or less: "Since the great sun of the French," which means king, "sent you here to govern the country, and he has found in you much valor and the necessary qualities to make you obey, we come here, with my nation, to present to you our fealty and assure you that, when you need our small services, we will always be ready to follow your orders, whether it is to second you in a war you may have against your enemies, as well as for any other thing that regards the usefulness of the French nation, which we have always loved, and which we continue to cherish."

This, briefly, is the style of his speech, which lasts more than one and a half hours because of the repetitions they make of the same thing. After the interpreter has given an account to Monsieur [131] de Périer of the content of the aforementioned speech, a servant presents a chair to the great chief, who sits down, and the other chiefs come

---

244. Dumont de Montigny provides a detailed description of the calumet ceremony in *Regards sur le monde atlantique*, 360–63. On the calumet and its role in diplomatic relations in the colonial Southeast, see Gallay, *Indian Slave Trade*, 102–11.

one after the other to make their speeches, too, which do not last more than a half of a quarter of an hour.

When they have finished making their speeches, four worthies get up, along with four Indians, and dance the calumet dance, all painted and ornamented with different types of feathers, to the sound of an earthen pot covered with a deerskin, ornamented with many bells and accompanied by their voices. This makes a music as bizarre as their movements and dances. When they have danced for a while, by making extraordinary contortions that make you want to die laughing, they sit down again on their bottoms, whereupon one of them gets up and takes the calumet, which he fills with an excellent herb that in France is called *feneque*. He presents it to his chief, who lights it with a firebrand. After this chief has smoked his puff, he presents it to Monsieur de Périer for the second time, and then to the whole company. After this ceremony, he presents the gifts, which he puts at the governor's feet, and withdraws with his troop. The next day, Monsieur de Périer meets him at the company headquarters, where he tells his thoughts to the chief, who comes there accompanied by his people, and then, in exchange for the approximately one hundred pounds of pelts they have given, he has distributed to this chief, as well as to the others, more than one thousand écus' worth of merchandise, as much in red and blue cloth as in combs, mirrors, muskets, vermilion, etc. When they return to their village, the chief has it all divided.

Fish That Are Found in the Mississippi River

The freshwater drum, a fish more or less like the perch of France, is very common. It is ordinarily two to three feet long, and sometimes longer, and weighs up to seventy pounds. This fish has very firm flesh, even a bit too firm, in my opinion. It is very active; its flesh is very white but it decays very quickly. As soon as this fish is out of the water in the sun for an instant, it dies.

[132] The freshwater catfish is also very common. This fish has the opposite fault of the freshwater drum, for it is extremely soft, but otherwise it is very delicate, especially the female when she is fat. It has the same flavor as eel. The largest ones are not the best. They often catch some that weigh as much as 100 and 120 pounds.

They eat excellent eels there as fat as one's leg.

The carp there is monstrous and has fat on its back of two thumbs' thickness; one would say it was lard. They smell a bit like mud; the strongest are four and a half feet long and twenty-two to twenty-three inches across. They weigh eighty to ninety pounds.

They also catch a type of shark that is very good. There are also congers as big as my leg.[245]

As far as little fish, there is sun perch, which is very good fried, and gudgeon,[246] but ordinarily they are very large, for there are some that weigh up to fifteen pounds. They are like the ones in France as far as shape and flavor.

There is yet another small fish, the bowfin, which is good only if it is salted. They eat a fish called a stingray, which is shaped the same as a ray and has the same flavor. This fish is found in freshwater and in salt water.[247]

The Mississippi also produces two fish and a third kind that are eaten only as a last resort. The first is an armored fish[248] whose scales are so hard that it is rare for a musket ball to pierce it at twenty paces. It is called an armored fish as much for its scales as for its kind of beak, which has three rows of very sharp teeth that make it feared by all the other fish. It is quite good when well boiled, since its eggs are poisonous, for it has killed several people who ate some of them. The second is the cayman, or crocodile.[249] There are a huge number of them, and they are monstrous in size. Their excrement smells a bit musky. There are some in the river that have pulled cattle into the water, which they devoured. This is why the Negroes who lead the livestock to drink take great care to look and see if there are any around. They killed one that, after it had pulled in a woman who was doing her washing along the edge of the water, came back for her baby, who was crying, and ate the baby too. They killed it, and upon weighing it they found that it weighed seven hundred fifty pounds. This animal has meat that is very lean and quite white, and it smells [133] musky too. Here is what happened to me concerning this animal.

One day I was on a pleasure excursion with some of my friends on Bayou Saint John, of which I spoke previously. We had brought as provisions some good paté, a few dozen bottles of good wine, and some cured meat from the butcher's in order to spend the day at the home of a certain Joseph Bon, inhabitant of said place, who lived on the other side of the aforementioned bayou. In order to go to his house, we got into a little pirogue with our provisions. We were only halfway when, all of the sudden, a huge crocodile came and put his two front feet on the edges of our little boat, which he almost turned over, to get our meat. We were in a great deal of trouble, so, in the meantime, having loaded our muskets, together we all shot him in the head and blasted out his eyes. He left us,

---

245. A conger is a type of marine eel.

246. Gudgeon, a freshwater fish found in Europe, not North America, is related to the carp.

247. The Atlantic stingray is primarily a saltwater fish but is also sometimes found in freshwater rivers and estuaries, especially during the summer months.

248. The fish Caillot described as armored fish were alligator gar.

249. Caillot used the term "*cocodrilles*," or "crocodiles," when describing American alligators found in Louisiana.

making a dreadful turbulence in the water. Not knowing where he was going anymore, he beached himself on the bank. The Negroes from the plantation, seeing that he had been wounded, ran and pulled him out of the water. We measured him and discovered that he was twenty-two feet long. Nevertheless, the armored fish is his master, for no matter how big he might be, the armored fish kills him. When this animal sleeps, the armored fish approaches him and cuts off his tail, which causes him to die.[250]

The third fish that is not eaten at all is the cutlass fish, which actually has the shape of a cutlass.

When the river is quite low, it is full of little creatures they call prawns, shaped more or less like our crawfish. There are prodigious numbers of them. They are very good for purifying blood. They are eaten like crawfish.

There are beavers, but only in the Natchez area. It is a delight to see their little houses built on tree branches that touch the water. The way in which they build them is curious. They go look for soil, which they carry on their tail, and then, using their paws and tail, they build. Each of these animals has three to four rooms in which to live, and two exits. One is for leaving when they are not afraid about anything, and the other, which opens into the water [134], where they dive when they are being hunted without the hunters being able to see them. You would say that it was a little village built on the water when seeing them.

In Bayou Saint John there are fish, namely mullet, sun perch, angelfish, which have two sorts of wings, magnificent crawfish, and little turtles. At the end of the bayou is Lake Pontchartrain, in which there are swordfish. These animals fight the whale, even though they are much smaller. At the end of their head they have, in effect, something like a sword blade, which is ten to twelve inches wide and about seven to eight feet long. With this they cut fish cleanly as a razor. They are not worth eating. What they are good for is oil for burning. In this lake there are fish called flounder, salmon trout,[251] a type of sardine, *passeau*, rays, and even porpoises.

Land and Forest Animals

The bison is in appearance like ordinary oxen, except its hair is finer and is as soft as the beaver's. The skin of this animal is also very supple. It is excellent for putting on a

---

250. The armored fish, or alligator gar, is not, in fact, a predator of the American alligator. The opposite is true: the adult alligator gar's only known predator is the American alligator.

251. Also known as rainbow trout, or steelhead, salmon trout is a Pacific Ocean fish. Caillot may have been referring to speckled trout.

bed in winter; there is nothing warmer. The Indians paint them marvelously. It has a little hump on its back.

The bears and tigers[252] are very big, but not very bad. Nevertheless, when you shoot at these animals you must take good care not to miss them, for otherwise they charge you and devour you. In the beginning, when I first arrived in the colony, I would go hunting with one of my friends almost every day. One day, after going a little way away from him, I, in fact, found a tiger, which I took aim at and wounded. As soon as this animal felt himself wounded, he became angry and came at me. I had only just enough time to throw down my musket and quickly climb the closest tree. I was no sooner up it when, looking down, I saw the animal, which was climbing after me. I took my knife in my hands to defend myself. While waiting, I called to my friend, who was not long in finding me, and he got me out of [135] the difficult situation I was in. Since that time, I have not had the desire to hunt them anymore; on the contrary, I have left them in peace. The meat of a young tiger is as good as a lamb's; there is no difference. As far as bear goes, it has more or less the flavor of beef, except for a wild taste that is not too disagreeable. It has two uses: the first is that it is eaten, and the second is that very good oil is extracted from it, depending on its size.[253] This oil is used in salads and for everything. You can get sixty to eighty pints of oil from a big bear.

The fox is more or less like the fox in France. There are some that are all white.

The hare and the rabbit are not as big and as good as the ones in France. Rabbits do not burrow; they go into the hollows of decaying trees to make their homes, because, if they were to burrow, they would drown in the water, which is at a depth of one foot.

There are many wildcats.[254] They most closely resemble badgers. They have large claws, very sharp teeth, black flesh, and smell like wild animals.

As far as the roe deer goes, it is quite good and very common, the same with does and harts, which are in no short supply.

You still find wolves, but smaller than the ones in France. They have very short legs, black fur, and are very bad. They often wreak havoc among the cattle.

There is a certain little animal called the wood rat, which is quite peculiar.[255] The females have a bag under their belly that astonishes those who see these animals in the

---

252. Caillot and other contemporary memoirists often referred to cougars as *tigres*, or tigers. See the entry for "Pichou" in Read, *Louisiana Place Names*, 114–15.

253. The Louisiana black bear (*Ursus americanus luteolus*) was quite common during the French colonial period, when Indians and settlers alike hunted it for meat and oil.

254. Caillot, like Le Page du Pratz, used the term "*chats sauvages*" to describe raccoons. See "Raccoon," in Read, *Louisiana Place Names*, 88.

255. "Wood rat" ("*rat de bois*") here referred to the opossum. See "Opossum" in Read, *Louisiana Place Names*, 86.

woods. When they are surprised and they have babies, when these little animals hear or see something, they flee toward their mother, who just opens a hole like she was swallowing them. They go into a kind of pouch, which hangs under her belly, and after she goes farther away to bring them to safety, she just opens this hole, and the little ones come out again, as easily as they went in.

The bobcat is an animal that is not as tall as the tiger, nor as mean.[256] It is a tiger all the same.

There is also a little beast, which resembles the marten, that is called [136] the stinky beast.[257] This beast can be smelled in the woods from half a league away because of its stench. The odor is very disagreeable, and when, by chance, they piss on travelers' things when people are forced to camp in the woods for the night, even if they only barely pass over something, you nevertheless have to cut off that part if you do not want to always have that dreadful stink under your nose.

There are two types of crawfish: some never leave the water and the others are in the ground. The latter are very different from the others, not because of their flavor, but because they have stronger claws than the water variety. During a certain period of time, their bodies are very soft. They make something like little earthen chimneys that they build to a height of eight to nine inches. There is such a great number of them in a half arpent of land, you can find more than five to six thousand chimneys, inside of which they breathe air mornings and evenings. It is quite an odd thing to see. In Saint Domingue there are *tourlourous*, otherwise known as land crabs, which are in great number on the ground. Likewise, in the land of the Mississippi, crawfish are everywhere. There are no moles or earthworms.[258]

There are three types of beautifully colored mottled snakes. The one to fear the most is the rattlesnake, which some of the Indians worship. It is the worst one. Its bite is fatal, and, within four to five hours, if you do not promptly seek a remedy, you are as good as dead. This animal shows how many years old it is by the number of its little rattles, which are on the end of its tail. They are like little bells; this is why it has been given the name of rattlesnake. Its fat is very good for rheumatism, but it is also good to eat, and better than eel. There are a number of other animals of which I do not speak and with which I am not familiar.

---

256. Like Le Page du Pratz, Caillot differentiated between two types of wildcats in Louisiana—cougars and bobcats. Both authors referred to the animals as *tigres* (cougars) and *pichoux* or *pichaix* (bobcats). See "Pichou" in Read, *Louisiana Place Names*, 114–15.

257. "Stinky beast" ("*bête puante*") referred to a skunk.

258. Though Caillot may not have seen any moles or earthworms during his sojourn in the colony, both creatures can be found throughout the Mississippi Valley.

I forgot to talk about the female lizard that changes color when she wants. I have seen her change from green to black, then gray, then return to her first color, all in the space of a half hour. [137] They have blue feet, and under their neck they have a little skin, which they puff out from time to time, that is pink in color.[259]

Birds

The eagle is very common.

There are a great number of parrots, but, up to this point, no one has been able to make them speak. The Indians do not like them and say that they are spirits, but what they do not understand at all is seeing the ones that are brought from Guinea that speak.[260]

There are two kinds of squirrels in Louisiana. There are those that fly, and others like the ones in France, except for their fur, which is like a rabbit's. As far as the flying ones go, they have a very thin little piece of skin under their front legs, which extends to the belly, and it is like the skin of a bat's wings. They do not fly far. They are half as big as the others and are very easy to catch.

Partridges are abundant in the colony, but they are much smaller than in Europe and not as good. They perch in the trees.

The cardinal is a red bird, and there are a very great number of them. People have brought many of them on several ships. Even I had sixty of them, without being able to keep a single one alive during the passage between Bermuda and Newfoundland's Grand Banks, which is very cold for them.

There are also ravens the same as in France, except they are smaller and fewer in number.

Herons are in no short supply, but they are also very small.

There are some birds that are called egrets. They are all white and the size of a chicken. Their meat is not bad. They have a spray of plumes, which serves them as a tail, and it is from these animals that all the aigrettes are taken.[261]

---

259. This description refers to one or more types of anole lizards. Commonly misidentified as chameleons, which are found only in Old World environments, anoles are natives of the Americas' warmer climate zones.

260. Just as trade goods crisscrossed the globe on ships during the early modern period, so too did the flora and fauna of lands newly explored and colonized by Europeans. African parrots likely found their way to Louisiana on board slave ships from the Senegambian region, while New World birds were often transported back to Europe by passengers returning to France, many of whom hoped to sell the creatures as exotic pets to wealthy purchasers. Louise E. Robbins offers a fascinating look at the transport, trade, and maintenance of nonnative animals in eighteenth-century France in *Elephant Slaves and Pampered Parrots: Exotic Animals in Eighteenth-Century Paris* (Baltimore: Johns Hopkins University Press, 2002).

261. This usage of "aigrettes" refers to the tuft of feathers sometimes worn on hats, especially in military dress.

There are also many spoonbills. This is a bird about the size of a goose, but with pink-colored plumage. When freshwater falls down, [138] it makes spots on them. They have to bathe in seawater, where they become more beautiful than before. Their beak is the color of flesh, and actually looks like a spatula, and is six inches in length. They eat only while sweeping side to side, and they are very tasty.

The bustard is a bird as big as two geese.[262] Its neck and legs are very long. The pelican is the same size. Its beak is as wide as a fist against its head, and fourteen to fifteen inches long. It is seen only in winter.

The snakebird is grayish. What is odd about this bird is its beak, which truly resembles a lancet.[263]

There are three types of ducks: the French duck, which is the same thing as a regular duck; the wood duck, which is a perching duck; and the wild turkey, which is big and has magnificent plumage. Teals are quite numerous.

There is the nighthawk, which is a bird that appears only at dusk and eats only mosquitoes.

The screech owls are larger than in France and have a more dreadful cry. There are also other types of owls and many other birds of prey.

The woodpecker is the same as in Europe, along with the tit and the magpie, but the latter is very rare and different from the others. There are many starlings and thrushes. There is a bird called a white ibis, which really has a very hooked bill. They are also very good to eat. You can also see swans in great numbers near the Illinois.

The strangest of the birds, in my opinion and that of many others, is the hummingbird. It is two or three times as big as a cockchafer. It is called the *oiseau mouche* because of its smallness.[264] It has the most adorable birdsong in the world, especially when you hear it fly away. I brought some on board the ship to take to France, but neither I nor the others were ever able to keep a single one alive, in spite of all the care we took.[265] They are of many different colors at once: green, white, blue, yellow, red. The wing tips and tail are [139] golden.

Turkeys are in great number, but taste better and are bigger than the barnyard type.

As far as insects go, there are great numbers of them, especially mosquitoes, which they call *maringouins*. There are also gnats that are extremely small, and you get

---

262. There are no bustard varieties in North America. He may have referred to a turkey vulture, or one of several other buzzard varieties.

263. The French name for this bird is "*bec-à-lancette*," or lancet-beak.

264. The literal translation of "*oiseau mouche*" is "fly bird."

265. Caillot's references to his failed attempts to transport cardinals and hummingbirds from Louisiana to France make clear that the journal was completed sometime after he left the colony in 1731.

covered with them, even in your mouth, eyes, and nose.[266] They bite as fiercely as the maringouin, but its bite is not as venomous. When New Orleans was first beginning to be established, they saw many people die from the bites of these insects. Horseflies are also very bad, since, as soon as they land somewhere, they pinch off a piece, but I fear their effects less than those of the two other sorts of animals about which I have just spoken. I will not speak about a number of other crawling and flying beasts for fear of trying the reader's patience, but I will now pass to the subject of trees and other shrubs, both the most common and most rare.

Trees, Flowers, Herbs, and Roots [267]

Cypress, cedar, and pine trees grow perfectly well here. The persimmon is a tree that bears a fruit more or less similar to the medlar [268] and is good only when it is soft. It is yellow, the size of a plum, and Indians make bread from it.[269]

There is the cottonwood, which is a tree that grows very tall and bears only big white flowers and, after, produces a kind of little red log that is food for many birds and parrots too.[270] However, the real cotton plant is a bush, where the cotton is in a kind of sheath, like what you would say the horse chestnut comes in, except that there are no spikes. When the cotton is ripe, the sheath splits and opens in four. It is picked then, and is magnificent.

Laurel trees are of many types. There is a white kind and a red kind. They are named thus because one bears white flowers and the other [140] red ones. They are the same size as oaks. They are almost always green. The third laurel is the true laurel, which is also good for sauces and stews, as in France.[271]

---

266. Caillot was likely describing biting midges, or no-see-ums.

267. Useful reference guides to Louisiana's native flora are Walter C. Holmes, *Flore Louisiane: An Ethno-Botanical Study of French-Speaking Louisiana* (Lafayette: University of Southwestern Louisiana, 1990); Caroline Dormon, *Wild Flowers of Louisiana* (Garden City, NY: Doubleday, Doran, and Co., 1934); Dormon, *Forest Trees of Louisiana* (Baton Rouge: Division of Forestry, Louisiana Department of Conservation, 1941); and Charles M. Allen, Dawn Allen Newman, and Harry H. Winters, *Trees, Shrubs, and Woody Vines of Louisiana* (Pitkin, LA: Allen's Native Ventures, 2002).

268. A member of the rose family and a once-common European orchard fruit, the medlar produces a fruit similar in appearance to the persimmon, which is sometimes known as the American medlar.

269. The persimmon fruit—which Caillot referred to as "*placminier*," a Creole French variation on the Muskogean word "*piakimin*"—was commonly incorporated into bread by southeastern Indians. The Louisiana town of Plaquemine and parish of Plaquemines derive their names from the Creole French word and were so named because of the great number of persimmon trees found in the area. "Plaquemine," in Read, *Louisiana Place Names*, 52–53; Dawdy, "'A Wild Taste,'" 394–95, 397.

270. This description fits the southern magnolia, not the cottonwood.

271. Louisiana is home to two native bay laurel species: white (sweet) bay and red bay. The dried leaves of both trees are used in cooking.

The willow is the same as in Europe.

The mulberry tree has very good mulberries that are as long as a finger.[272]

The pecan is a big tree that bears pecans. This is a kind of little oval nut. From a single tree you can gather seven or eight cartloads. To harvest them, they bring the tree down so they do not have to bother climbing up.

Elms are like in France. There are no hornbeams in Mississippi.[273]

There are three types of oaks: oaks like the ones in Europe, white oaks, and live oaks. These trees have green leaves almost the whole year, especially the live oak.

The chestnut trees are very beautiful. They bear small chestnuts but of an excellent flavor.[274]

There are two types of walnut trees, the white and the red. The latter has a very brittle wood, but it is the better one to use.

The fig tree grows in abundance, but the figs are not the best. There are no white figs.

Peach trees bear little peaches that never mature. Even if you left them on the tree, they would go bad there rather than ripen.

Wild grapevines also grow alongside trees in the timber forests, and you find their fruit high up in the trees. There are two kinds of grapes. One grows in clusters, but the grapes are only as big as peas. The other has at most four grapes together, but these are as big as small plums. The skin is very hard and it has a rather wild flavor.[275] You can also find plum trees, but not often.

There are huge numbers of good and bad plants, among which there is poison ivy, which is very bad, for just by touching it, [141] any part of your body that you touch with your hand itches for many days. I can talk about this from experience, since upon arriving in the country I got into some of it. There are many others that are very pernicious and that have very subtle poisons. Those who are familiar with medicinal plants find excellent ones in this colony. There are many other shrubs and roots about which I will not speak, and which would be to no purpose. I am content just to let you know about the main ones.

As far as flowers go, there are many tuberoses and violets too, but they do not have any smell. Roses here have a lovely perfume, even more agreeable than those in France.

---

272. The red, or common, mulberry is found throughout the lower Mississippi Valley. The tree produces edible elongated aggregate fruits that resemble blackberries when fully ripened.

273. The hornbeam is a very hard-wooded tree, also known as ironwood.

274. Caillot may be referring to either the American chestnut or chinquapin. Both produce edible nuts and both suffered significant reduction of their numbers in the twentieth century due to chestnut blight, making these once-common species rare in present-day Louisiana.

275. Caillot mentioned just two of several species of wild grapes native to Louisiana. Though it is difficult to determine to which species the first description refers, the second variety is likely the muscadine grape. Allen, Newman, and Winters, *Trees, Shrubs, and Woody Vines*, 282–86.

The four o'clocks, amaranth, pomegranate flowers,[276] and also many more exist in great quantities, especially the four o'clocks.

Remarks

Indians never begin any exercise or undertaking without dancing beforehand, whether they want to go to war, go hunting, gather their grains or potatoes, and other things. All these different enterprises have their own specific dances.

They also have dances for pleasure, but one should note that men and women are separated from one another; that is to say, the men dance apart and the women do likewise.

Of all the Indian nations of North America, the Illinois and the Natchez are considered the best dancers. They are also very active and well built; their women are also very good looking.

Once they start dancing for fun, what often happens is that they dance for two to three days and nights in a row without eating. In order to provide illumination at night, they use big bunches of dried cane, which they light one after the other.

You can recognize the bravery of the Indians, and the number of men they have killed, by little circles pricked in black on their shoulders. For each man, they draw as many circles.

[142] The Chakchiuma are the ones who make the least amount of effort to find food.[277] They live off the sap of trees, like the cypress and others. They eat meat sometimes, but they prefer tree sap above all else. Indians do not have any hair on their bodies anywhere, except for the hair on their heads.

They are very jealous of their wives and do not wish for them to be touched. It is the opposite with their daughters, for, if you go see them and you drink with them, they offer you their daughters to take enjoyment of as long as you want to stay with them. This is the way with them, from the great chief to the least of his subjects, and, if you refuse, they regard that as a great insult that you have committed against them and their daughters, who are for the most part young and quite playful. Among the Choctaw, there is a war chief named Houakizouou who has three daughters of perfect beauty. I confess to you that I was astonished by their charms when I saw them. They

---

276. Since Louisiana has no native pomegranate trees, Caillot may have confused the colony's native hibiscus flowers with those of the pomegranate, which are similar in appearance.

277. In the eighteenth century, the Chakchiuma village was located near the confluence of the Yalobusha and Yazoo Rivers (north of present-day Greenwood, Mississippi).

have delicate manners, even though they are Indians, and certain airs of grandeur that I have not seen in any other Indian women. This is how Indians comport themselves.

I will now resume the continuation of my discourse, in which I will describe the most noteworthy thing that happened while I stayed in that colony.

On November 19, 1729, a Spanish bilander[278] arrived in New Orleans; its crew told us that the king of France was dead, and said that a French frigate, which had just anchored when they were ready to leave Havana, had told them this as if it were a very certain thing. News such as this soon spread sadness throughout the town, and, as they were making preparations for a Mass for the king eight days later, we learned of the arrival of three ships, of which two were French, one loaded with provisions and goods, the other a slave ship, and the third was Spanish.[279] The first thing that was done was to clarify the news that had just been disseminated. We found out from them that, in fact, the king had been ill, but [143] that he was doing well and had entirely recovered. This put joy in all of our hearts again, and mainly in mine, for such news had made me somber and withdrawn. No one was thinking about anything else except rejoicing and having the "Te Deum" sung,[280] when the next day, about five o'clock in the evening, a group of us who were friends were walking together along the levee, otherwise known as the quay, and saw a little pirogue coming down the river. We would not have paid any attention at all to that boat if not for the fact that we noticed that it was being rowed, and that it was going very fast. We stopped a moment to examine it, and, without giving it another thought, we continued along on our walk.

Nevertheless, since I was waiting for a pirogue that was supposed to be bringing several pieces of merchandise to me that a man with whom I had dealings was supposed to send me, I deluded myself that this might be it. I was already beginning to calculate to myself the profit I was going to make, when I saw that this pirogue had arrived at the river bank and that a great number of people were running there.[281] This made us

---

278. A bilander is a small, masted merchant ship.

279. The two French ships were the slave ship *Duc de Bourbon* and either the *Baleine* or *Alexandre*.

280. The "Te Deum," according to historian Daniel Roche, served three primary functions in ancien régime France. "First, it called attention to major events, distinguished by the king's presence. . . . Second, it indicated the king's intention to dominate all of French territory from the palace of Versailles to the most remote diocese. . . . Finally, the ceremony ritualized magnificence in a brief burst of consumption (of food, wood, candles, and fireworks), as if pressing a claim against nature and scarcity while at the same time upholding the established order." For more on the use of the "Te Deum," see Roche, *France in the Enlightenment*, trans. Arthur Goldhammer (Cambridge: Harvard University Press, 1998), 269–71.

281. Like many other inhabitants in colonial Louisiana, Caillot engaged in petty trade, relying on local barter and trade networks to satisfy needs and wants not met (or not met at an agreeable price) by company stores. Such trade often violated the company's trade monopoly, but the prohibition deterred few inhabitants. Even company employees took advantage of sideline trade opportunities. On colonists' dependence on the local frontier-exchange

quicken our pace toward that place, to find out why everyone was crowding around that boat. When we were quite close enough to be able to distinguish who these new arrivals were, we were very surprised to see some of these people completely naked, others in their drawers, maimed. This encounter left us somewhat bewildered, without, nevertheless, knowing what it might mean, but alas, how surprised we were to the contrary when we heard these people speak, so pale and disfigured, who told us without any preface that everything was on fire and covered in blood at Natchez, and that they thought they were the only ones who had been able to escape.[282] There was also in their group a Capuchin who had been wounded by a musket in his arm while escaping. The joy we were just beginning to feel again turned into the most abject sadness on that day.[283]

We followed these poor wretches to the house of Monsieur de Périer, governor of the province, to whom they told the following: that the whole Indian nation of the Natchez, those of the [144] Chis, and perhaps all the other nations had joined together, and, under false pretenses of bringing gifts to the commander of the Natchez colony, Monsieur de Chépart (who was indeed the cause of the downfall of that life, as you will see),[284] a party of them, being more loaded down than usual, as much with fowl as with grains, came into the town to bring their presents, while the others were

---

economy to satisfy their needs and sometimes advance themselves economically, see Usner, *Indians, Settlers, and Slaves*; and Sophie K. White, "'A Baser Commerce': Retailing, Class, and Gender in French Colonial New Orleans," *William and Mary Quarterly*, 3rd ser., 63 (2006): 517–50.

282. The Natchez war, also called the Natchez uprising, Natchez rebellion, Natchez revolt—and once commonly called the Fort Rosalie massacre—has been documented at length in primary and secondary literature. The Natchez's initial attack on the French occurred on November 28, 1729. No eyewitness accounts of the bloodshed have survived, but Caillot's narrative of the event complements several other contemporary accounts informed by survivors' tales and later interviews with Natchez prisoners of war, including those penned by Charlevoix, Delaye, Diron Dartaguiette, Dumont de Montigny, Le Page du Pratz, and Périer, for example. These secondhand accounts provide a basic outline of events. See Pierre-François Xavier de Charlevoix, *Charlevoix's Louisiana*, ed. Charles E. O'Neill (Baton Rouge: Louisiana State University Press, 1977), 81–84; Jean-Baptiste Delaye, "Lettre en forme de relation du S. de Laye au sujet du massacre des Français fait par des sauvages le 28 novembre 1729," 15 March 1730, ANOM, C13C 4, fo. 35v; Diron Dartaguiette to Minister of Marine Maurepas, 9 February and 20 March 1730, *MPA* 1:56–61 and 76–81; Dumont de Montigny (who provides a scathing indictment of the Company of the Indies), *Regards sur le monde atlantique*, 235–58; Le Page du Pratz, *Histoire de la Louisiane* 3:230–303; and Etienne Périer to Minister of Marine Maurepas, 5 December 1729 and 18 March 1730, *MPA* 1:54–56 and 61–70. More detailed recent interpretations can be found in Barnett, *The Natchez Indians*; Balvay, *Révolte des Natchez*; Hall, *Africans in Colonial Louisiana*, 100–5; George Edward Milne, "Picking Up the Pieces: Natchez Coalescence in the Shatter Zone," in Ethridge and Shuck-Hall, *Mapping the Mississippian Shatter Zone*, 388–417; and Gordon Sayre, "Plotting the Natchez Massacre: Le Page du Pratz, Dumont de Montigny, Chateaubriand," *Early American Literature* 37 (2002): 381–413.

283. On the conflicting accounts of who first arrived in New Orleans bearing news of the Natchez attack, see Balvay, *Révolte des Natchez*, 133–34. According to Périer, news of the attack reached the city on December 2, 1729. Périer to Maurepas, 18 March 1730, *MPA* 1:61–70.

284. Natchez Commandant Sieur de Chépart arrived in Louisiana as a commissioned lieutenant in 1719. He was universally faulted by contemporary observers for bringing tensions between the Natchez and the French to a boil in 1729 by ordering the evacuation of one of the Natchez villages (White Apple) and claiming the land as his own. De Chépart was also blamed for ignoring multiple warnings of the coming attack. Balray, *Révolte des Natchez*, 160–64; Barnett, *Natchez Indians*, 101–2; Passenger list, *Duc de Noailles*, 12 September 1719, ANOM, G1 464.

outside of town, hidden in the woods with all their muskets. No one paid any attention because this is the way they saw them do things every day, except, in truth, not such a great number of them. Thus, they told Monsieur de Périer that these Indians had then entered into the town and had dispersed into each house, three or four of them together, according to the people who were there, under the pretext of trading chickens for gunpowder. They had been given the signal that, at the first musket shot they heard inside the fort, they would begin firing, too, everywhere, right to the plantations.[285] This was very precisely executed, for one hundred fifty or two hundred had entered the fort to sing the calumet to Monsieur de Chépart and give him their presents, as was their custom. They carried out their plans so well that, when their great chief went to place his hand in the commander's as a mark of peace after the ceremony, he turned away, and, without acting like anything was wrong, he went off to the side, seeing that no one was on their guard, not even the sentinels. He profited from this moment and had his war chiefs and the others strike immediately. They did not have much trouble destroying everyone in the fort, where the most important people of the town had come to pay their respects.

At about ten thirty, while he was at the commander's during the offensive, the chief was at the head of the Indians and signaled them to fire on everyone. It was Monsieur de Chépart who was killed first. The same thing was carried out in the town, where they killed all the Frenchmen and some of the Frenchwomen. The other Indians, who were still hidden in the woods outside the town, struck the plantations, so that, in less than an hour, the coup was over. In addition, these people said that, as far as the women went, the Indians had assembled all of them [145] in a house, where they were being guarded.[286]

When they had killed everyone, they went to the riverbank right away, where they surprised all those who were in a galley that had arrived there the day before, in the evening. They massacred all of them except two men, who resisted them for a half hour, fighting courageously. But they were forced to yield, which they did by throwing themselves through a hail of musket balls into a little pirogue, where, when they were in the middle of the river, they bound their wounds. One had been hit in his arm and leg, and the other in the middle of his stomach.[287] That is how they escaped.

---

285. After killing the officers and soldiers at Fort Rosalie, the Natchez moved east, away from the Mississippi River, toward the plantations lining Sainte Catherine's Creek.

286. Between 230 and 240 French settlers were killed in the Natchez attack of November 28, 1729. Many of the victims were men. More than 60 surviving Frenchwomen and children, 2 Frenchmen, and at least 106 slaves were held captive by the Natchez following the attack.

287. Contemporary reports suggest that between twenty and thirty Frenchmen and a handful of African slaves escaped the Natchez's wrath altogether, fleeing into the woods or managing to escape by pirogue downriver.

When the Indians did not find any more obstacles to prevent them from going into the ship, they took possession of it and opened the hatches to take the booty, which was, for the most part, brandy, flour, and the rest in dry goods, like shoes, hats, powder, musket balls, etc., which amounted to three hundred thousand livres.[288] They had the casks of brandy brought to shore, broke them open, and they all got drunk for as long as the drink lasted, and, when they were quite full, they all left in turns to see the Frenchwomen, where they satisfied their sordid passion by fair means or by force. As far as the goods went, as they had seen that we would give our orders in writing to the storehouse to those who wanted some, they did the same: the great chief had a little piece of charcoal and some paper on which he scribbled, and then he gave it to the Indians to go get what they needed. The women were the ones who told us they had all seen this, and many other equally apish tricks.

When all of the Indians who were part of the plot were all assembled together, the great chief named Apple Chief, because the village where he lived had this name, sat in the middle of all the rest and gave the order that, since there were no French who were not known by them, they bring him their heads from their corpses. This was done immediately, and in doing this they finished killing the ones who were still languishing. When all the heads were lined up in front of him, he had the bodies of the most important ones placed in a circle, each one holding the next by the hand, stretched out on the ground. The great chief made orations to them, even though they were dead, [146] and told them that it was not worthy to tyrannize them and take their goods and other things like that. This lasted a good hour. In the end, out of three hundred men who were in that town, only twenty-one of them escaped alive. It was their Negroes who had warned them to flee, for otherwise not a single one of them would have escaped.

When these poor people had finished speaking, Monsieur de Périer sent them to rest, ordered for them to be given what they needed, and—because of the report that they had just given—he sent off two pirogues right away: one to go try to find out if the Choctaws had anything to do with the plot, and the other, in the event that they had not, to give them the order to march against the Natchez so that they could go destroy them. The two boats left, one shortly after the other. That same day, around midnight,

---

This last group may have included the "pale and disfigured" survivors Caillot reported seeing. Balvay, *Révolte des Natchez*, 131–32, 138.

288. In addition to killing much of Natchez's French population and taking the rest of the population hostage, the Natchez seized the entire cargo of the half-galley that had arrived on November 27 from New Orleans, contents destined for the Indian trade. The loss of these trade goods had far-reaching ramifications. North and east of Natchez, the French were in stiff competition for Indian allies with their better-supplied English neighbors in Carolina. The disruption of the Indian trade undermined French administrators' abilities to engage Indian allies in retaliatory attacks against the Natchez.

he also armed a half-galley with fifty soldiers, including the officers, which he sent as a detachment to the Taensa, where the rendezvous with the Choctaws was supposed to be, in order to mount an attack all together and, at the same time, strike these savages, who appeared to be enemies of the Choctaws.

While everything was in this state, to cap it all, we were warned that the Negroes of the colony wanted to turn against us too. There were at least fifteen hundred or two thousand of them, which frightened us a great deal, because they are good fighters, more formidable than ten thousand Indians. In a brief space of time, we found ourselves surrounded by misfortunes without hope of any rescue, since there were only three to four hundred men to hold off so many enemies, of which Monsieur de Périer had detached about two hundred to go fight the Natchez, and the rest were used to guard the city. Meanwhile, the war against the Indians began. Not four days had passed since the war had begun, when we were visited in town by many Indians from the *petites nations*,[289] some bringing scalps of Indians they had killed. Others came to try to get presents, still others came to offer their services to us, and all of this was only to observe what we were doing and how they could strike us.[290]

The Monday after Three Kings Day,[291] six pirogues came downriver with eight Indian prisoners [147] who had wanted to bribe the Tunicas to turn against us. The same day, a Jesuit also arrived, who was coming from the Illinois country, who told us what had happened that Sunday. While saying Mass on the riverbank upstream from Natchez, and knowing nothing about what was going on, he saw about twenty Indians coming, all armed, who knelt and pretended to be paying attention to Mass. Not being suspicious about a thing, as he was close to the elevation of the Sacred Host, he turned around and saw the Indians, who were behind his people, taking aim at them. He got hit by a musket ball in his arm, and by some lead shot, from which he got a few pellets in his mouth and on his lips. In spite of this, he had the presence of mind to take the chalice and the Host and to escape in his pirogue. Since he was with his people, except for two, who were dead on the ground, they quickly pushed off and escaped in that way.[292] That same day we got a warning from some Indians that,

---

289. Literally, "small nations," "*petites nations*" was used to describe the small Indian groups along the Gulf Coast who traded and were allied with the French.

290. Conspiracy theories and rumors of additional plots to kill and overthrow the French were rampant in the days and weeks following the Natchez attack. Many Louisiana administrators, including Périer, believed that the English in the Carolinas had instigated the violence, and feared the actions of the Natchez were part of a larger, pan-Indian conspiracy. Balvay, *Révolte des Natchez*, 133–37; Barnett, *Natchez Indians*, 106–9.

291. Three Kings Day, also known as Epiphany, falls on January 6, the twelfth night of Christmas.

292. While en route from the Illinois country to New Orleans, Jesuit Father Stephen Doutreleau stopped to celebrate Mass with his fellow travelers, on January 1, 1730. A crowd of Yazoos opened fire on the celebrants, killing one of the Frenchmen and wounding four others, including Doutreleau. Two weeks before this ambush, the

before eight days were out, we would be destroyed. This did not fail to have some effect on how the city was guarded.

From December 1, 1729, to February 15, 1730, every day at eleven in the evening, there appeared a sort of comet. It would depart from the south and go toward the north.[293]

We found out, almost as soon as the Natchez massacre had been carried out, that Monsieur de Kolly, who had a concession in a place called Terre Blanche, at a distance of three-quarters of a league from the town of the Natchez, had been killed. This man had come to the colony to try to recover losses he had incurred in France for an agio, which had forced him to dispose of his goods and servants. His affairs were going quite well; he was just trying to finish them by selling his possessions so that he and his son, whom he cherished a great deal, could go rejoin his wife, whom he loved more than himself, and allow her to resume the way of life she had been forced to abandon.[294] Then, having gone up to Natchez, he and his son (who was a very fine youth, of a very gentle nature, who knew how to conduct himself and was admired by the whole town) went to their place at Terre Blanche to rest, after arriving there from Natchez. Afterward they went by horseback to go to the fort to see Monsieur de Chépart, commander of the town.

After they had arrived and had just gotten off their horses to go into [148] the fort, they heard at that very instant a great deal of shooting inside, and all over the town, and they saw a man named Baillif, a councilor in that place who was coming out to greet them, fall backward, dead, in front of their eyes.[295] That made them realize there was something extraordinary going on, and it frightened them into taking flight, even though Monsieur de Kolly was a very brave man. But, nonetheless, on that occasion he got very confused. They immediately got back on their horses and left at full gallop to go to their concession to fortify it, in case of need, and to find out the extent of this continual shooting in safety, having seen for sure that it was an alarm caused by the Indians. As they had some cannon, they got them ready for firing, but all of their

---

Yazoos and Koroas, taking their cue from the Natchez, had killed Jesuit missionary Jean-François Souel and all of the troops stationed at Fort Saint Pierre. These attacks fueled colonists' fear of a pan-Indian conspiracy. Thanks to George Milne for sharing his summary of the attack on Doutreleau and his escape, "Right in the Jesuit's Eye: Partisan Perspectives in French Louisianan Travel Narratives," unpublished manuscript, 1–2.

293. The Comet of 1729, also known as Comet Sarabat, was first sighted by Jesuit Father Nicolas Sarabat on August 1, 1729, in Nîmes, France. One of the brightest ever recorded, the Comet of 1729 was a nonperiodic, slow-moving comet that remained visible to observers for more than five months. Gary W. Kronk, *Cometography: A Catalog of Comets*, vol. 1, *Ancient to 1799* (New York: Cambridge University Press, 1999), 394–96.

294. Jean-Daniel de Kolly suffered significant financial losses in the stock market crash that followed the collapse of the Mississippi Bubble. In the following passage, Caillot describes the ordeal of de Kolly and his son, who were in Natchez to check on the Sainte Catherine, not the Terre Blanche (White Earth), concession. According to Dumont de Montigny, de Kolly, who had a stake in several Louisiana concessions, including the Sainte Catherine concession (one league's distance from Terre Blanche), had arrived in Natchez the night before the attack via the half-galley from New Orleans. Dumont de Montigny, *Regards sur le monde atlantique*, 150–51, 239.

295. Charles Bailly (not Baillif) arrived in Natchez, where he served as judge and councilor, in November 1728.

precautions were useless because, unfortunately for them, their minds were extremely mixed up, and even more so at the sight of two hundred fifty or three hundred Indians, who they saw coming toward them carrying scalps at the end of many canes, all of them armed to the teeth. That sight disturbed them so much that, instead of pointing their cannon at them, they hid themselves. Monsieur de Kolly hid himself stuffed down inside a large cask, where the brutes found him and killed him without his putting up any resistance. As far as his people, who were fleeing every which way, there were many that were killed.[296]

When his son saw that the savages were killing his father, he threw himself on them, sword in hand, and killed seven or eight of them, but he was prostrated by his loss of blood, which was flowing copiously everywhere. They took him and bound his wounds to make him suffer longer. At the end of two days, when he was doing a bit better, they started in on him again, making him suffer new torments. They took off all of his clothes, until he was naked as the day he was born, and made a fire to burn him, sometimes on an arm, sometimes on a leg, etc. They made him suffer for eight days, at the end of which he died, in his nineteenth year.

What frightened the Indians a great deal was that, after dividing the spoils among themselves, they found his watch, which was ticking. This movement surprised them greatly, without their being able to comprehend a thing. Finally, not [149] knowing what to think about it, and all of them having remained completely still, they put the watch on the ground, and they all gathered around it. They then had a discussion about what they should do about it. Some said that it should be burned and that it was the spirit of the young man that was moving around inside. Others said that they should leave it there. In the end, one of them took it upon himself to look and see what was inside it. This was a sign of great bravery for him, and he was applauded and regarded by the others as a great warrior. Thus he undertook the task of opening it, and, not succeeding, he took his tomahawk and struck it to make it open. The first blow he made broke the chain, which all of the sudden made a noise that seemed so extraordinary to them that they all took flight. This adventure saved the lives of two people who were still hidden in the house and who, without a doubt, would have been discovered next. Nonetheless, they later went to hide in the woods, where they covered themselves with leaves as best as they could while waiting for nightfall, such that the Indians were passing back and forth close to them without being able to see them.

---

296. The 1726 census lists twelve *engagés*, or indentured servants, and twenty-nine slaves on the Sainte Catherine concession, and seven indentured servants and thirty-one slaves at Terre Blanche. Since Caillot confuses the two concessions throughout this section, it is difficult to determine which concession's laborers he referred to here as de Kolly's people.

When night fell, they heard some noise in the woods, about a musket shot away. They saw a man dressed in the French fashion, who was coming toward them. They were on the verge of calling out to him to come hide with them until it was darker, thereby escaping together. Luckily for them, they waited until this person was closer so they could call out to him without making much noise, but when they saw him from a closer distance, they realized it was an Indian dressed in the clothes he had taken from the governor, and they were very glad they had kept their silence.[297]

When the night was completely dark, they crept along, little by little, up to the edge of the wood, to listen and see if they could hear anything that might ruin the plan they had made for escaping. However, they did not hear anything, so they ran to the edge of the water to get on a boat. When they got there, they did not find any boat into which they could throw themselves, except for a little pirogue, which they knew was tied up at the back of the galley, where [150] the Indians were drinking. Seeing that there were no other boats, they drew lots to see which of the two would go to untie it. The lot inevitably fell to one of them. He went to try his luck, and was fortunate enough to succeed in his plan. They both got into the boat and, by rowing, were able to escape. The Indians, hearing them fumbling about, fired their muskets a great many times, but it was useless, because it was completely dark. In this way, they escaped without either one of them getting hurt. They are the ones who told us what had happened concerning their masters.[298] They told us that, if fear had not seized them, they would have easily been able to untie the galley and close the hatches, where some of the Indians were, and bring it to New Orleans, but their only thought was to save their lives.

On the January 19 we had an alarm, around eleven in the evening. It was the second one, because we had already had one a few days previously. However, it did not take long for it to be confirmed as false. This one was caused by the departure of fifty Choctaws who were going off to war for us against the Natchez, and who, before leaving, shot their muskets into the air, even though they had been expressly forbidden to do so. This caused a mortal fright among the women, who were already making the air reverberate with their cries. Some were already packing their bags in order to go escape on the ships; others were running around crazed in the streets. They armed all the soldiers

---

297. By "governor" Caillot was referring to Commandant de Chépart.

298. The two survivors who managed to escape from the White Earth concession, according to Caillot, were indentured servants. Dumont de Montigny's relation of their escape differs slightly. In his account, only one of the two Frenchmen made it out alive. Dumont de Montigny stressed that the other man entered the French munitions storehouse, where he was killed by Indians dressed in the French style. Dumont de Montigny, *Regards sur le monde atlantique*, 245–46.

and dispatched four well-mounted officers to go scouting about and find out what it could be. They came back a half hour later and returned calm to the city, saying that it was the people mentioned above. As there had already been many alarms, Monsieur de Périer made a decision how to proceed in view of everything that could happen. He had the drums sound the alarm to have all the inhabitants assemble, and he formed four companies [151] of militia from them,[299] of which the captains and officers were the following,

Namely:

Monsieur Bruslé, then first councilor, was the first captain. The second company was the one led by Monsieur Prat, physician and botanist. The third was led by Monsieur Fleuriau, the king's prosecutor, and the fourth was led by Monsieur d'Hauterive,[300] fourth councilor and fourth captain.

The major of the militia, who is the hospital steward, was chosen to lead the councilors and their commander.[301] It is quite an amusing thing for a steward to have power over the councilors and thus over the rest of the other officers, who were for the most part surgeons and apothecaries, all wearing the gorget.[302]

When these four companies were created, the inhabitants were upset to see that the employees were not mounting the guard at all, and that they were simply patrolling.[303] They got so worked up that, in the end, they complained to Monsieur de Périer, who, to appease them (not being able to do otherwise for not having a force at hand), promised them to make us mount the guard. Upon this word they had just been given, they jeered us, so that not a day passed that we were not in fights with them. We went to see the governor, to whom we protested that, if we were to mount the guard with the inhabitants, we would never agree with them. Thus he was good enough to give different orders. The next Sunday, they beat the drums to call us to assemble, and, when we

---

299. This assembly took place in the Place d'Armes (now Jackson Square). Périer organized four units of one hundred fifty men each with the intent of supplementing the colony's existing French troops and Choctaw allies. Périer to Minister of Marine Maurepas, 18 March 1730, *MPA* 1:71; Dumont de Montigny, *Regards sur le monde atlantique*, 260.

300. Renauld d'Hauterive did serve as captain of one of the four militia companies formed to defend New Orleans, but he was never a councilor.

301. Caillot referred to Henri de Louboey, whose primary duties were to the colonial military but who also served as the New Orleans hospital's record keeper.

302. Originally made of metal or leather and used beginning in the medieval period to protect the neck and throat in battle, gorgets were, by the eighteenth century, worn primarily as ornamental accessories on military uniforms.

303. In the colonies, the term "employee," or "*employé*," referred exclusively to low- or midlevel white-collar workers, including clerks, like Caillot; bookkeepers; storehouse keepers; et cetera. The formal process of relieving the standing guard, or sentries, is known as mounting the guard.

were all gathered together, the governor formed a company of cadets from us, which numbered forty.

It was when the inhabitants saw that we would not be with them that they grumbled, and much more when they saw that we were a step above them, for we were the colonel's company. We chose a captain from among us because no one could command us anymore, since Monsieur Bruslé was captain of the militia. Thus we chose the storehouse keeper to be our captain, who, on the Sunday following [152] our first review for his first day in that capacity, presented to each of us a white cockade and gloves. We began to distinguish ourselves from the inhabitants by this, and the following week we appeared on the parade ground, armed, all dressed the same. We had a *justaucorps*[304] of red camlet, a hat edged with silver, a waistcoat of white dimity, the trousers as well, white silk stockings, and each with muskets costing forty-six livres *tournois*, everything brand-new. Our captain was the one who advanced us this gear, for which we paid him a twenty-livre reduction per month. To celebrate his appointment, he provided a breakfast for the whole company, where, drinking to the king's health and to his, we fired celebratory shots.

This was how we were incorporated, and for this reason we had no connection with the inhabitants. We did not just go out onto the parade grounds, we did our drills there and passed in review near the government building, and also when we mounted the guard, the whole company did so together.

On February 25 we received news about the Natchez, from which we learned that someone named Madame, a Frenchman who frequented that nation, having found out that the galley was coming up the river, told the Natchez: "Here is the galley that is coming up the river charged with powder, ammunition, and muskets to kill all of you." The Natchez, upon hearing this Frenchman say these things, took fright at his words and resolved to destroy the French people who were living at Natchez. That is what they did, even though Monsieur de Chépart, who was commanding there, had been warned more than eight days previously about their evil plan, yet nevertheless still refused to heed any warning from anyone at all, and even went as far as putting fetters on some of his friends who warned him. The Indians said, "Since the Frenchman is a dishonorable man and wants to harm us, we must strike first."

The wife of the great chief, who heard about the plot, and not lacking in spirit, in her own way protested to her husband [153] as best she could, being a very good wife

---

304. The *justaucorps*, popular from the late seventeenth through the eighteenth century, is a knee-length coat with a fitted bodice that flares below the waist.

who was very disposed toward the French.[305] But everything she thought to tell him was useless, for, having already made an agreement with the other nations to utterly destroy all the Frenchmen in the colony, they fixed their sights on the task of executing their hideous plan, which, luckily for us, did not have all the success they were hoping for. Having been mistaken in their calculations, they struck three days too soon, which exposed them and prevented the other nations from striking, to the effect that no one believed that those nations were part of the plot at all, and so only the Natchez were suspected, just like in the war they had declared six years previously.

This is how Indians count. First of all, they do not count by number, month, and days. Their manner is that, when they want to carry out an attack, they take a fistful of little pieces of wood, which they call rods, and they put them to one side. Each day they take one away, and, when there are no more of them, they execute what they have planned.[306] They also count by moons, so they say, "In one, two, or three moons we will do such and such."

To return to the great chief's wife: when she had seen that her nation had attacked us in spite of her protestations, she went to throw herself at her husband's feet, to whom she made yet another long speech, saying that he should not burn the women whom he had taken as slaves. She said to him, "You have killed the Frenchman, who gave you everything you asked for, without any reason, for he was not dishonorable. But," she said, "it is Madame himself who is more evil than you, and the Yazoos whom you have made strike the blow. Thus it is right for me to make him an oration." She took a tomahawk and ran off to find him and said, "You were dishonorable to turn against the Frenchman, who is your brother. I am coming to rebuke you for your betrayal and to make you see that I love them more than you. It is worthy for me to avenge his death." At that moment, she struck him in the face with her tomahawk, and, when she struck him, about thirty more Indian women came, each with a pointed length of cane, with which they stabbed out his eyes, and pierced him a thousand times through his body.[307]

---

305. According to Le Page du Pratz, this woman was Tattooed-Arm (Bras-Piqué), the mother (not the wife) of the great sun of the Natchez. After being captured and taken to New Orleans in 1730, Tattooed-Arm provided to Le Page du Pratz her version of what happened. As Gordon Sayre and Arnaud Balvay have pointed out, however, the imprisoned Tattooed-Arm had good reason to paint her actions in a pro-French light. Le Page du Pratz, *Histoire de la Louisiane*, 3:244–51; Sayre, "Plotting the Natchez Massacre," 400; and Balvay, *Révolte des Natchez*, 155.

306. Le Page du Pratz posited that there was in fact a pan-Indian conspiracy to attack the French, but that Tattooed-Arm prevented multiple Indian groups from attacking simultaneously by removing some rods from the bundle the Natchez used to count the days until the attack. In doing so, she caused the Natchez to strike the French prematurely. *Histoire de la Louisiane*, 2:250.

307. Given that Tattooed-Arm was held in New Orleans prior to being sold into slavery in Saint Domingue, it is possible that she relayed more than one version of what transpired at Natchez to visitors, including Le Page du Pratz and Caillot. The prison that held her and the other Natchez captives was on the Place d'Armes, facing the river, just steps from Caillot's office.

[154] The Natchez then went back to their home, having thought about what had just happened and realizing their mistake, but too late. They started to cry and resolved to destroy the nations who had attacked us, which were the Yazoos and the Chakchiuma. Concerning the latter, they even slaughtered babies at the breast. That is what we found out on February 25.

We were already quite far along in the Carnival season without having had the least bit of fun or entertainment, which made me miss France a great deal. The Sunday before Mardi Gras, upon returning from hunting, where I had gone to try and dissipate my boredom, I found a friend waiting for me in order to invite me to a supper he was giving for a few people. He told me that I would have all the diversions there that one could partake of in the city. Indeed, that very evening, I began to savor the first pleasures in the colony, where I had already been for a few months. We spent not only an evening but the whole night, too, singing and dancing. When I returned home, I was certain that those would be the last pleasures I would partake of during the Carnival season, since it was already quite near the end, but, no matter the sadness one feels, it seems that those days are dedicated to pleasures and to having fun. The next day, which was Lundi Gras, I went to the office, where I found my associates, who were bored to death. I proposed to them that we form a party of maskers and go to Bayou Saint John, where I knew that a lady friend of my friends was marrying off one of her daughters.[308] They accepted, but the difficulty of finding appropriate clothes made us just talk about it. However, since I myself was desirous of finding out how people would have fun at this wedding party, I proposed this excursion for a second time, that evening at supper. But, upon seeing that no one wanted to come along, I got up from the table and said that I was going to find some others who would go, and I left.

I was, in fact, in a house where I did not delay in [155] assembling a party, composed of my landlord and his wife, who gave me something to wear. When we were ready and just about to leave, we saw someone with a violin come in, and I engaged him to come with us. I was beginning to feel very pleased about my party, when, by another stroke of luck, someone with an oboe, who was looking for the violin, came in where we were, to take the violin player away with him, but it happened the other way around, for, instead of both of them leaving, they stayed. I had them play while waiting for us to get

---

308. Having spent much of his life in and near Paris, Caillot would have participated in Carnival events at home, and he may even have been a member of one of the many informal bands of masked and costumed young men who took to the Paris streets each year. The following description of Lundi Gras (Fat Monday) masking and revelry constitutes the earliest documented account of Carnival being celebrated in Louisiana. The wedding Caillot proposed to attend at the Bayou Saint John home of Widow Antoinette Fourier de Villemont Rivard was that of François Antoine Rivard and his fifteen-year-old stepsister, Jeanne Antoinette Mirebaize de Villemont. Marriage of Antoine Rivard and Jeanne Antoinette de Villemont, 20 February 1730, SLC, M1, 189.

ready to leave. The gentlemen I had left at the table, and who had not left the house, came quickly upon hearing the instruments. But, since we had our faces masked, it was impossible for them to recognize us until we took them off. This made them want to mask, too, so that we ended up with eleven in our party. Some were in red clothing, as Amazons, others in clothes trimmed with braid, others as women. As for myself, I was dressed as a shepherdess in white. I had a corset of white dimity, a muslin skirt, a large pannier, right down to the chemise, along with plenty of beauty marks too.[309] I had my husband, who was the Marquis de Carnival; he had a suit trimmed with gold braid on all the seams. Our postilion went in front,[310] accompanied by eight actual Negro slaves, who each carried a flambeau to light our way.[311] It was nine in the evening when we left.

When we had gone a distance of two musket shots into the woods, our company was soon separated at the sight of four bears of a frightful size, which our postilion, passing close by them without even seeing them, had woken by snapping his whip. These animals, at the light of the flambeaux, went running, just like we did from the fear we felt, without knowing where we were going or what we were doing. Nonetheless, after our first movements, they went away, and we continued on our way, laughing about the little comedy [156] we had just seen, which had really given us a fright.

When we got to the bayou, we sent a slave to go find out what was going on, namely, if people were dancing and what they were doing. During this time, we prepared ourselves, and upon returning the slave told us that they had just gotten up from the table and they were dancing. Right away, our instruments began playing, the postilion started cracking his whip, and we walked toward the house where the wedding celebration was taking place.

The whole gathering seemed very satisfied with our visit, and no sooner had we entered than they made us all dance. Afterward, in order for us to take some refreshments, they asked us in earnest to take off our masks. Until then, we had not been recognized, except for our postilion, because of his height. After we had been asked for a bit, we took off our masks. They recognized the other people almost immediately, because they were better known and had been in the country longer than I.[312] What also made it hard for people to recognize me was that I had shaved very closely that

---

309. As Caillot's costuming choice makes clear, Carnival revelers of both sexes have long displayed a penchant for cross-dressing, a tradition still embraced by modern-day celebrants.

310. A postilion is the front rider who goes in advance of the carriage or other horsemen as a guide. In this case, the "postilion" may simply have walked in advance of the maskers, who may have been traveling on foot.

311. Flambeaux are torches that were used to light paths before the advent of gas lights or electricity. Beginning in the mid-nineteenth century, flambeaux were used to light Carnival parades. This practice persists in some modern nighttime Carnival parades, though the traditional wax-wicked torches have mostly been replaced with those lit by portable oil or propane torches.

312. By February 1730, Caillot had been in Louisiana only seven months.

evening and had a number of beauty marks on my face, and even on my breasts, which
I had plumped up. I was also the one out of all my group who was dressed up the most
coquettishly. Thus I had the pleasure of gaining victory over my comrades, and, no
matter that I was unmasked, my admirers were unable to resolve themselves to extin-
guishing their fires, which were lit very hotly, even though in such a short time. In fact,
unless you looked at me very closely, you could not tell that I was a boy.

I did not enjoy for long the pleasure of having put most of the people of this assemblage in my chains, for I, too, soon saw myself enchained by very tightly tied knots. I felt
a fire that immediately made me lose my freedom, which I had guarded for a long time.

It was after I was unmasked that, having more easily the freedom to look around
from side to side, I perceived, while perusing a number of [157] beauties, one who right
away reduced me to the most pitiful state in the world.[313] I turned over in my mind
how I should play it to go approach her, when someone came to ask me to dance. When
I had finished my dance, I did not miss the opportunity to go ask her. I noticed that
she accepted my hand with pleasure. We danced, but I was unable to explain my feelings toward her, and what her charms were making me suffer (because of her mother,
who was plaguing her continually). But my eyes knew how to beseech, since my mouth
could not. When we stopped dancing, I went to take her to the person she chose. Then
I took myself to one of the corners of the room, where, at my leisure, I had the satisfaction of contemplating her delicate and well-formed figure, her snow-white skin, her
beautiful rosy cheeks, her incomparably blue eyes. In short, she seemed perfect to me.

I managed to approach one of her friends, and she did not take long to come over.
When I had the pleasure of having her near me, I unburdened my heart without
constraint, and told her everything I was feeling for a person of her consideration. She
answered me with naiveté, modesty, and a joyful spirit capable of piercing the most
insensitive heart. You decide what effect she produced in mine, which had already
belonged to her for some time, without knowing it, as you will see.

While continuing to converse with this adorable young lady, I asked her very insis-
tently that this not be the last meeting I would have with her in the future. At the same
time I asked her where she was living in the city. She answered me that, as long as she
was staying where she was, she did not know of any way that I could hope to see her.
I did everything I could to persuade her to the contrary, and told her again that, even
if she was strictly watched, I would still find a way to talk with her in private. After all
my [158] entreaties, I finally found out that she was at the Ursuline convent. At these

---

313. This most recent object of Caillot's affection was likely the daughter of one of the wealthy Carrière brothers
(André, Joseph, or François), whose families maintained plantations downriver from New Orleans.

words I was left surprised at this lucky encounter, calling to mind many particulars, and, when I had examined the features of her face, I recognized her to be the same person, who I had seen the first time I had gone to the convent, as being the one who, among many other lodgers, had inspired in me an extreme love, without ever having been able to see her again since then, even a single time.[314]

I leave you to imagine the pleasure I felt in renewing the acquaintance with a person to whom I had not been able to speak, except with my eyes, and for whom I had been searching for a long time. I let her know the reason for my silence with a much more ardent passion than before. It is quite true that, when I first saw her upon entering the ball, her face struck me, without my being able to figure out where I had seen her. I even thought it had been in France.

Little by little, the hour passed, and, unfortunately for me, it was time for me to go back, as it was close to four o'clock in the morning. I had the most difficult time in the world to bring myself to leave her. Nevertheless, it had to be done, and, taking leave of her, she was kind enough to let me know that there would be a tomorrow. I expressed to her the joy I felt, and promised her not to miss an occasion so favorable for me. We thus said good-bye to everyone there who had extended all their hospitality to us, especially the father and mother of the groom and of the bride, who expressed to us the pleasure that we had given them and invited us to come back and spend the day with them the next day.[315]

We left with our musicians, not as joyful as we had arrived, and I noticed that we had gone almost half of the road home without any of us saying a single word. I could not prevent myself from exploding with laughter, which woke my companions from the half slumber into which they had fallen. Unable to keep from [159] thinking continuously about the place I had just left, I took a slave to light the way for me and stayed a bit behind the others, in order to abandon myself more profoundly to the pleasures I had had in conversing with my adorable sweetheart, and to the pleasure I would have the next day, upon seeing her again.

I was not the only one who was wounded by Cupid's arrows, for the first lieutenant of the *Duc de Bourbon*, who was walking a little ahead of me, had a much sadder

---

314. Beginning in November 1727, the Ursulines housed and educated female boarders. In the spring of 1728, there were twenty girls of European descent and seven enslaved girls residing at the temporary convent, a house the Ursulines rented from Jean-Daniel de Kolly. The property had no perimeter walls, making the boarders more visible than they would be in a typical convent. Its location on the corner of Chartres and Bienville Streets also meant that nuns and boarders likely walked through the streets to Mass at St. Louis Church on the Place d'Armes. Though no register of the early boarders survives, Emily Clark details a typical day in their lives in *Masterless Mistresses*, 54–57.
315. During this period, French wedding celebrations often included feasting and dancing that could span several days and nights.

and much more lovesick air about him than I did.[316] I wanted to find out who the beloved was for whom he was wearing chains, so, for this reason, I doubled my pace and caught up with him. I asked him to tell me the reason for his sadness, which I was very concerned about, for apparently something must have happened to make him unhappy, either something that the people at the party had done or that the others of us had done. He told me no in quite an aloof manner. I kept on tormenting him, so much that he was forced to tell me the truth. He told me that I was the one who was the cause of his affliction. Hearing such a statement, I was quite surprised, being unable to figure out the reason why. He continued and told me that the person with whom I had had many conversations held him in her chains, but that, being friends, he did not want to let her know, since I loved her and had the good fortune to be loved by her, according to all appearances.

I thanked him for being so obliging and told him right away that he was wrong to believe that I could do him harm, since the young lady was my first cousin and that, if he had thought I was making her advances, it was that we were just joking around, and I was only asking her to do me a favor. Since he had been in town only two days, and I knew that he would not be staying long in New Orleans, I kept my head. He was reassured by what I had very convincingly just told him, and from that moment he began to be much friendlier with me than before, and asked me to return there the next day with him. I promised him, but, far from keeping my word to him on this matter, I was planning from that very moment what I [160] should do to keep him out of the way, for the sincere confession he had just made to me concerning his love for my charming sweetheart was only too suspect to me, and not at all to my taste. I was not so pleased about it as I made him think I was, and, in the meantime, we entered the city, which brought our conversation to an end. We spoke of going to have breakfast, whereupon each of us went our own way to get some rest.

About half past noon, while we were eating as a group and talking about returning to Bayou Saint John, he came in. We finished our conversation in such a way that he did not hear anything about it. After he had said hello to the gentlemen, he came to sit down near me, and spoke to me about returning to the wedding (being all dandied up). I told him I was quite vexed that I could not go out that day, having a group of friends with whom I had made plans to go have some fun. I told him it would not be polite to leave them and that, if he wanted to do us the honor of remaining with us, he would make us truly happy. Luckily I gave this excuse, which he very easily accepted. He told

---

316. The first lieutenant of the *Duc de Bourbon* was forty-one-year-old Louis Le Roy de Fortière of Port Louis, France. Crew Register, Armament of the *Duc de Bourbon*, 1729–30, FML, 2P23 III.7.

us that he was quite obliged to us, that he would go to his ship, and then he would come back to see us again. By a stroke of luck, when he reached his ship, his captain told him to stay aboard the whole day.

When he left us, the first thing that occurred to us was to leave immediately, which we did, without finding any obstacle to impede us from doing so. There was not a single one of us who had not made different conquests. Among these, one of my friends had made one of an adorable provincial, I mean a girl from Languedoc, whose name was Mademoiselle de Lussert, an intimate friend of Mademoiselle Carrière, who was the object of my tender affection.[317] They were both lodgers at the Ursuline convent, about sixteen or seventeen years old, with cheerful dispositions and expressive, ardent eyes.[318] In short, we got ready to return there in our normal clothes. Since I knew that at the wedding there had only been [161] some Bordeaux, I suggested we bring along four dozen bottles of Frontignan,[319] for which I advanced the money. When we were all agreed upon it, seeing nothing else was missing, we were about to leave, when we saw the first lieutenant of the *Bourbon* enter. That sight surprised us, thinking he was going to be a reason for our party to get broken up. But luckily, after he had had a drink with us, he promptly got us out of our difficulty by saying that he had come to look for his snuffbox and his handkerchief, which he had left at our place, and that he was going to be leaving right away because he had left the ship without any officers. When he went out, we told the violins and oboes to play, and we left.

I believe, without a doubt, that that day was made for lovers. It was neither hot nor cold. The sun was covered by a few small clouds that only made it delightful. Various odors drifted through the woods, along with a confused murmur of diverse birds that seemed to share their love with us. I will let you imagine what state we were in. As for myself, I was burning with impatience to get there, and, if ever a road had seemed graceful, it was that one. When we were one musket shot away from the house, we saw that some of the wedding party was on a balcony that wrapped around the outside of the room where the others were dancing. As soon as they saw us with our two violins and the oboe, all the people gathered there came out to meet us. After, we greeted

---

317. Mademoiselle de Lussert may have been related to Captain Joseph-Christophe de Lusser, a Swiss military officer who lived with his wife, Marguerite Bouras, and family in Mobile. Both were guests at the home of Widow Antoinette Fourier de Villemont Rivard. Marriage of Antoine Rivard and Jeanne Antoinette de Villemont, 20 February 1730, SLC, M1, 189.

318. Given that the women of the Rivard and Carrière families were great supporters of the Ursulines—they helped found the laywomen's confraternity Ladies Congregation of the Children of Mary in 1730—it is possible that the widow Rivard's daughter was also an early boarder at the convent, before her marriage. Clark, "'By All the Conduct of their Lives,'" 779–80; and Clark, *Masterless Mistresses*, 76.

319. Frontignan lies along France's Mediterranean coast, in the Languedoc region. The town and its surrounding area are best known for wine made from the muscat doré grape.

everyone and paid our little compliment to the bride, who expressed her true pleasure at seeing us return, for, without us, they would have been bored.

We went into the house, where our instruments and the others got everything going again, especially when we had given these young ladies the Frontignan to drink, which we told them was cider from Normandy. Only the beautiful girl from Languedoc was not fooled. This gave them a cheerful and delightful disposition. Monsieur de Périer, who had heard some talk about our previous night's masquerade, came and paid us the honor of tasting the wine, danced two minuets, and [162] then left. I danced a *passepied* with Mademoiselle Carrière, and after the dance I went to situate myself in the midst of those young ladies, whom I made to play several little games, when I figured out how to slip away, and then I had the chance to speak to my dearly beloved and reiterate to her what I did not weary of telling her. My friends did not miss the opportunity of these precious moments to do the same with their sweethearts.[320]

We were all very tranquil and were spending our time very agreeably without any trouble, all of us being well matched (since the oldest of the men and the oldest of the ladies was no more than twenty-four to twenty-five years old.)[321] When we had spent three hours like this, and supper was ready, we had to think about going away. This separation was causing me great anxiety, when the mother of the bride pulled me aside to a room with two other friends of mine and proceeded to invite us to supper. According to the natural inclination of my heart, I would not have needed to hear another word said about it, but, in order to follow the rules of etiquette, I put up some resistance. Finally, when she saw that we were still persisting in wanting to leave, she told us that she was quite mortified that we refused to grant her this favor and that apparently we had another party in town, or that the one where we were was boring us, and a thousand other things like that. We told her that she was going to too much trouble for us, that, if we wanted to go away, it was only for fear of inconveniencing those gathered there.

Right away she took my hat from me and closed it up in an armoire. I did not need any more prodding, so I went to inform my friends, who were overwhelmed with joy and went to thank Madame Rivard (that is the name of the woman who had invited us to stay) for the hospitality she had shown us. I began again to taste new pleasures, but, when I thought again about how the next day I was going to lose my dearly beloved, or that, at the very least, even if I had hope of seeing her again, I would be deprived of the

---

320. The minuet was a couple's dance set to three-four time that was popular throughout Europe—and, by extension, colonial America—between 1650 and 1750. Adapted from a Breton folk dance, the *passepied* (translated as "passing feet") became popular as a couple's dance during the reign of Louis XIV.

321. Caillot himself was twenty-two at the time.

satisfaction of talking with her, this prompted a terrible change of feelings in me. When they came to tell us that supper was served, we sat down at the table, where there were forty-six of us. I took great care to sit down at one of the corners of the table between Mademoiselle Carrière [163] and Mademoiselle de Lussert, who were out of view of their relatives. We spent this meal, between five to six,[322] very agreeably, but, after we left the table, we had a great deal of fun, for Bacchus, having left his kingdom to go find Venus, suggested endless pleasures to us, but do you know, seigneur, that the time seemed short and charming to me, that of all the allurements that have been shown to my eyes, nothing under heaven could compare to the charms of that adorable girl.

The hour of our departure finally arrived, and we said good-bye to the lovely company and to the bride and groom. We left around five thirty in the morning, lamenting the end of the Carnival season. This is how I spent those days in the land of Mississippi. Now we will get back to the description of the Indian war.

On March 6, nine women who had been taken as slaves by the Natchez arrived in New Orleans unexpectedly. They told us that the Indians had sent them to look for wood, and they had taken advantage of the situation to flee to the French camps.[323] But, unfortunately for them, their children had stayed behind in the Indian fort, which made them wail with grief. Among these women there was one named Madame La Sonde, an officer's wife who had twice been attached to the post to be burned.[324] To her good fortune, she was saved from this fate because the Indians found themselves in need of wood. They also told us that, the same day the army arrived at Natchez, they were supposed to have all been burned, that the oldest among them had already died. It was a horrible thing to see the sad state of affairs of these wretched women, and to hear them speak about it.

The next day, we saw a boat arrive, coming downriver under full sail and being rowed as well. After they had landed, we realized [164] it was Monsieur de Périer's son with Monsieur Le Baron, astrologer and engineer, who were coming back from Natchez.[325] They brought with them Madame Desnoyers, who was the most important woman of said place, in terms of rank, and had escaped quite differently than the aforementioned

---

322. It is unclear in this instance whether Caillot meant that he and his party shared an early meal together "between five to six" in the evening or that there were five to six people present.

323. These may have been the women who escaped from the Natchez forts on February 15. Barnett, *Natchez Indians*, 115.

324. Catherine Notas was the wife of Laurent La Sonde, who served as surgeon major at the Natchez post until he was killed during the Natchez attack. Marriage of Laurent Hurlot La Sonde and Catherine Notas, 15 November 1728, SLC, M1, 164.

325. Sieur Chambellan Graton was the stepson of Governor Périer (not the son-in-law, as Marcel Giraud stated in volume 5 of *A History of French Louisiana*). He arrived in Louisiana with his mother and stepfather in 1727.

women.[326] There were two more women with them as well. Upon coming ashore, when they saw many of their friends, they could not keep from bursting into tears, seeing the state they all were in, with bare feet, bare heads, hair all tangled, ruined shifts ripped to shreds, and black as ink. In brief, they were pitiable, but they did not remain that way for long. They told us that the Indians were a good five to six hundred strong in the fort, and that, every time one of them died, these savages would bury a live white woman with the dead man, and even for their children they would kill a white one, but in a very cruel way.

This is how they would kill them: they would take the first child they happened upon and throw him into the air, and other Indians would catch him on pointed cane spears, and they would bury him like this, or else they would take them by their feet and strike their heads against the ground. This is how they acted toward these poor little innocent babes.

They told us they had seen another atrocity even more terrible, or at least as terrible, which was the following: upon the death of a young Indian woman, those vile brutes took a young German woman who was ready to give birth at any moment. They took her, cut off her nose, lips, and ears, which they put in her mouth, then they opened her belly with a knife, from which they pulled out the baby, cutting off his head and putting him back in the body of this hapless woman, who was making horrid cries. They sewed up her belly, then they all pissed in her mouth, and buried her alive in this state.

[165] They told us how they had set about saving themselves. Madame Desnoyers told us that, as for herself, since she spoke the Indian language quite well, they made her one of their interpreters. Then one day the Indians, having asked for peace, and capitulating to us, had her brought to their Fort de la Valeur [see plate 22],[327] which was the farthest along on our side, in order to negotiate terms with the interpreter of our army. Turning around to see if there were any Indians behind her, she saw only one, who was listening. She approached him, and, under the pretext of wanting to whisper in his ear, she stabbed him with her knife. Being near the fort's entrance, she escaped by coming out and throwing herself into the army. However, she had one bitter regret, and that was leaving behind her twelve-year-old daughter, who was as beautiful as she could

---

326. Marie-Angelique Chariron, wife of Martin Desnoyers, manager of the Terre Blanche concession and adjutant major at Natchez's Fort Rosalie, spoke and wrote the Natchez language fluently. She later served as an interpreter for the French during retaliatory attacks.

327. Fort de la Valeur is marked as site A on plate 22. Fort de la Valeur was one of two fortified sites—the other was Fort de la Farine (site B)—occupied by the Natchez during the French-Natchez war of 1730. Both forts were stocked with cannon and powder looted from Fort Rosalie.

be.[328] The Indians, seeing that she had escaped, asked for her return, and promised to give back all the other women to get her back again.[329]

The others told us that they had twice been attached to the frame to be roasted, with the wood all ready to be set on fire. But, luckily for them, they had had the ability, even though they were attached like that, to persuade the Indians that there was no point in killing them like that; rather, they wanted to fight against us, and if it happened that they were defeated, they wanted to die with them. They cut them free that time, but, since they were not so young, they reattached them to the stake a second time. Since they no longer had any hope of escaping, and were preparing themselves to die, the great chief's wife happened to pass by where they were, and, as they had already begun to set fire to their legs, she made them stop and untie them, to take them as slaves for herself. A few days after, the Indians, constrained by famine to make another peace treaty, gave back all the women, and these too, but naked as the day they were born.[330] They would not even have made that treaty if they had not [166] run out of food. Some poisoned themselves; others conjured with such a frightful force that they died at once.

Monsieur Le Baron also brought five Negroes with him who had manned the cannon against us for the Indians, and who had taken Madame Desnoyers by force, had made her mill rice, and had done to her—as well as to others—what they wanted. As recompense, when they did not want her anymore, they made a fire with which to burn her, but fortunately the great chief's wife stopped them, and the next day they were captured by us.

The next day, at six in the morning, the remainder of the women and orphans arrived, who assuredly would have made even those with the most hardened hearts shed tears, to hear how those poor creatures were crying out. The air was filled with the sounds of people lamenting their deplorable fate; you would have to have been there to comprehend the sorrow that overwhelmed everyone. We learned from that boat that the Indians had asked for peace yet again, for the third time, and that we had not been able to refuse them, lacking ammunition. They also told us that every day the Choctaws

---

328. Though there is no extant record verifying the existence of Desnoyers's twelve-year-old daughter, she did have a three-and-a-half-month-old son, Antoine-Laurent Desnoyers, born August 9, 1729. It is unclear what became of him, though he is not listed in Father Philibert's 1730 list of those killed during the Natchez and Yazoo attacks. Birth of Antoine-Laurent Desnoyers, 10 August 1729, SLC, B1, 89; Father Philibert to Minister of Marine Maurepas, 9 June 1730, ANOM, C13A 12, fo. 57–58v.

329. Caillot's account of Madame Desnoyers's escape differs significantly from that of Dumont de Montigny, who stressed Desnoyers's role as a negotiator between the opposing parties, rather than as an escapee. See Dumont de Montigny, *Regards sur le monde atlantique*, 250–52, 255–56.

330. A French-allied Choctaw raiding party recovered the first French hostages from the female great sun's cabin on January 27, 1730. The Choctaw kept these hostages as slaves until the French compensated them for their recovery. The remaining women, children, and African slaves were recovered by Major Louboey on February 26, 1730. Balvay, *Révolte des Natchez*, 138–41.

were mutinying, and going off one by one to return to their villages very unhappy, pillaging from us what they could grab. Consequently, they lifted the siege. However, even though peace had been declared, it did not prevent people from always staying on their guard, and it was well worth it, for the Natchez, a few days later, made a sortie from within the canebrake without our being able to see them.[331] They did not have too much trouble in routing the army, whereupon, being surprised, they cried out, "Run! Run for your life!" The army found itself entirely pushed back, due to the delinquency of many officers who were lazy cowards who had never seen action. There was only one, named Monsieur Dartaguiette, a captain in New Orleans and brother of Monsieur Dartaguiette, director of the Company of the Indies, who took seven willing men with him and jumped into the trench, which they won back. As far as the other [167] 125 Frenchmen who were there, they had such a fright that some had thrown their arms down to more easily run away, and others had hidden themselves. It was only when they saw the trench won back that they returned to their post.

I have spoken above about the Negroes who had manned the cannon for the Indians. They were burned along with two others, who had killed the Jesuit who lived in Natchez and were wearing his clothes.[332]

None of the French who had gone upriver to Natchez came back. They stayed there to keep the enemy in sight while waiting for help to come, but, as munitions were being taken to them, the army came back on March 11 and informed us that the Indians had abandoned their two forts, due to lack of provisions, and had gone to distant nations to ask for help, bringing them presents of the booty they had taken from us in order to bring them over to their side. Meanwhile, they burned their forts so they could not be used anymore, and they built two more for the safety of the detachment that remained there, as well as for the post. A few days after, we found out that they had taken refuge in the mountains, and that the chief of the Tunicas (one of our Indian friends) had gone there with forty of his warriors to conquer them and try to bring some of them back alive. This chief has been baptized and is almost Frenchified.[333]

---

331. During the November attack, the Natchez pillaged trade goods intended for the southeast Indian trade from the recently arrived half-galley and a company warehouse at Natchez. In doing so they undermined French administrators' ability to adequately compensate French-allied Choctaw raiding parties. Sometime during the night of February 25–26, hundreds of Natchez who had been holed up in their forts escaped into the night while supposedly being under French and Choctaw watch. The Choctaw may have been complicit in the Natchez's escape. By turning a blind eye to the escape in exchange for the release of French hostages, the Choctaw better positioned themselves to negotiate compensation for the captives.

332. The Natchez kept only two men of European descent alive as slaves: a carter named Mayeux and a tailor named Le Beau. Le Beau was tasked with fashioning new clothes from cloth raided from the warehouse and galley and refitting clothes taken from French victims. Le Page du Pratz, *Histoire de la Louisiane* 3:260–61.

333. Caillot likely referred to Tunica Chief Cahura-Joligo, a French ally noted for his adherence to Catholicism and dressing in the French manner.

Gallery 3

Pages from Marc-Antoine Caillot, *Relation du Voyage de la
Louisianne . . .,* drafted between 1729 and 1758; The Historic
New Orleans Collection, *2005.0011*

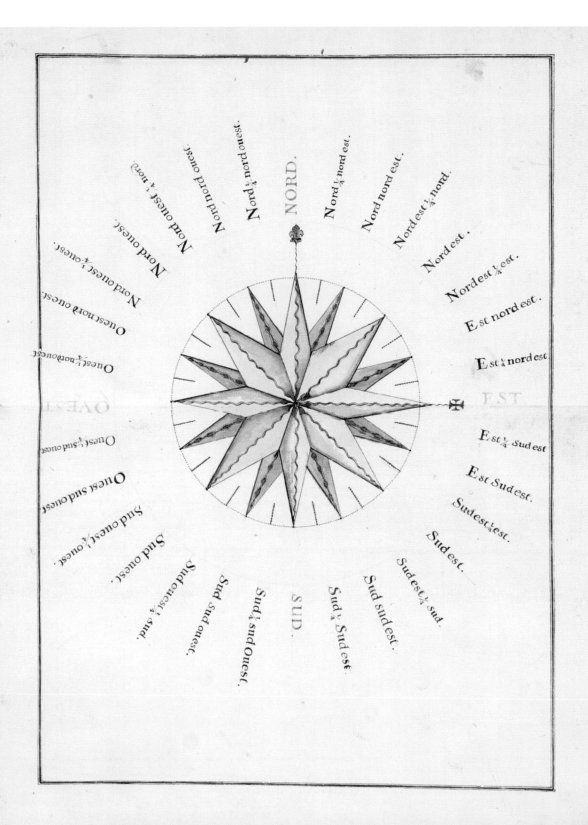

NORD.

Nord ¼ nord ouest.

Nord nord ouest.

Nord ouest ¼ nord.

Nord ouest.

Nord ouest ¼ ouest.

Ouest nord ouest.

Ouest ¼ nord ouest.

OUEST

Ouest ¼ sud ouest.

Ouest sud ouest.

Sud ouest ¼ ouest.

Sud ouest.

Sud ouest ¼ sud.

Sud sud ouest.

Sud ¼ sud Ouest.

SUD.

Sud ¼ Sud est.

Sud sud est.

Sud est ¼ sud.

Sud est.

Sud est ¼ est.

Est Sud est.

Est ¼ Sud est

EST.

Est ¼ nord est

Est nord est.

Nord est ¼ est.

Nord est.

Nord est ¼ nord.

Nord nord est.

Nord ¼ nord est.

NORD.

PLATE 4

PLATE 15

PLATE 16

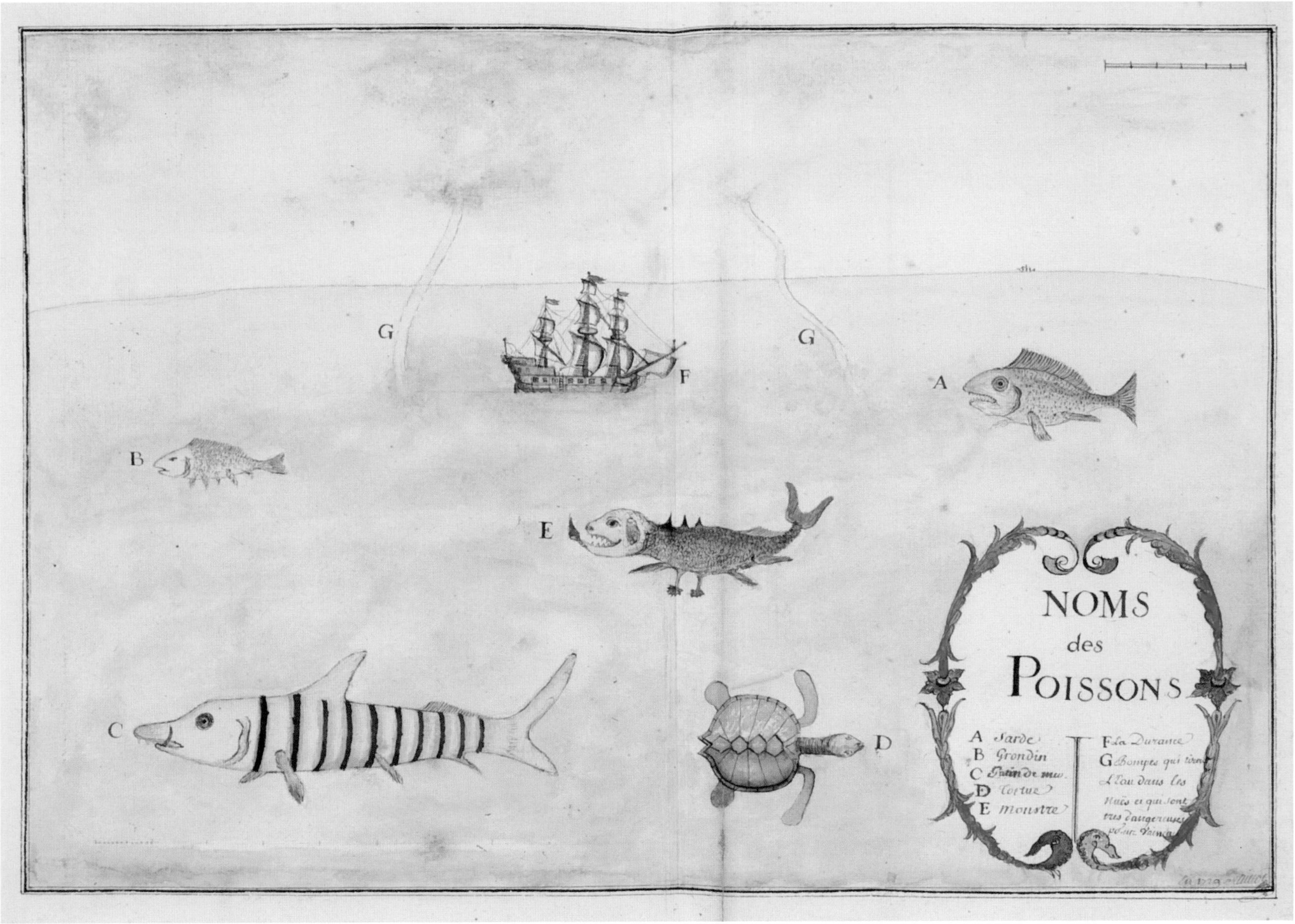

PLATE 17

NOMS
des
POISSONS

A Sarde
B Grondin
C Bonite ou
D Tortue
E micouille

F a Durande
G Bonique qui sont
Ce Poissons las
Voici ce qui sont
tous d'argent aux
pêche Pinn'a

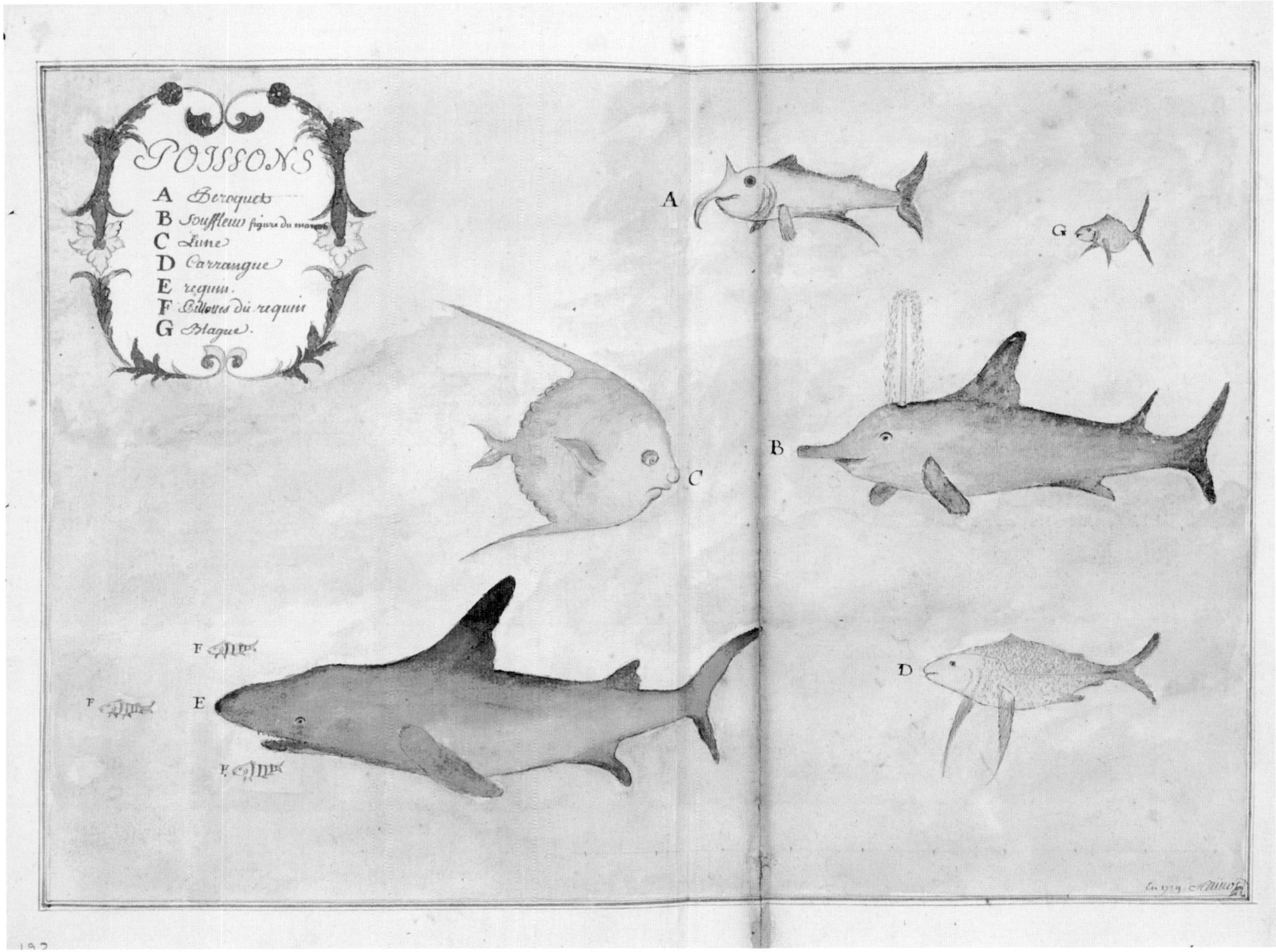

POISSONS
A Beroquets
B Soufleur figure du marsouin
C Lune
D Carrangue
E requin.
F Pillotes du requin
G Blague.
A
B
C
D
E
F
F
F
G
En 1729 A. Nino

PLATE 18

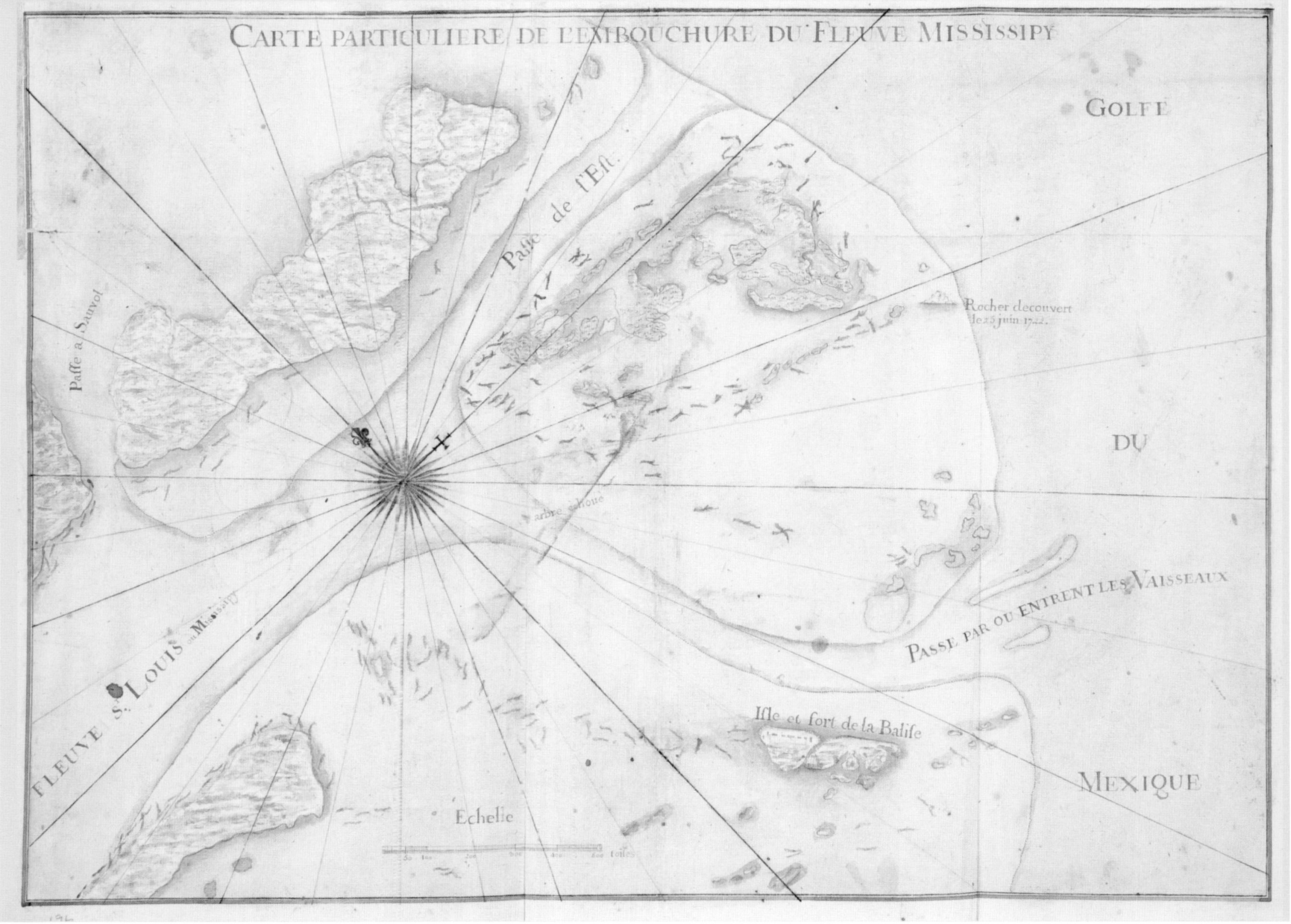

CARTE PARTICULIERE DE L'EMBOUCHURE DU FLEUVE MISSISSIPY

GOLFE

DU

MEXIQUE

PASSE PAR OU ENTRENT LES VAISSEAUX

Rocher decouvert le 23 juin 1722.

Isle et fort de la Balise

Passe de l'Est

Passe a Sauvol

FLEUVE S.t LOUIS

Echelle

PLATE 20

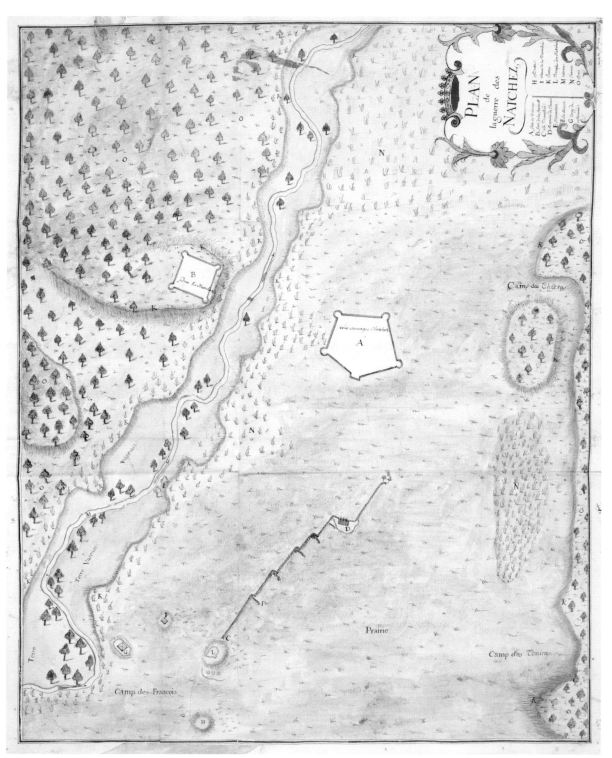

PLAN
de
la guerre des
NAICHEZ,

Camp des Chatcas

A les Sauvages Naichez

Camp des Francois

Praine

Camp des Tonicas

PLATE 22

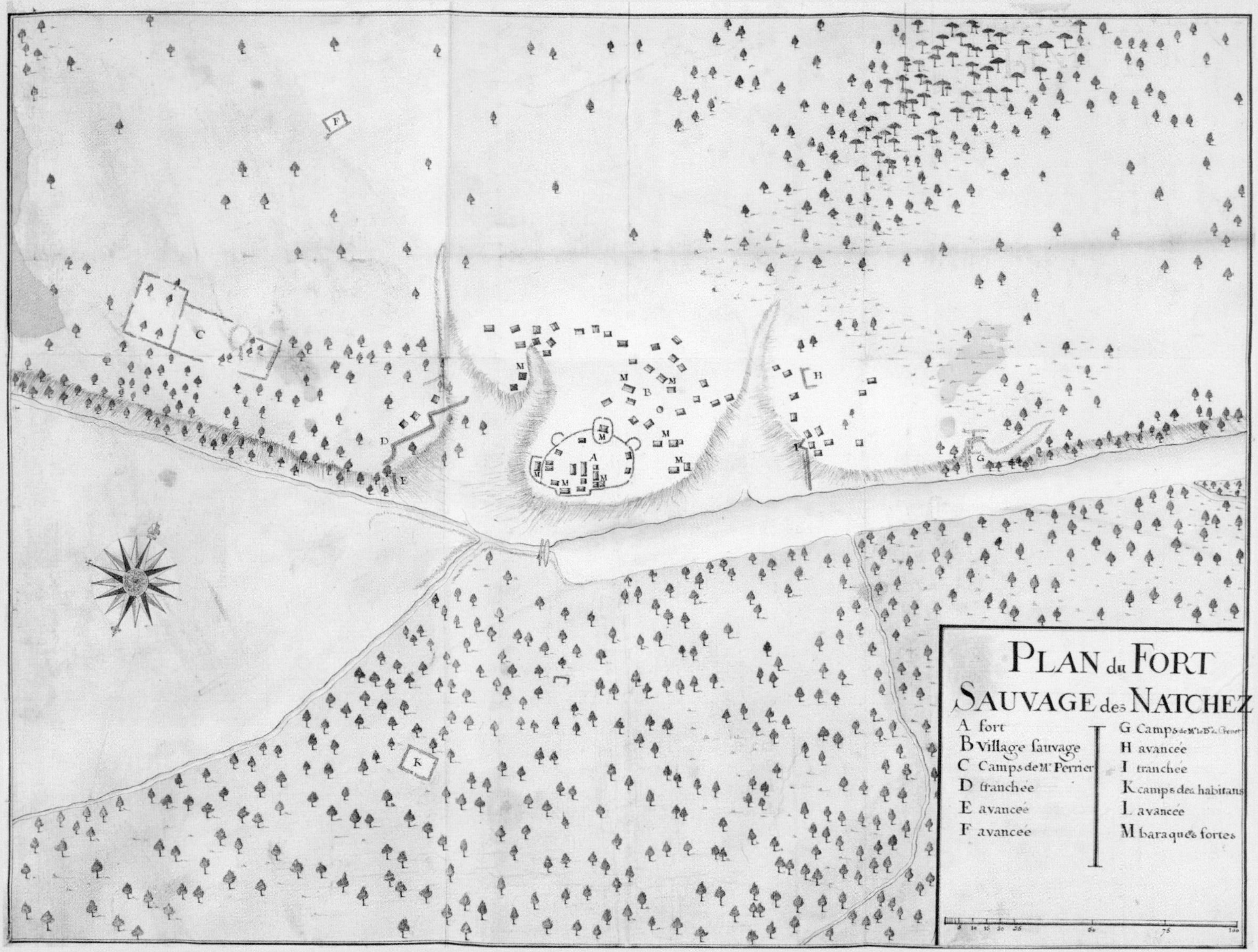

PLATE 23

PLAN du FORT
SAUVAGE des NATCHEZ

A fort
B village sauvage
C Camps de M Perrier
D tranchee
E avancee
F avancee

G Camps
H avancee
I tranchee
K camps des habitans
I avancee
M baraques fortes

Every night, from March 15 to 18, we heard something in the air that sounded like a confusion of wailing voices. They started in the east and went to the west. We were not able to find out what it might have been. The feelings of many were that it was bears and tigers that were howling, but the Biloxi Indians who were in New Orleans, upon hearing these cries, told us they had never heard anything like it, that it was not good to stay in that city any longer, and the Negroes told us the same thing. This made us realize that it was something extraordinary, since people had heard it in different places.

On the 22nd of the same month, about ten o'clock in the morning, we had a third [168] alarm, which scared three-quarters of the city, who thought that the Indians were attacking without our being able to see them. What made us persist in our error was the musket fire that could be heard all over the city. It was the inhabitants who were shooting their firearms to get them ready. They were, in fact, shooting at the back of the city next to the woods, which made us not doubt one bit that we had been taken by surprise, along with the tumultuous noise of the cries the women were making. Some had their luggage in hand, others had three or four little children around them and were praying to all the saints, and there were some who were running to throw themselves onto the ships. It was a touching thing to see even the sick people, who had not even been able to move either hand or foot, find the strength to flee. As for us and the inhabitants, we armed ourselves, the inhabitants in the parade ground, and the rest of us at the advance posts, waiting for a decision on this false alarm, which we all thought quite real. Even Monsieur de Périer, who was at the company headquarters, left promptly at the sound of the general alarm, which they were beating on the drums.

When we had all gotten ready for combat, we saw three men coming, who told us that someone named Sans Regret, a sergeant of the militia, while leaving the tavern quite plastered, had imagined that he had heard the Indians' death cries, and that they had shot and even killed the Negroes. Because of that vision, he commandeered ten men to go with him to find out how many of them there were, and, at the same time, he had cried out the alarm, which did not take long to spread throughout the whole city. Thus it was that fear took hold of everyone's mind, and to such a degree that I met two young ladies by the surname of La Chaise, who were losing all hope of being able to escape. Having run into them, I brought them to the ship the *Duc de Bourbon*. They confessed to me later that, since they did not know where they were going, and if I had not brought them to the ship, they would have gone to hide themselves in the woods. The nuns fled [169] to the Jesuits, who were quite well fortified.

On the 23rd of the same month, we were warned that the Biloxi Indians had been chased from their village by the Choctaws, who had killed two of them in order to capture a party of Frenchmen, and that they were coming to take refuge near us. The Choctaws had also told them that in a while they would come sack us.

On April 10, the day before Easter, they burned a Natchez Indian woman whom the Tunicas had captured, and whom they had brought to us so we could avenge ourselves by making her suffer the torments that her nation, and she herself, had employed against the French. This is how they killed her.

Monsieur de Périer did not want the French to get mixed up in it, so for that reason he turned over that unfortunate woman to the Tunicas, who had brought her to do what they wanted to with her. When they first found out that she was at their disposal, they prepared themselves the night before by dancing the dances and singing the calumet of death, which is sung only when they intend to kill someone or declare war against them. This calumet is painted black.

The next day, around noon, once they had made their preparations, a group of them went to the woods to look for the driest canes, and the others put two poles together in the manner that they in fact call the burning frame [see plate 6], to which the wretched woman was to be attached.

When they had finished, they painted themselves. After, they made the death cries around this frame, and began to run around as if they had been possessed by the devil, and, still crying out (this is their custom), they went to the watchhouse, where she was in fetters, adjusting a ribbon to plait her hair, which most Indian women wear [170] very long. They took off her fetters, and the Indians immediately took hold of her. They tied her by her hands, and came back as quickly as they had gone. The one among them who offered to burn her was a Natchez, who was supposed to have died along with the great sun at the time of his death, since he was one of his friends. When they presented the cord with which he was to be strangled as an honor (like I pointed out in my description of the ceremonies that they held for the death of this sun), and when he saw that he was going to die, even though he did not want to die, he did not say anything. However, when the war chief approached him, he got up abruptly, took a tomahawk, which was at hand, and killed him. Then he deserted them for the Tunicas, where the chief received him as one of his worthies, that is to say, as a manservant. That is how she was burned, by one of her own tribe and one who was even one of her relatives.

She recognized him, for she told him that, if he returned to the Natchez, they would make him pay dearly for all the torments she was going to suffer, that he deserved it more than she did, and that at least she had never killed any of her own kind, but, as for him, he was a dog for killing her. That did not prevent him from continuing. He attached her as you see, and began by burning the hair of her •••, then one breast, then her buttocks, then back to the left breast. Up until then, she had endured the pain

Figure 20. Tunica Chicf Bride les Boeufs with the scalps of three
Natchez men. Bride les Boeufs is pictured with the widow and child of
his predecessor, Chief Cahura-Joligo, who was killed by the Natchez
in 1731. *Sauvage matachez en Guerrier*, by Alexandre de Batz, 22 June
1732. (Courtesy of the Peabody Museum of Archaeology and Ethnology,
Harvard University, 41-72-10/19)

with a steadfastness that absolutely only Indians can maintain (they are known as great warriors when they sing up until their death). She began, then, to jerk about a little, blood flowing everywhere. Nevertheless, she became even more assured than before. She looked insolently from one side to the other. When she noticed some Indians who were watching her being burned from afar, she called to them to come get tortured, too, after her. This is, in my opinion, the most frightful spectacle one could ever see—you could see fat mixed with blood flowing copiously onto the ground.

When they decided that they had burned her enough on all the parts of her body, the Tunica chief's worthy took his tomahawk [171] and cut a ring around her head where her hair was, and then he scalped her and threw her scalp in the air [see fig. 20]. As it was falling back down, it fell on the head of a woman, who had such a great fright that, at that very instant, fever took her and stayed with her more than two months without her getting any better. I assure you that you must have a very steady heart to see spectacles such as these. As they were going to kill her, the Frenchwomen who had found themselves in the hands of the Natchez each took a pointed piece of cane and ran her through repeatedly. Then she became like an enraged beast, and expired two or three minutes later.

What I found most detestable and abominable was a soldier who, when she was dying, cut off a piece of her ••• and ate it. As punishment, he was put in irons and made to run the gauntlet. This is how that wretched woman died. According to her crime, she had to remain in the frame fifteen days, since she was the reason a Frenchman had been burned and suffered for three days in succession. She was with the Indians who threw the children in the air and caught them on the tips of pointed cane spears. Afterward, she put these innocent children on a spit and forced their mothers to turn them, and so forth.

Five days after this affair, those of us in New Orleans learned that there were seven Choctaw villages plotting against us, by means of a letter brought to us by six Choctaws from their interpreter to Monsieur de Périer. These same Indians, while making their oration, let it be known that the English were giving them many presents. The interpreter also wrote that a chief named Ouachilly, upon hearing bad things said about us, had the ill-intentioned Indian who said this chopped up into little pieces.

All this news served only to make us extremely unsettled, and mainly Monsieur de Périer, who, as soon as he had found out about the defeat of the French in Natchez, at once sent the frigate *Saint-Michel* to go to France to ask for prompt assistance. But, the 30th [172] of the above-mentioned month of April, a Spanish boat arrived, and they told us that this frigate had put into port at Havana, two days before they left. They said they had sold a lot of goods, and, if they had stayed another half day longer, their boat was going to be seized as an interloper (that is to say, a vessel that trades without permission or letters of commission).[334] You should know that this vessel, after arriving on the coast under the pretext of a leak, and having been found to be an interloper, was seized along with all of its goods, which remained in the storehouses of New Orleans.[335]

---

334. It is unclear from Caillot's account whether the "frigate" described as selling contraband goods in Havana was the *Saint-Michel* or another vessel. Given the urgency of the *Saint-Michel*'s mission, however, it is difficult to imagine its captain would have authorized an illicit trading stop in Havana en route to France.

335. Throughout the eighteenth century ships carrying contraband goods often made unauthorized stops in foreign ports under the pretext of needing repairs.

That left only the personal effects of the officers and others who were expelled, of which the company had no knowledge, which were sold in Havana under the same pretext of having a leak.

On May 3, upon receiving the warnings, about which I have spoken here above, the Biloxi Indians, neighbors of the Choctaws, came to warn us that that nation held it against them for having attacked them, and that they were not going to delay attacking the French. We did not want to let them know that we were paying attention to this and that this was troubling us. But this *petite nation*, seeing that we were barely listening to them, returned to their village, where they made the decision to go join up with the Choctaws, not knowing which way to turn. That resolution they had just taken was then detrimental to us, due to our lack of distrust toward them. We saw them come more often than usual, without having any suspicions about it, still believing them to be friends of ours. However, seeing that they were asking too pointedly when our big pirogues (that is to say, our ships) were leaving, and even that they wanted to trade deerskins for our dogs, saying that these animals would prevent the French from sleeping at night—from discourses such as these, we concluded that there was something very suspicious going on, and that made us spread the word to everyone.

Monsieur de Périer [173] got two of these Indians drunk, who announced the Choctaws' plan, and said that they assembled together every day and were making preparations to come at the Green Corn (which means when the corn is ripe), July 3, to scalp the French. This made us take precautions. The next day, when they wanted to leave, they asked for gunpowder and musket balls, but we refused to give them any. That very day, some of the French set out to go on the lookout. What made us fear that they had already come and were hiding in the woods was the report of an inhabitant named Monsieur Dalcourt,[336] who related that he had seen several broken branches in the woods that were painted red below and black above, which are the Indians' signs of war.

The next day a man was dispatched to go take some gunpowder and musket balls to the petites nations upriver, to try and engage them to go attack the remaining Natchez, but it was like giving them switches to whip us with, since they are not any better than the others.

---

336. Etienne de Lalande Dalcourt arrived in Louisiana as a company cashier in 1722 but was dismissed by La Chaise in 1725 on suspicion of his having pilfered company stores. By 1730 Dalcourt's fortunes had improved. The 1731 census captures him living on a medium-sized plantation downriver from New Orleans. Minutes of the Superior Council of Louisiana, 21 April 1722, *MPA*, 2:269; Jacques de La Chaise to the directors of the Company of the Indies, 6 September 1723, *MPA* 2:327–29; Maduell, "Census of Inhabitants along the River Mississippi, 1731," in *The Census Tables*, 115.

On May 7, a party from the detachment that we had left at Natchez came downriver and told us that everything was quite calm there. Nevertheless, a few days before they had come down, a party of forty Natchez had come, in order to try to get some goods they had hidden, but a Negro who was working in the cypress grove, with his musket next to him, saw them and charged after them, and had them running for their lives as he chased after them for three hours. They believed, because of the fear they had, that this Negro was not the only one, which scared them a great deal, for they greatly dread Negroes, whom they call black Frenchmen.

On the 8th of the month of June, ten Choctaws came to ask Monsieur de Périer for some pirogues to use to go see their brothers who were on the other side of the lake and numbered eight hundred, under the pretext of going to war against the [174] Chitimachas. But he took care not to give them these, since he knew it was us they were coming to attack. He agreed for the chiefs to pass by, and had presents given to them.

As the time marked for our loss approached, and the green corn was ripe, we all kept ourselves on guard. We had already passed July 4 and 5 without seeing anything yet, when on the 9th we saw 110 Indians arrive, both Bayogoulas and Colapissas, whom we thought were Choctaws, and, to all appearances, in great number. We found ourselves in a bit of a fix, but, in order not to let them see that we were afraid of them, no one took up their arms and we put on brave faces. When they were a little closer, they came to tell us that it was the petites nations, who were leading prisoners: three Natchez, four Yazoo men, and one Yazoo woman. We were overjoyed at this report, and we appeared steadfast before them. They went right away to the governor's house to make their oration and to deliver the prisoners to him, whom he had locked up immediately.

Those wretches did not languish for long because, the next day, Monsieur de Périer had four of them burned by the very ones who had brought them. These Indians took their scalps, and afterward they split their skulls and backs with blows from their tomahawks. There was one of these four who, after he had been scalped, continued to sing, right up until his death, which is a mark of valor. He said, singing, that he was upset at having killed only one Frenchman, and that in a while we would receive news that his brothers would avenge his death. (The other four were sent to the islands, where they were sold for the profit of the Company of the Indies.)[337]

In fact, the next day a pirogue came, which brought news that the Natchez had attacked ten soldiers and thirty Negroes who had gone to the cypress swamp well armed in order to work. But, unfortunately, they went to sleep, and they were surprised

---

337. These four captives were likely sent to Saint Domingue and sold as slave laborers.

by the Indians, who had been there for eight days [175] on their bellies, spying on them at a distance of a musket shot. Finding them all laid out for the taking, they had killed all of them, with the exception of this soldier, who had hidden himself in the hollow of a tree during the attack, from where he had seen all his comrades killed. When the Indians had nothing else to fear, they stripped the corpses completely naked and put them into the pirogue in which they had come, which they let drift with the current so it would pass in front of the French fort, to mock them. These Natchez pulled back after this attack, into two stone forts they had made for themselves among several little islands, which made them impregnable.

From this soldier we also found out that there were easily more than three to four hundred of them, along with five to six hundred Chickasaws who had united with them. The latter are very good warriors who fight relentlessly on foot and on horseback.

On July 15, many inhabitants were warned by their Indian women slaves to flee or to be well on guard, because the Indians were going to attack the French the following Tuesday, and that before then, on Sunday, they would bring presents of watermelons to Monsieur de Périer, on Monday some chickens, and Tuesday they would attack with five to six thousand men.

In fact, when on that Sunday the watermelons arrived, brought by the Biloxis, there was then great dread, not knowing what should be done. You could hear women wailing. You would have said that it was a hex, for even though we had the most beautiful devices in the world with which to fortify ourselves, we did nothing with them. The cannon stayed in their places, even though they had first been loaded with wadding. Monday the chickens were brought by the same nation. Seeing that, in the meantime, things were becoming serious, Monsieur de Périer had the drums sound the general alarm that day to call an assembly of the inhabitants, where they also interrogated the Indian women, who said that the Choctaws, having returned very unhappy with the French, had said that.

[176] The whole city stayed on guard, and spent the night in the square bearing arms, and they closed the women up in the ships with their children and the sick people. As far as the rest of us, we were all resolved to fight before relegating ourselves to the ships, which we would have done as a last resort. But what we feared turned out to be nothing.

On August 8, a boat from Mobile arrived, from which we found out that there was an English frigate at the coast, loaded with cheese, herrings, and beer, and distributing these provisions in the colony. We also learned that this frigate was coming to spy on what was happening among us, and we were then certain that they were the ones who had incited the Indians, by means of their presents, to start a general insurrection against us, so they could become the masters of the whole colony after our destruction.

There was no one in New Orleans who did not buy some of these provisions, but, a few days later, someone who imagined they had been poisoned by what had come from the English ship spread the rumor, which gave the apothecary great pleasure, because everyone who had eaten some—in other words, the whole city—got some of the antidote and purged themselves. In the meantime, the ship *Prince de Conty* arrived, which made our minds a bit more tranquil, as much for the news of the fifty soldiers they had aboard as for the response from the *Saint-Michel*. The *Saint-Michel* specified that two company ships were being armed with troops, and that the king had loaned one of his ships to the company for one year, armed with three hundred men.

That news did us a world of good, because there were at that moment in the city about three hundred fifty Indians, who, upon seeing the *Prince de Conty* arrive, asked what that great pirogue was. They were told that it was many Frenchmen who were coming [177] and that, shortly, as many Frenchmen as there are trees would be coming. Upon hearing such a discourse, they appeared dumbfounded, and, without saying a word, the next day they took off. They went to bring this news to their villages, where they said that Frenchmen had just arrived in New Orleans, lots of them, and that in a half moon more would be arriving, as many as blades of grass.

On September 5, we finally learned of the arrival of the king's ship, from a soldier from the Balize who came to bring us this news.[338] From that moment, you could hear cries of joy throughout the city, which had been deprived of joy for so long. From that point on, everyone seemed to be renewed and to gain new energy. As recompense, that soldier received one hundred écus and was made a sergeant.

We worked to furnish some apartments in the government building for all the officers, such that you heard more than jubilation, and as many women who had cried out in fear now cried out for the joy they felt.

Monsieur de Périer went to see his brother at the Balize, in order to bring him back, but he refused to leave his ship before it was anchored at New Orleans. It took them only eight days to get there, while the company ships sometimes took one and two months to get up the river. When he was a cannon shot away from the city, he saluted the shore by firing the cannon eleven times, flags and pennants flying. The shore returned his salute, shot for shot. The ships that were in the port raised their flags, which they undertook with a cannon shot, and then they saluted the king's ship by firing the cannon thirteen times.

---

338. The king's frigate *Somme* arrived in New Orleans on September 15, 1730. The ship bore two hundred troops of the marine under the command of Governor Périer's younger brother Lieutenant Commander Antoine-Alexis Périer de Salvert.

When Monsieur de Salvert was anchored in front of the company headquarters, he left his ship and came ashore in his yawl (it is a type of very light English boat), where, as he was setting foot to shore, he was saluted by eleven cannon shots, with the troops lined up on both sides, from the shore to the government building, where the whole assemblage [178] was leading him. The king's ship made a second discharge, which was answered by those on shore and by the two company ships.

The next day, which was Sunday, the commander had the drums sound the general alarm, and gave the order that evening for everyone to arm themselves and present themselves at the parade ground. Our company, in fact, was on watch that night. We nevertheless had to appear bearing arms when coming off guard. When the inhabitants were lined up on the parade ground to the left, the troops to the right, and our company near the government building, Monsieur de Salvert came out, leading the one hundred fifty soldiers from his ship to the sound of the drum, and came to the parade ground, where he was recognized as first lieutenant general of the province of Louisiana. After doing a few quarter wheels in formation, they went back. For eight days there was nothing but joy and continuous merriment in the whole city.

From that point, they began preparations for the war, so they could destroy the rest of the mutinous Indians. When everything was ready—like tents, sandbags, gunlock covers, gaiters, etc.—and Monsieur de Périer was getting ready to leave with his brother, they received news from travelers from the Illinois country that the Arkansas, with Frenchmen leading them, had vanquished a party of Foxes, our enemies and one of the cruelest of nations. They told us that fifty had been destroyed. This news brought great pleasure, for the trade in provisions and other merchandise began from that point on to be abundant in New Orleans, something that previously no traveler had undertaken except with great danger, because of these savages. The next day the "Te Deum" was sung to give thanks to God for the grace he had just shown us by having delivered some of our enemies to us, and also to pray for him to give us [179] great success in the war we were getting ready to undertake. There was a grand procession from the parish church to the nuns' convent, and during the procession there were three discharges, of both muskets and cannon.

Two days later, which was December 9, the troops of the navy departed, commanded by Monsieur de Salvert, and on Monday, December 11, 1730, the army and militia departed, commanded by Monsieur de Périer.

Eight days after the army's departure, the major of the parade grounds had the remainder of the inhabitants assemble there, so that new procedures for the guards could be established, and also to appoint four officers to replace four who had been dismissed. They mutinied and at first refused to receive them, so they would be allowed to choose the ones they wanted. The major, seeing this mutiny, called the guard, who came, but they had no sooner arrived in the parade ground, wanting to put the mutineers to the sword, than the whole bourgeoisie surrounded them, being ready to revolt entirely. The guard pulled back, seeing that they were too few to be able to put up resistance on the major's behalf, and not one of the four officers would have been appointed if not for a man named Monsieur de Martonne, who luckily, in the meantime, had come back. This Monsieur de Martonne, who served and was second in command on the king's frigate named the *Somme*, had seen from his ship what was going on in the parade ground, and reprimanded the major. He told him that he did not know how to use his authority, and that he should bust the head of the first one to move. At the same time, he called the guard and advanced, sword in hand, toward the bourgeoisie, who did not say the least word. He had two of them taken, and they were put in prison, where he had fetters put on their feet and hands while waiting for the return of Monsieur de [180] Périer. As for the others, despite the fact that they were upset, he made them accept the appointed officers without another grumble. This showed the cowardice of the inhabitants and their malignant schemes.

On February 2, 1731, Monsieur de Périer came back from the Natchez war. He told us that he was victorious over the Indians, that he had taken four hundred fifty of them as slaves, who his brother was leading, escorted by the army, which was composed of six hundred Frenchmen.[339] They were also bringing fifty Negroes who had been captured with the Indians, who had fought five days against the army, when, in the end, they were forced to surrender, seeing they were entirely destroyed by the grenades and bombs, the mortars of which were wood encircled by iron. They shot very far.

When the Indians saw the first bomb explode in the air, they jeered, saying the French had gone mad, sending them rotten cannonballs. They were still making fun of us when we sent them a second one, which made a terrible roar in their midst and killed a good number of them. This astonished them to the extreme, and they started to conjure and said that it was the Great Spirit, who was with the French. A few days after it happened, we in New Orleans received word that the Foxes, nine hundred in number, had been destroyed by the Illinois and the Arkansas. This news had the effect of returning perfect tranquility to the inhabitants. At the end of the week, Monsieur de

---

339. Périer's forces took approximately 450 Natchez women and children and more than 45 warriors captive in January 1731. The captives were brought downriver to New Orleans, where many of them died due to overcrowding and poor sanitary conditions in the jail. On May 28, the surviving 280 captives were boarded onto the company ships *Vénus* and *Aurore*, bound for Cap Français, Saint Domingue, where they were to be sold as slaves to the profit of the company. One hundred twenty-seven Natchez perished en route to Saint Domingue. Contemporary reports suggest that at least several hundred Natchez men, women, and children escaped Périer's 1731 campaign, taking refuge with various Indian groups in the lower Mississippi Valley.

Périer had the "Te Deum" sung as an expression of gratitude. The troops of the army, navy, and militia all bore arms, and our company was there too. Three discharges were fired, both from the muskets as well as the cannon. They fired the cannon 324 times that day. After the service, Monsieur de Périer stood at the head of our company and thanked us on behalf of the king and the company for the fine service we had rendered. From that day we no longer appeared bearing arms.

[181] Following this, peace and calm were entirely reestablished in the colony, except for fifty Natchez Indians who had escaped, whom we feared as evildoers and who got several nations on their side, principally the Choctaws. I have already said in the past that they are a very bad people, numbering five to six thousand, and are, fortunately, very cowardly. We are waiting for some troops to come to the country to declare war on them.

I profited from the opportunity of having ships that were going to be sailing for France to ask the directors for my passage, which I had not wanted to ask for previously, during wartime, in order to see its success, and also so that no one would suspect me of being cowardly. To the contrary, I did not let any opportunities pass to offer my services to our general. So when I asked him to honor my request to return to France, he encouraged me to stay, with a promise of rendering some service to me in the country. But knowing that he would ruin himself by these promises, and he would get rich by not keeping any, made me tell him that I could not promise him anything, and I asked him only to have the kindness to give me fifteen days to think about what decision I should make. Four days later, I had completely arranged my affairs on this matter. One evening, when I had gone to supper at my inn, the fire, which, according to the masons' report, had been smoldering in the chimney of my bedroom for five or six days, took hold. It burned the house and all that I had, with the exception of the things I had on myself and my bed, which were saved, so that in a very short space of time I found myself faced with having nothing. Fortunately for me, although I lost everything, I had the consolation of not owing anything to anybody. Nevertheless, it made me feel quite sick to my heart, especially all the money, which amounted to 217 livres that I no [182] longer possessed. Since I was getting over a serious illness, which had cost me a lot, I did not know what decision to make, whether to remain or pull up my stakes.

I remained undecided a few days, but this last incident had the effect of making up my mind entirely, with the advice of several people whom I consulted, who had until then tried to influence me to stay on behalf of Monsieur de Périer. Seeing me beaten down, they declared their feelings to me as friends, which, after examining all things for my advancement, they advised me, if I could, to get myself away from that unlucky colony, which I had a great deal of trouble leaving. Meanwhile, presenting requests to the council, to whom I explained that some very pressing affairs concerning me were calling me back home to France without delay, in addition to the illness of the country, which I pretended to have, these reasons resolved them to grant me my request. Once I had it signed by the council, I soon forgot the losses and troubles I had suffered there, because of the pleasure I was feeling in leaving that unfortunate country. I very quickly prepared myself to leave. There were no friends, neither male nor female, who could keep me from leaving. I left New Orleans on April 1 in the year 1731, as happy to the same degree as I had been sad upon arriving there. We boarded a boat to go downriver to the mouth, where the Balize is. After arriving there, we stayed on land several weeks, waiting for the ships to pass a sandbar where there was shallow water, and where almost all the ships run aground very easily. The *Prince de Conty,* on which we were supposed to travel, after running aground like the others, passed with a great deal of trouble. When it was offshore, we were taken to go aboard, and we left that day.

We had already spent two days, and were twenty leagues or so from land, when, during the course of dinner, a great noise arose in the [183] ship. We were not long in finding out what our misfortune was. They came to tell the captain that the ship was foundering. We immediately left the table and had time only to put the ship's boat into the sea and get ourselves aboard. We were not two musket shots away when there was no longer any ship.

It was assuredly a sad spectacle to see the disorder everything was in. On one side you saw cattle drowning; on the other, casks, chests, planks, chairs, beds, and ten to twelve men whom we could not save, because the sea was too agitated and our only thought was how to get back to the Balize, from where we had left. We related our misfortune to the director,[340] who was quite stunned and sympathetic to the situation we found ourselves in, having been unable to save anything from this shipwreck other than our own selves. He wrote to Monsieur de Périer, as much to inform him of this accident as to know what decision we should make, and, while waiting to hear his reply, he kept us at his house.

At the end of the week, we received Monsieur de Périer's decision. He wrote us what he would do regarding our misfortunes. He gave us the choice of boarding the ship called the *Américain,* otherwise called the *Saint-Louis* [see plate 21], or returning to New Orleans.[341] We wrote him that we wished fervently for him to provide us passage

---

340. Louis-Auguste de La Loire Flaucourt replaced Bernard Duvergé as port director and overseer at the Balize in 1731.

341. The *Saint-Louis* was a slaving vessel commissioned by the company to bring bound laborers from Africa to Louisiana. Commanded by Etienne Bréban, the *Saint-Louis* was preparing for its return voyage to France when the *Prince de Conty*'s demise forced Bréban to take on nine of its passengers including Caillot. The shipwreck of

on said ship, even though it was in very bad shape. Things were thus concluded. He had some provisions for us, given to the captain, and reimbursed the director of the Balize what he had used up in provisions on our behalf.

When the *Saint-Louis* came down the river after the king's ship and passed the sandbar without trouble, we took our leave of Monsieur de La Loire Flaucourt (that is the name of that director), thanked him for [184] the consideration he had so generously shown us, and we went to go aboard ship a second time.

One thing that was quite odd is that the ship on which we reembarked had almost been condemned in New Orleans, for it was no good, so consequently the captain and the officers were supposed to have made the crossing with us on the *Prince de Conty*. But, instead, it turned out that we and the officers of the *Prince de Conty* were only too happy in our misfortune to make the crossing on that ship. We left the Balize May 4, 1731, at five and a quarter hours in the evening, after enduring many gales while in a roadstead, which caused dreadful seas for us for five days.

---

the *Prince de Conty* is clearly marked on Callot, "Plan et Veüe General du Fort de la Balize," April 1733, ANOM, 04DFC115A. See also admiralty court records, "Rapport du *Saint-Louis* de 1729 à 1731," Archives départementales de Morbihan (ADM), bundle 9 B 99.

Bibliography

Archival Repositories

ADHS   Archives départementales des Hautes-de-Seine, Nanterre, France
ADM   Archives départementales du Morbihan, Vannes, France
AN   Archives Nationales, Paris, France
ANOM   Archives nationales d'outre-mer (formerly the Centre des archives d'outre-mer), Aix-en-Provence, France
BAnQ   Bibliothèque et Archives nationales du Québec, Quebec City, Canada
BnF   Bibliothèque nationale de France, Paris, France
FML   Fonds de la Marine à Lorient, Service historique de la Défense, Lorient, France
SLC   Sacramental Records of the Saint Louis Church/Cathedral, Archives of the Archdiocese of New Orleans, Louisiana
THNOC   The Historic New Orleans Collection, New Orleans, Louisiana

Technical Reference Works

Alembert, Bossut, La Lande, Condorcet, and Charles. *Encyclopédie Méthodique. Dictionnaire des jeux, faisant suite au tome III des Mathématiques.* Paris: Panckoucke, 1789.

Aubin, Nicolas. *Dictionnaire de marine.* Amsterdam: Brunel, 1702.

Falconer, William. *An Universal Dictionary of the Marine; or, a Copious Explanation of the Technical Terms and Phrases Employed in the Construction, Equipment, Furniture, Machinery, Movements, and Military Operations of a Ship.* London: T. Cadell, 1776.

Heilbrunn Timeline of Art History. New York: The Metropolitan Museum of Art, 2000–, www.metmuseum.org/toah.

O'Neill, E. Wesley, Jr. "French Coinage in History and Literature." *French Review* 39 (1965): 1–14.

Parlett, David. *The Oxford Dictionary of Card Games.* New York: Oxford University Press, 1996.

Read, William A. *Louisiana Place Names of Indian Origin: A Collection of Words.* Tuscaloosa: University of Alabama Press, 2008.

Rowlett, Russell. "How Many: A Dictionary of Units of Measurement." The University of North Carolina at Chapel Hill, 2004. http://www.unc.edu/~rowlett/units/index .html (accessed 2009–2012).

Published Primary Sources

Bossu, Jean-Bernard. *Nouveaux voyages aux indes occidentales.* Paris: Le Jay, 1768.

Challe, Robert. *Journal d'un voyage fait aux Indes orientales.* 3 vols. Rouen: Jean Baptiste Machuel Le Jeune, 1721.

———. *Journal d'un voyage fait aux Indes orientales (Du 24 février 1690 au 10 août 1691).* Edited by Frédéric Deloffre and Jacques Popin. Paris: Mercure de France, 2002.

Charlevoix, Pierre-François Xavier de. *Charlevoix's Louisiana: Selections from the History and the Journal.* Edited by Charles E. O'Neill. Baton Rouge: Louisiana State University Press, 1977.

Cockburn, William. *Sea Diseases; or, A Treatise of Their Nature, Causes, and Cure.* London: G. Strahan, 1736.

Dumont de Montigny, Jean-François Benjamin. *Mémoires historiques sur la Louisiane.* Paris: C. J. G. Bauche, 1753.

———. *Regards sur le monde atlantique, 1715–1747.* Edited by Carla Zecher, Gordon Sayre, and Shannon Lee Dawdy. Quebec: Septentrion, 2008.

Eltis, David, Stephen Behrendt, David Richardson, and Herbert S. Klein, eds. *The Trans-Atlantic Slave Trade: A Database on CD-ROM.* Cambridge: Cambridge University Press, 1999. (*TASTDB*).

Estienne, René, ed. *Les armements au long cours de la deuxième Compagnie des Indes, 1717–1773.* Lorient: Service historique de la Marine, Archives du port de Lorient, 1996.

Hachard, Marie-Madeleine. *Relation du voyage des dames religieuses Ursulines de Roüen à la Nouvelle-Orléans, parties de France le 22 février 1727 et arrivez à La Louisienne le 23 juillet de la même année.* Rouen: A. Le Prevost, 1728.

———. *Voices from an Early American Convent: Marie Madeleine Hachard and the New Orleans Ursulines, 1727–1760.* Edited by Emily Clark. Baton Rouge: Louisiana State University Press, 2007.

Iberville, Pierre Le Moyne d'. *Iberville's Gulf Journals.* Edited and translated by Richebourg Gaillard McWilliams. Tuscaloosa: University of Alabama Press, 1981.

Labat, Jean-Baptiste. *Nouveau voyage aux isles de l'Amérique.* Vol. 1. The Hague: P. Husson, T. Johnson, P. Gosse, J. Van Duren, R. Alberts et C. Le Vier, 1724.

———. *Nouveau voyage aux isles de l'Amérique.* Vol. 5. Paris: Guillaume Cavelier, fils, 1722.

Laval, Antoine. *Voyage de la Louisiane.* Paris: Jean Mariette, 1728.

Le Page du Pratz, Antoine-Simon. *Histoire de la Louisiane.* 3 vols. Paris: De Bure, l'aîné, 1758.

Maduell, Charles R., Jr., ed. and trans. *The Census Tables for the French Colony of Louisiana from 1699 through 1732.* Baltimore: Genealogical Publishing Co., 1972.

Martineau, Alfred, ed. *Correspondance du Conseil Supérieur de Pondichéry avec le Conseil de Chandernagor.* 3 vols. Pondicherry, India: Société de l'histoire de l'Inde française, 1915–27.

———. *Correspondance du Conseil Supérieur de Pondichéry et de la Compagnie.* 6 vols. Pondicherry, India: Société de l'histoire de l'Inde française, 1920–35.

Mississippi Provincial Archives: French Dominion. Vols. 2–3, edited and translated by Dunbar Rowland and A. G. Sanders. Jackson: Press of the Mississippi Department of Archives, 1932. Vols. 4–5, edited and translated by Dunbar Rowland and A. G. Sanders; revised and edited by Patricia K. Galloway. Baton Rouge: Louisiana State University Press, 1984. (*MPA*).

Pénicaut, André. *Fleur de lys and Calumet: Being the Pénicaut Narrative of French Adventure in Louisiana.* Edited and translated by Richebourg Gaillard McWilliams. Tuscaloosa: University of Alabama Press, 1988.

Pradel de Lamase, Jean-Charles de. *Le chevalier de Pradel: Vie d'un colon français en Louisiane au XVIIIe siècle d'après sa correspondance et celle de sa famille.* Edited by A. Baillardel and A. Prioult. Paris: Maisonneuve frères, 1928.

Thwaites, Reuben Gold, ed. *The Jesuit Relations and Allied Documents: Travels and Relations of the Jesuit Missionaries in New France, 1610–1791.* Vol. 67. Cleveland: Burrows Brothers, 1900.

Valette de Laudun, M. *Journal d'un Voyage à la Louisiane, fait en 1720 par M.***, capitaine de vaisseau du Roi.* The Hague: Musier, Fils et Fournier, 1768.

Secondary Sources

Allain, Mathé. "L'Immigration française en Louisiane." *Revue d'histoire de l'Amérique française* 28 (1975): 555–64.

———. "*Manon Lescaut et Ses Consoeurs*: Women in the Early French Period, 1700–1731." In *Proceedings of the Fifth Meeting of the French Colonial Historical Society,* edited by James J. Cooke, 6–26. Lanham, MD: French Colonial Historical Society, 1980.

Allen, Charles M., Dawn Allen Newman, and Harry H. Winters. *Trees, Shrubs, and Woody Vines of Louisiana.* Pitkin, LA: Allen's Native Ventures, 2002.

Baird, W. David. *The Quapaw Indians: A History of the Downstream People.* Norman: University of Oklahoma Press, 1980.

Balvay, Arnaud. *La Révolte des Natchez.* Paris: Editions du Félin, 2008.

Banks, Kenneth. *Chasing Empire Across the Sea: Communications and the State in the French Atlantic, 1713–1763.* Montreal: McGill-Queen's University Press, 2002.

Barnett, James F., Jr. *The Natchez Indians: A History to 1735.* Jackson: University Press of Mississippi, 2007.

Biver, Paul. *Histoire du Château de Meudon.* Paris: Jouvé et Cie, 1923.

Brain, Jeffrey P., George Roth, and William J. De Reuse. "Tunica, Biloxi, and Ofo." In Fogelson, *Handbook of North American Indians,* 14:586–97.

Burton, H. Sophie, and F. Todd Smith. *Colonial Natchitoches: A Creole Community on the Louisiana-Texas Frontier.* College Station: Texas A&M University Press, 2008.

Campanella, Richard. *Bienville's Dilemma: A Historical Geography of New Orleans.* Lafayette: Center for Louisiana Studies, 2008.

Campisi, Jack. "Houma." In Fogelson, *Handbook of North American Indians,* 14:632–41.

Cellard, Jacques. *John Law et la Régence: 1715–1729.* Paris: Plon, 1996.

Christopher, Emma. *Slave Ship Sailors and Their Captive Cargoes, 1730–1807.* New York: Cambridge University Press, 2006.

Clark, Emily. "'By All the Conduct of Their Lives': A Laywomen's Confraternity in New Orleans, 1730–1744." *William and Mary Quarterly,* 3rd ser., 54 (1997): 769–94.

———. *Masterless Mistresses: The New Orleans Ursulines and the Development of a New World Society, 1727–1834.* Chapel Hill: University of North Carolina Press, 2007.

Cordingly, David. *Seafaring Women: Adventures of Pirate Queens, Female Stowaways, and Sailors' Wives.* New York: Random House, 2007.

Creighton, Margaret S., and Lisa Norling, eds. *Iron Men, Wooden Women: Gender and Seafaring in the Atlantic World, 1700–1920.* Baltimore: Johns Hopkins University Press, 1996.

Crété, Liliane. *La traite des Nègres sous l'Ancien Régime: Le nègre, le sucre, et la toile.* Paris: Perrin, 1989.

Dawdy, Shannon Lee. *Building the Devil's Empire: French Colonial New Orleans.* Chicago: University of Chicago Press, 2008.

———. "The Burden of Louis Congo and the Evolution of Savagery in Colonial Louisiana." In *Discipline and the Other Body: Correction, Corporeality, Colonialism,* edited by Steven Pierce and Anupama Rao, 61–89. Durham: Duke University Press, 2006.

———. "*La Ville Sauvage*: 'Enlightened' Colonialism and Creole Improvisation in New Orleans, 1699–1769." PhD diss., University of Michigan, 2003.

———. "'A Wild Taste': Food and Colonialism in Eighteenth-Century Louisiana." *Ethnohistory* 57 (2010): 389–413.

Deiler, J. Hanno. *The Settlement of the German Coast of Louisiana and the Creoles of German Descent.* Philadelphia: Americana Germanica Press, 1909.

Deloffre, Frédéric, and Jacques Popin. "Le *Journal de voyage* de 1721." In *Journal d'un voyage fait aux Indes orientales (Du 24 février 1690 au 10 août 1691),* by Robert Challe, 71–88. Paris: Mercure de France, 2002.

Dennis, John V. *The Great Cypress Swamps.* Baton Rouge: Louisiana State University Press, 1988.

Deveau, Jean-Michel. *La France au temps des négriers.* Paris: France-Empire, 1994.

Dormon, Caroline. *Forest Trees of Louisiana*. Baton Rouge: Division of Forestry, Louisiana Department of Conservation, 1941.

———. *Wild Flowers of Louisiana*. Garden City, NY: Doubleday, Doran, and Co., 1934.

Druett, Joan. *Hen Frigates: Wives of Merchant Captains Under Sail*. New York: Simon and Schuster, 1998.

Duval, Kathleen. "Interconnectedness and Diversity in French Louisiana." In Waselkov, Wood, and Hatley, *Powhatan's Mantle*, 133–62.

Eccles, W. J. *The French in North America, 1500–1783*. East Lansing: Michigan State University Press, 1998.

Edmunds, R. David, and Joseph L. Peyser. *The Fox Wars: The Mesquakie Challenge to New France*. Norman: University of Oklahoma Press, 1993.

Edwards, Philip. *The Story of the Voyage: Sea-Narratives in Eighteenth-Century England*. New York: Cambridge University Press, 1994.

Ethridge, Robbie Franklyn. *From Chicaza to Chickasaw: The European Invasion and the Transformation of the Mississippian World, 1540–1715*. Chapel Hill: University of North Carolina Press, 2010.

Ethridge, Robbie Franklyn, and Charles Hudson, eds. *The Transformation of the Southeastern Indians, 1540–1760*. Jackson: University Press of Mississippi, 2002.

Ethridge, Robbie Franklyn, and Sheri M. Schuck-Hall, eds. *Mapping the Mississippian Shatter Zone: The Colonial Indian Slave Trade and Regional Instability in the American South*. Lincoln: University of Nebraska Press, 2009.

Favier, René. "Jouer dans les villes de province en France au XVIII siècle." *Histoire Urbaine* 1 (2000): 65–85.

Fingerson, Laura. *Girls in Power: Gender, Body, and Menstruation in Adolescence*. Albany: State University of New York Press, 2006.

Firth, Raymond. *Symbols: Public and Private*. Ithaca: Cornell University Press, 1973.

Fogelson, Raymond D., ed. *The Handbook of North American Indians*. Vol. 14, *Southeast*. Washington, DC: Smithsonian Institution, 2004.

Freundlich, Francis. *Le Monde du jeu à Paris: 1715–1800*. Paris: A. Michel, 1995.

Galán, Francis X. "Last Soldiers, First Pioneers: The Los Adaes Border Community on the Louisiana-Texas Frontier." PhD diss., Southern Methodist University, 2006.

Gallay, Alan. *The Indian Slave Trade: The Rise of the English Empire in the American South, 1670–1717*. New Haven: Yale University Press, 2002.

Galloway, Patricia. "'The Chief Who Is Your Father': Choctaw and French Views of the Diplomatic Relation." In Waselkov, Wood, and Hatley, *Powhatan's Mantle*, 345–70.

———. *Choctaw Genesis, 1500–1700*. Lincoln: University of Nebraska Press, 1998.

Galloway, Patricia, and Jason Baird Jackson. "Natchez and Neighboring Groups." In Fogelson, *Handbook of North American Indians*, 14:598–615.

Galloway, Patricia, and Clara Sue Kidwell. "Choctaw in the East." In Fogelson, *Handbook of North American Indians*, 14:499–519.

Garraway, Doris. *The Libertine Colony: Creolization in the Early French Caribbean*. Durham: Duke University Press, 2005.

Garrigus, John D. *Before Haiti: Race and Citizenship in French Saint-Domingue*. New York: Palgrave Macmillan, 2006.

Gay, Daniel. *Les Noirs du Québec, 1629–1900*. Quebec: Septentrion, 2004.

Giraud, Marcel. *Histoire de la Louisiane française*. Vol. 3, *Epoque de John Law, 1717–1720*. Paris: Presses Universitaires de France, 1977.

———. *Histoire de la Louisiane française*. Vol. 4, *La Louisiane après le système de Law, 1721–1723*. Paris: Presses Universitaires de France, 1974.

———. *A History of French Louisiana*. Vol. 5, *The Company of the Indies, 1723–1731*. Translated by Brian Pearce. Baton Rouge: Louisiana State University Press, 1991.

Goddard, Ives. "Bayogoula." In Fogelson, *Handbook of North American Indians*, 14: 175–76.

———. "Colapissa." In Fogelson, *Handbook of North American Indians*, 14:177–78.

———. "Washa, Chawasha, and Yakni-Chito." In Fogelson, *Handbook of North American Indians*, 14:188–90.

Greenwald, Erin M. "Company Towns and Tropical Baptisms: From Lorient to Louisiana on a French Atlantic Circuit." PhD diss., The Ohio State University, 2011.

Grussi, Olivier. *La Vie quotidienne des joueurs sous l'Ancien Régime à Paris et à la Cour*. Paris: Hachette, 1985.

Hagan, William T. *The Sac and Fox Indians*. Norman: University of Oklahoma Press, 1958.

Hall, Gwendolyn Midlo. *Africans in Colonial Louisiana: The Development of Afro-Creole Culture in the Eighteenth Century*. Baton Rouge: Louisiana State University Press, 1992.

Hahn, Steven C. *The Invention of the Creek Nation, 1670–1763*. Lincoln: University of Nebraska Press, 2004.

Hann, John H. *Apalachee: The Land between the Rivers*. Gainesville: University Presses of Florida, 1988.

Hardy, James D., Jr. "The Superior Council in Colonial Louisiana." In *Frenchmen and French Ways in the Mississippi Valley*, edited by John Francis McDermott, 87–102. Urbana: University of Illinois Press, 1969.

———. "The Transportation of Convicts to Colonial Louisiana." *Louisiana History* 7 (1966): 207–20.

Harms, Robert. *The* Diligent: *A Voyage Through the Worlds of the Slave Trade*. New York: Basic Books, 2002.

Haudrère, Philippe. *La Compagnie française des Indes au XVIIIe siècle, 1719–1795*. 2 vols. Paris: Les Indes Savantes, 2005.

Haudrère, Philippe, and Gérard Le Bouëdec. *Les Compagnies des Indes*. Rennes: Editions Ouest-France, 2005.

Higginbotham, Jay. *Old Mobile: Fort Louis de la Louisiane, 1702–1711*. Tuscaloosa: University of Alabama Press, 1991.

Holmes, Walter C. *Flore Louisiane: An Ethno-Botanical Study of French-Speaking Louisiana*. Lafayette: University of Southwestern Louisiana, 1990.

Hudson, Charles. *The Southeastern Indians*. Knoxville: University of Tennessee Press, 1976.

Kavanagh, Thomas. "The Libertine's Bluff: Cards and Culture in Eighteenth-Century France." *Eighteenth-Century Studies* 33 (2000): 505–21.

Kelton, Paul. *Epidemics and Enslavement: Biological Catastrophe in the Native Southeast, 1492–1715*. Lincoln: University of Nebraska Press, 2007.

Kettering, Sharon. "Patronage and Kinship in Early Modern France." *French Historical Studies* 16 (1989): 408–35.

Kniffen, Fred B., Hiram F. Gregory, and George A. Stokes. *The Historic Tribes of Louisiana, from 1542 to the Present*. Baton Rouge: Louisiana State University Press, 1987.

Koda, Harold, and Andrew Bolton. *Dangerous Liaisons: Fashion and Furniture in the Eighteenth Century*. New Haven: Yale University Press, 2006.

Kronk, Gary W. *Cometography: A Catalog of Comets*. Vol. 1, *Ancient to 1799*. New York: Cambridge University Press, 1999.

Langlois, Gilles-Antoine. *Des Villes pour la Louisiane française: Théorie et pratique de l'urbanistique coloniale au 18e siècle*. Paris: l'Harmattan, 2003.

Lankford, George E. "Chacato, Pensacola, Tahomé, Naniaba, and Mobilia." In Fogelson, *Handbook of North American Indians*, 14:664–68.

Laverny, Sophie de. *Les Domestiques commensaux du roi de France au XVIIe siècle*. Paris: Presses de l'Université de Paris-Sorbonne, 2002.

Le Conte, René. "The Germans in Louisiana in the Eighteenth Century." In *A Refuge for All Ages: Immigration in Louisiana History*, translated and edited by Glenn R. Conrad, 31–43. Lafayette: Center for Louisiana Studies, 1996.

Lindemann, Mary. *Medicine and Society in Early Modern Europe*. New York: Cambridge University Press, 2010.

Linon-Chipon, Sophie. *Gallia Orientalis: Voyages aux Indes orientales, 1529–1722: Poétique et imaginaire d'un genre littéraire en formation*. Paris: Presses de l'Université Paris-Sorbonne, 2003.

Livet, Georges. "La route royale et la civilisation française de la fin du XVe au milieu du XVIIIe siècle." In *Les Routes de France depuis les origines jusqu'à nos jours*, edited by Guy Michaud, 57–100. Paris: L'Association pour la diffusion de la pensée française, 1959.

McClellan, James E., III. *Colonialism and Science: Saint Domingue in the Old Regime*. Baltimore: Johns Hopkins University Press, 1992.

Merians, Linda Evi. *The Secret Malady: Venereal Disease in Eighteenth-Century Britain and France*. Lexington: University Press of Kentucky, 1996.

Milne, George Edward. "Picking Up the Pieces: Natchez Coalescence in the Shatter Zone." In Ethridge and Shuck-Hall, *Mapping the Mississippian Shatter Zone*, 388–417.

———. "Right in the Jesuit's Eye: Partisan Perspectives in French Louisianan Travel Narratives." Unpublished manuscript.

―――. "Rising Suns, Fallen Forts, and Impudent Immigrants: Race, Power, and War in the Lower Mississippi Valley." PhD diss., University of Oklahoma, 2006.

Moreau, François. "La littérature des voyages maritimes, du Classicisme aux Lumières." In *La Percée de l'Europe sur les océans vers 1690–vers 1790*, edited by Etienne Taillemite and Denis Lieppe, 223–64. Paris: Presses de l'Université de Paris-Sorbonne, 1997.

―――. *La plume et le plomb: Espaces de l'imprimé et du manuscrit au siècle des Lumières*. Paris: Presses de l'Université de Paris-Sorbonne, 2006.

Moreau, François, ed. *La Communication manuscrite au XVIII siècle*. Paris: Universitas, 2003.

Morgan, M. J. *Land of Big Rivers: French and Indian Illinois, 1699–1778*. Carbondale: Southern Illinois University Press, 2010.

Mousnier, Roland. *The Institutions of France under the Absolute Monarchy, 1598–1789*. Vol. 2, *The Organs of State and Society*. Translated by Arthur Goldhammer. Chicago: University of Chicago Press, 1984.

Murphy, Antoin E. *John Law: Economic Theorist and Policy-maker*. Oxford: Oxford University Press, 1997.

Nières, Claude. *Histoire de Lorient*. Toulouse: Privat, 1988.

O'Brien, Greg. "The Coming of Age of Choctaw History." In *Pre-removal Choctaw History: Exploring New Paths*, edited by Greg O'Brien, 3–25. Norman: University of Oklahoma Press, 2008.

Ogle, Gene E. "Slaves of Justice: Saint Domingue's Executioners and the Production of Shame." *Historical Reflections* 29 (2003): 275–93.

O'Neill, Charles Edwards. *Church and State in French Colonial Louisiana: Policy and Politics to 1732*. New Haven: Yale University Press, 1966.

Parthesius, Robert. *Dutch Ships in Tropical Waters: The Development of the Dutch East India Company (VOC) Shipping Network in Asia, 1595–1660*. Amsterdam: Amsterdam University Press, 2010.

Perret, André. "René Montaudoin, armateur et négrier nantais (1673–1731)." *Bulletin de la Société Archéologique et Historique de Nantes et de la Loire-Inférieure* 88 (1949): 78–94.

Pétré-Grenouilleau, Olivier. *Nantes au temps de la traite des Noirs*. Paris: Hachette, 1998.

Pollock, Linda A. "The Practice of Kindness in Early Modern Elite Society." *Past and Present* 211 (2011): 121–58.

Popin, Jacques. "Le *Journal de voyage* destiné à Pierre Raymond: Ecriture et Réécriture." In *Autour de Robert Challe*, edited by Frédéric Deloffre, 49–62. Paris: H. Champion, 1993.

Pratt, Mary Louise. *Imperial Eyes: Travel Writing and Transculturation*. New York: Routledge, 1992.

Rediker, Marcus. *Between the Devil and the Deep Blue Sea: Merchant Seamen, Pirates, and the Anglo-American Maritime World, 1700–1750*. Cambridge: Cambridge University Press, 1987.

———. *The Slave Ship: A Human History*. New York: Viking, 2007.

———. *Villains of All Nations: Atlantic Pirates in the Golden Age*. Boston: Beacon Press, 2004.

Robbins, Louise E. *Elephant Slaves and Pampered Parrots: Exotic Animals in Eighteenth-Century Paris*. Baltimore: Johns Hopkins University Press, 2002.

Roche, Daniel. *France in the Enlightenment*. Translated by Arthur Goldhammer. Cambridge: Harvard University Press, 1998.

Rogers, J. Daniel, and George Sabo III. "Caddo." In Fogelson, *Handbook of North American Indians*, 14:616–31.

Sayre, Gordon M. *The Indian Chief as Tragic Hero: Native Resistance and the Literatures of America, from Moctezuma to Tecumseh*. Chapel Hill: University of North Carolina Press, 2005.

———. "Natchez Ethnohistory Revisited: New Manuscript Sources from Le Page du Pratz and Dumont de Montigny." *Louisiana History* 50 (2009): 407–36.

———. "Plotting the Natchez Massacre: Le Page du Pratz, Dumont de Montigny, Chateaubriand." *Early American Literature* 37 (2002): 381–413.

Spear, Jennifer M. *Race, Sex, and Social Order in Early New Orleans*. Baltimore: Johns Hopkins University Press, 2009.

Stein, Robert Louis. *The French Slave Trade in the Eighteenth Century: An Old Regime Business*. Madison: University of Wisconsin Press, 1979.

Strayer, Brian. Lettres de Cachet *and Social Control in the Ancien Régime, 1659–1789*. New York: Peter Lang, 1992.

Surrey, Nancy Miller. *The Commerce of Louisiana during the French Régime, 1699–1763*. New York: Columbia University Press, 1916.

Swanton, John R. *Indian Tribes of the Lower Mississippi Valley and Adjacent Coast of the Gulf of Mexico*. Washington, DC: Government Printing Office, 1911.

Thomas, Daniel H. *Fort Toulouse: The French Outpost at the Alabamas on the Coosa*. Tuscaloosa: University of Alabama Press, 1989.

Usner, Daniel H., Jr. *American Indians in the Lower Mississippi Valley: Social and Economic Histories*. Lincoln: University of Nebraska Press, 1998.

———. *Indians, Settlers, and Slaves in a Frontier Exchange Economy: The Lower Mississippi Valley Before 1783*. Chapel Hill: University of North Carolina Press, 1992.

Vaillé, Eugène. *Histoire générale des Postes françaises*. 6 vols. Paris: Presses Universitaires de France, 1947–53.

Vidal, Cécile. "Antoine Bienvenu, Illinois Planter and Mississippi Trader: The Structure of Exchange between Lower and Upper Louisiana." In *French Colonial Louisiana and the Atlantic World*, edited by Bradley G. Bond, 111–33. Baton Rouge: Louisiana State University Press, 2005.

———. "French Louisiana in the Age of the Companies, 1712–1731." In *Constructing Early Modern Empires: Proprietary Ventures in the Atlantic World, 1500–1750*, edited by L. H. Roper and B. Van Ruymbeke, 133–62. Leiden, Netherlands: Brill, 2007.

Vignols, Léon, and Henri Sée. "Les Ventes de la Compagnie des Indes à Nantes, 1723–1733." *Revue de l'histoire des colonies françaises* 13 (1925): 489–534.

Villefosse, René Héron de. *Histoire des grandes routes de France.* Paris: Librairie Académique Perrin, 1975.

Viviès, Jean. *English Travel Narratives in the Eighteenth Century: Exploring Genres.* Surrey, UK: Ashgate Publishing, 2002.

Waselkov, Gregory A. *Old Mobile Archaeology.* Tuscaloosa: University of Alabama Press, 2005.

Waselkov, Gregory, Peter H. Wood, and Tom Hatley, eds. *Powhatan's Mantle: Indians in the Colonial Southeast.* Lincoln: University of Nebraska Press, 2006.

Waugh, Norah. *Corsets and Crinolines.* London: Batsford, 1987.

Weber, David J. *The Spanish Frontier in North America.* New Haven: Yale University Press, 2009.

Weilbrenner, Bernard. "Les Archives du Québec." *Revue d'histoire de l'Amérique française* 18 (1964): 3–13.

Weyler, Karen A. "'The Fruit of Unlawful Embraces': Sexual Transgression and Madness in Early American Sentimental Fiction." In *Sex and Sexuality in Early America*, edited by Merril D. Smith, 283–314. New York: New York University Press, 1998.

White, Douglas R., George P. Murdock, and Richard Scaglion. "Natchez Class and Rank Reconsidered." *Ethnology* 10 (1971): 369–88.

White, Richard. *The Middle Ground: Indians, Empires, and Republics in the Great Lakes Region, 1650–1815.* Cambridge: Cambridge University Press, 1991.

White, Sophie K. "'A Baser Commerce': Retailing, Class, and Gender in French Colonial New Orleans." *William and Mary Quarterly*, 3rd ser., 63 (2006): 517–50.

Woods, Patricia Dillon. *French-Indian Relations on the Southern Frontier, 1699–1762.* Ann Arbor: UMI Research Press, 1980.

Index

Contributors

Erin M. Greenwald is curator and historian at The Historic New Orleans Collection. Since joining The Collection in 2007, she has edited numerous exhibition catalogues and a book, *In Search of Julien Hudson: Free Artist of Color in Pre–Civil War New Orleans*, for which she also wrote the introduction. She is currently working on a book about the history of the French Company of the Indies in the Atlantic and Indian Ocean worlds, and on an exhibition entitled *Pipe Dreams: Louisiana under the French Company of the Indies, 1717–1731*. She received her PhD in history from the Ohio State University.

Teri F. Chalmers is a translator of French and Italian and a former professor of practice in Tulane University's Department of French and Italian. She has translated articles for *Bonsai* and essays for Cambridge University Press, and has worked with The Historic New Orleans Collection since 2006. Chalmers earned a BA in Italian and linguistics from Newcomb College, an MA in Italian from UCLA, and a PhD in medieval Romance languages and literatures, with a concentration in French, from Tulane University. She also studied in France at the Université de Strasbourg, and in Italy at the Università degli Studi in Florence.

Praise for A Company Man

"A wonderful, careful, informed, and loving job of editing. The translation is well written and sensitive to nuances. I learned a lot, especially the determined merriment in the face of horrors which remains characteristic of New Orleans."

—Gwendolyn Midlo Hall, author of *Africans in Colonial Louisiana: The Development of Afro-Creole Culture in the Eighteenth Century*

"What a remarkable find, this mislaid memoir by a skirt-chasing clerk in John Law's Company of the Indies. Marc-Antoine Caillot's mishaps on land and water as he travels from Paris to New Orleans by way of Saint Domingue seesaw between harrowing and hilarious. It's a fine translation, too, whose annotation and introduction alone are worth the price of the book. *A Company Man* will delight general readers and specialists for years to come."

—Lawrence N. Powell, author of *The Accidental City: Improvising New Orleans*

"One of the most important finds on colonial Louisiana in many decades. Its uniqueness lies in the personable context this company clerk provides for his journey to America. Expertly translated and annotated with wonderful illustrations, this is a book that readers will return to again and again."

—Alan Gallay, author of *The Indian Slave Trade: The Rise of the English Empire in the American South, 1670–1717*

"A remarkable achievement . . . In this journal historians of colonial Louisiana receive a gift of surprises and opportunities that will influence many interpretations to come. With language oftentimes lusty and witty, Caillot vividly captures everyday life as well as dramatic events during his two years in New Orleans. The introduction and notes add immeasurably to the value of this rare document, situating this clerk's career—and the manuscript itself—firmly within the context of French colonial experience and history."

—Daniel H. Usner Jr., author of *Indians, Settlers, and Slaves in a Frontier Exchange Economy: The Lower Mississippi Valley before 1783*

"Caillot's narrative is more than a refreshing and provocative departure from the well-known formal memoirs of his contemporaries. It is a richly informative window onto colonial consciousness and behavior that draws readers in and plunges them into the raucous and terrifying eighteenth-century Atlantic world. Greenwald's thoughtful and informed introduction and notes are a revelation of the mundane bureaucratic and human sinews that defined a French colonial project, a welcome and informative portrait for scholars and general readers alike."

—Emily Clark, author of *Masterless Mistresses: The New Orleans Ursulines and the Development of a New World Society, 1727–1834*

Publication of this book was made possible in part through the generosity of the Laussat Society of The Historic New Orleans Collection.

Caillot's original manuscript, *Relation du voyage de la Louisianne ou Nouvelle France fait par le Sr. Caillot en l'année 1730*, is housed in the Williams Research Center of The Historic New Orleans Collection, where it is the capstone of the institution's rich archival holdings documenting life in French Louisiana.

Le landemain nous nous r[...]

Berrier. qui en command[...]

[...] Louisianne ou nous fume[...]

[...]ue de tout ce qui dependroit de l[...]

[...]il le feroit de bon coeur, nou[...]

[...]ouvernement nous fumes a la d[...]

[...]eneral et Mlles ses filles nous[...]

[...]emis des lettres de leurs parents[...]

[...]Caffé apres avoir causé pend[...]

[...] le landemain nous primes [...]

[...]Voila la relation de mon voy[...]

[...]Louisianne; je vais mainte[...]